Value and the World Economy Today

Also by Richard Westra and Alan Zuege

PHASES OF CAPITALIST DEVELOPMENT (co-edited with Robert Albritton and Makoto Itoh)

Value and the World Economy Today

Production, Finance and Globalization

Edited by

Richard Westra
Pukyong National University
South Korea

Alan Zuege
York University
Canada

palgrave
macmillan

First published 2003 by
PALGRAVE MACMILLAN
Houndmills, Basingstoke, Hampshire RG21 6XS and
175 Fifth Avenue, New York, N.Y. 10010
Companies and representatives throughout the world

PALGRAVE MACMILLAN is the global academic imprint of the Palgrave Macmillan division of St. Martin's Press, LLC and of Palgrave Macmillan Ltd. Macmillan® is a registered trademark in the United States, United Kingdom and other countries. Palgrave is a registered trademark in the European Union and other countries.

ISBN 1–4039–0002–7

This book is printed on paper suitable for recycling and made from fully managed and sustained forest sources.

A catalogue record for this book is available from the British Library.

Library of Congress Cataloging-in-Publication Data
Value and the world economy today : production, finance and globalization / edited by Richard Westra, Alan Zuege.
p. cm.
Includes bibliographical references and indexes.
ISBN 1–4039–0002–7
1. Value. 2. Capitalism. 3. Marxian economics. 4. Production (Economic theory) 5. International economic relations. 6. Globalization—Economic aspects. 7. Financial crises—History—21st century. 8. Economic history—21st century. I. Westra, Richard, 1954– II. Zuege, Alan, 1968–

HB201.V347 2003
335.4′12—dc21 2003053641

10 9 8 7 6 5 4 3 2 1
12 11 10 09 08 07 06 05 04 03

Printed and bound in Great Britain by
Antony Rowe Ltd, Chippenham and Eastbourne

Contents

Notes on the Contributors

Robert Albritton is Professor of Political Science at York University in Toronto, Canada. His recent publications include *A Japanese Reconstruction of Marxist Theory; A Japanese Approach to Stages of Capitalist Development; Dialectics and Deconstruction in Political Economy* and the co-edited volumes, *Phases of Capitalist Development; New Dialectics and Political Economy.*

Suzanne de Brunhoff is Honorary Research Director at Centre National de la Recherche Scientifique, Paris, France. Her books include *Marx on Money; State; Capital and Economic Policy*; and *L'heure du marché: critique du libéralisme.* She has also written extensively on monetary policy, theories of finance, and the regulation of international finance.

Dick Bryan is Associate Professor in the Political Economy Program, Faculty of Economics and Business, University of Sydney, Australia. His books include *The Chase Across the Globe: International Accumulation and the Contradictions for Nation States* and (with M. Rafferty) *The Global Economy in Australia.* He has written extensively on the theory of competition, the internationalization of capital and global finance.

Simon Clarke is a Professor of Sociology, University of Warwick, United Kingdom and Scientific Director, Institute for Comparative Labour Relations Research, Moscow. His books include *Keynesianism, Monetarism and the Crisis of the State; Marx, Marginalism and Modern Sociology; Marx's Theory of Crisis; The State Debate* and *Management and Industry in Russia* (four volume series).

Gérard Duménil is a Research Director at the Centre National de la Recherche Scientifique, MODEM, University of Paris X-Nanterre. He is the author of *Le Concept de loi économique dans Le Capital; Marx et Keynes face à la crise* and (with D. Lévy) *The Economics of the Profit Rate; La Dynamique du capital* and *Au delà du Capitalisme.*

Ben Fine is Professor of Economics, School of Oriental and African Studies, University of London. His books include *Marx's Capital;* (with L. Harris) *Rereading Capital; The Value Dimension; Women's Employment and the Capitalist Family; The Political Economy of Diet, Health and Food Policy; Labour Market Theory; Social Capital versus Social Theory* and *The World of Consumption.*

Alan Freeman is Visiting Fellow, University of Greenwich and Economist, Greater London Authority. He has published several books including the co-edited volumes, *Ricardo, Marx, Sraffa*; *Marx and non-Equilibrium Economics* and *The New Value Controversy and the Foundations of Economics* and is a co-organizer of the International Working Group on Value Theory. He is also the author of numerous articles on value theory, economic crises and uneven development.

Andrew J. Kliman is Associate Professor of Economics at Pace University. He is co-editor of *The New Value Controversy and the Foundations of Economics* and is a co-organizer of the International Working Group on Value Theory. He has also written extensively on value theory and the falling rate of profit, including 'The Profit Rate Under Continuous Technical Change' (*Review of Radical Political Economics*, #20/4) and (with T. McGlone) 'The Transformation non-Problem and the non-Transformation Problem' (*Capital & Class #35*).

Dominique Lévy is a Research Director at the Centre National de la Recherche Scientifique, CEPREMAP, Paris. Recent books include (with G. Duménil): *The Economics of the Profit Rate: Competition, Crises and Historical Tendencies in Capitalism*; *La Dynamique du capital: un siecle d'economie americaine* and *Au delà du Capitalisme*.

Fred Moseley is Professor of Economics, Mount Holyoke College at South Hadley, Massachusetts. His books include *The Falling Rate of Profit in the Postwar United States Economy*; *International Perspectives on Profitability and Accumulation*; *Marx's Method in Capital*; *Heterodox Economic Theories: True or False* and *New Investigations in Marx's Method*.

Thomas T. Sekine was a Professor of Economics and Social and Political Thought at York University from 1968 to 1994 and currently teaches at the School of Commerce, Aichi-Gakuin University, Japan. His books include *A Japanese Approach to Political Economy: Unoist Variations* and *An Outline of the Dialectic of Capital* (two volumes).

Ajit Sinha is at Gokhale Institute of Politics and Economics, India. He has served on the editorial board of the *Review of Radical Political Economics* (RRPE) and the book series *Encyclopedia of Political Economy*. His publications include 'A Critique of Part One of *Capital* Volume One: The Value Controversy' (*Research in Political Economy*, 1996) and 'Transformation Problem' (in *Encyclopedia of Political Economy*, Routledge).

Richard Westra is Assistant Professor of Political Economy at Pukyong National University, Republic of Korea. His publications include the co-edited volumes, *Phases of Capitalist Development: Booms, Crises and Globalizations* and *New Socialisms: Futures Beyond Globalization*. He has also recently published articles treating the future institutional configuring of socialist societies and the current Japanese economic crisis.

Alan Zuege is at the Department of Political Science, York University in Toronto, Canada. He is co-editor of the books, *Phases of Capitalist Development: Booms, Crises and Globalizations* and *The Globalization Decade: A Critical Reader*, and is a contributing editor of the *Socialist Register*. He has also recently published articles in *Monthly Review, Socialist Register* and in the collection, *Die Strategie der Neuen Mitte*.

Introduction

Richard Westra and Alan Zuege

The aim of this collection is to advance and encourage cross-fertilization between two literatures: the conceptual debate over the foundations of political economy and concrete research on the world economy today. In meeting this challenge, the volume assembles original and innovative work from leading scholars who have written on both topics. The contributors hail from eight countries – Australia, Canada, France, India, Japan, South Korea, the UK and USA – and represent important schools of thought in political economy. Together, they bring a rich variety of intellectual traditions and critical perspectives to bear on this historical turning point in the global system.

The seeds of the modern debate over the theory of political economy lie in the development of capitalism in the eighteenth and nineteenth centuries. The political and social ferment of this period generated a variety of intellectual responses seeking to comprehend this radical social transformation and to explain the basic workings of the capitalist market which had emerged. The theories of Adam Smith and David Ricardo, as well as the fundamental 'critique of political economy' developed by Karl Marx, advanced alternative frameworks which, for all their differences, shared the assumption that beneath the surface of everyday market exchange lies a process of determination which had to be revealed by theory. The debate over the theory of 'value' however, both then and now, has encompassed more than just the determination of market prices of commodities. Rather, the controversy goes to the very heart of our understanding of the historical modalities of the distribution of power and production of wealth in society.

The evolution of the first 'value debate' was thus closely bound up with the flux of social relations in which it was embedded. The sharpening of class struggles and the appropriation of Ricardo's labor theory of value by the socialist movement soon generated a broad challenge to classical political economy, one which would lay the basis for modern day neo-classical economics.[1] What the 'Marginalist Revolution' of the 1870s accomplished, in one sleight of hand, was to shift the terms of debate from the concern with the social relations of the production of wealth – the source and distribution of value – to the narrow question of the optimal allocation of resources under conditions of scarcity. The centerpiece of the ascendant neo-classical school was a theory of relative prices which purports to explain the allocation process based on the 'opportunity cost' of market participants. The broad applicability of this price theory and its ideological role in rationalizing the capitalist system in terms of free and voluntary market exchange secured for neo-classicals a central place in the discipline they redefined as a 'separate science' of Economics, pushing the theory of value and critical political economy to the margins of debate.

Despite its diminished position, Marxist and radical political economy developed and transformed throughout the twentieth century.[2] But the last 25 years in particular have seen an international resurgence of work in critical economic theory and a reopening of the value debate, culminating most recently in a remarkable diversification of research on quantitative and qualitative aspects of political economy. A genuine plurality of positions – some old, some new – have emerged. Included among these are various attempts to defend, develop or critique Marx's conceptual and mathematical framework connecting values and prices.[3] New approaches to the philosophy and method of political economy have also been proposed, with particularly intense debate focusing on the role of dialectical logic and the value form in Marx's *Capital*.[4] Meanwhile, others have sought to reconstruct or strengthen central pillars of political economy, such as the theories of exploitation, money, competition and 'unproductive' labor.[5] Collectively, these contributions at the theoretical, methodological and empirical frontiers of political economy have helped to rejuvenate interest in heterodox approaches, especially in the rediscovery and development of Marx's project, and to establish firmer foundations for progressive research. To this extent the contemporary value debate – prominent contributors to which are featured in the present volume – has arguably produced some of the most original and sophisticated advancements in critical economic theory to appear for almost a century, developments that bring a new level of analytical rigor to the challenge to mainstream economics.

The revitalization of debate in political economy may have expanded and deepened the critique of conventional economic thought, but it has also yielded a number of *competing* theories of value – theories which offer alternative conceptions of capitalism and diverging explanations of the observable movements of actually existing capitalist societies. The controversies in value theory include but are by no means limited to textual disputes, philosophical controversies and mathematical formalizations. While the value debate retains a focus on the consistency and rigor of rival conceptions of value, a crucial challenge for the new approaches remains to demonstrate their explanatory potential against real world developments. The essays in this collection represent a development of the debate on both of these fronts.

The contributors to this volume articulate and develop a number of unique approaches which have staked out key positions in recent value-theoretic debate. In the course of doing so, the distinctions between different interpretations come into sharper focus, and these distinctions can be seen to inform different readings of the tendencies of contemporary capitalism: the changing technical and social organization of production, the process of capitalist globalization and international competition, the development of global finance, the anatomy of market breakdown and mechanisms of economic crisis, and the impact of consumerism on human subjectivity, among other themes discussed. These dramatic structural transformations of the past two decades are not mere objects of analysis for the new thinking in political economy. The growth of economic instability and social polarization, and the upheavals which follow in their wake, place new demands on theory to make sense of a changing reality. The renewal of critical political economy as such is more than just an 'internal' debate or ongoing dispute with orthodox economic theory; it gives intellectual expression to a growing chorus of resistance to the concrete policies and practices inspired by that orthodoxy.

The interest in the role of value theory in economic explanation has grown amidst rising dissatisfaction with the ability of neo-classical economics and mainstream perspectives to account for changes in the global economy. The propensity for crises that beset the advanced capitalist economies throughout the last three decades; the wild policy swings by capitalist states (administered by political parties of both right and left) initially committed to full employment and massive social expenditure, now defending neo-liberal austerity programs and attrition against workers; the emergence of international financial markets that operate more like global casinos than providers of liquidity for investment or trade; the growing international balance-of-payments asymmetries and global polarization of wealth – all of this is far removed from the mathematically 'elegant' models of orthodox economics with its fossilized assumptions of perfect competition, static equilibrium, factor price equalization, and so forth. Consequently, even economists in the mainstream academy have struggled to adapt, revising neo-classical methodology and extending the scope of their work to encompass areas, such as corporate governance, the global financial architecture, and various dimensions of institutional change and 'economic sociology,' that were previously the domain of critical traditions and research at the fringes.[6]

This volume hopes to contribute to the advancement and relevance of political economy in a number of ways: to present side-by-side a number of developed schools of thought emerging from recent theoretical, methodological and empirical debates; to relate them more explicitly to analysis of the inner workings of capitalism today; and to promote further dialogue across perspectival and disciplinary boundaries.[7] The contributors demonstrate how across complex and topical spheres of research – the impact of new financial instruments such as 'derivatives'; the relationship between money, global finance and economic crises; the role of managerial labor in corporate governance; globalization and neo-liberal economic policy; the precise dynamics of capitalist crisis and economic cycles; the limits of freedom and equality in the age of consumerism; and the lessons and relevance of the theory of value for today – critical economics can be a key which opens the door to rich and elucidative analysis. And it is hoped that, by bringing closer together the intertwined projects of honing political economists' conceptions of capitalism in theory and drawing out their implications for the current conjuncture, this volume will play an underlaboring role for debate in political economy for years to come.

We are bombarded today with a new and expanding 'common sense' economic vocabulary: international competitiveness, flexibility, the new economy, financial 'flu,' market 'correction,' downsizing, cutbacks, claw-backs and deregulation (to name but a few buzzwords) are bandied about in academic circles and the popular press with reckless abandon. To assess the inner connections and implicit claims that underlie this vocabulary it requires a proper theory. The contributors to this volume share the view that the gateway to rendering intelligible the complex and often hidden workings of the world economy today is critical political economy.

Notes

1. See for example Dasgupta (1985: Chapter 6).
2. Howard and King (1992) provide a detailed history.
3. Surveys from various perspectives may be found in: Fine (1986; and his contribution to this volume); Freeman and Carchedi (1996), Callari, Roberts and Wolff (1998), Foley (2000a), and Saad-Filho (2002).
4. For a tiny sampling of this voluminous literature, consult the following sources: Reuten and Williams (1988), Mohun (1994a), Moseley (1993a), Moseley and Campbell (1997), Albritton (1999), Albritton and Simoulidis (2002), Brown *et al.* (2002), Arthur (1998, 2002: Chapter 1), and Saad-Filho (2002: Chapters 1, 2).
5. Just a few examples of the diverse efforts which have opened up new vistas in value analysis and empirical research include: the disparate approaches – from Roemer's (1986) earlier work to Saad-Filho's (2002) recent writings – taking up the concept of exploitation; the growing literature on value and the theory of money (for recent surveys and discussions see Itoh and Lapavitsas 1998; Nelson 1999; Williams 1999; Freeman 2001a); applications of a developed Marxist theory of competition by Bryan (1985, 1986, 1995a), Botwinick (1993) and others; and the systematic empirical work by Moseley (1991), and Shaikh and Tonak (1994) incorporating the distinction between productive and non-productive labor.
6. On these developments, see Fine (1997).
7. In this sense, the present collection follows upon a previous volume (Albritton *et al.* 2001) in the effort to bring various schools of critical political economy into dialogue over the central questions of applied and theoretical political economy.

Part I

A Retrospective on the Value Debate

1

Value Theory and the Study of Contemporary Capitalism: A Continuing Commitment

Ben Fine

The dialectics of debate

Controversy has raged over Marx's labor theory of value from the time that it was first put forward. The debate has had two closely related aspects. One has concerned how value should be interpreted. For example does Marx's theory differ from Ricardo's and, if so, how and why? Is it a matter of definition or method? On the other hand, assuming agreement on the nature of Marx's value theory, there is the question of whether it is valid or not.

Here the debate has exhibited a paradox. For those who reject the labor theory of value often do so by appealing to exactly the same factors that endear it to its supporters. This is most notable in the so-called transformation problem. Critics of Marx suggest that the divergence between value and price, in the presence of wages and profits (and differing compositions of capital) undermines the labor theory of value. But supporters argue that it is the very divergence between value and price that makes value theory essential. Not surprisingly, these differences reflect methodological and theoretical issues. But the paradox in the realm of debate is not accidental for the reason that the economy, and society more generally, evolve on a contradictory basis. As society becomes more developed and complex, does this undermine the validity and necessity for value theory, or does the latter remain essential as the abstract basis on which to reconstruct and comprehend complex outcomes?

It is important to recognize that two separate, but closely related, methodological factors are involved here. The first is whether the features of the capitalist economy that are common across all of its history are amenable to explanation by reference to value theory – do we need the labor theory of value to explain wages and profits, or the course of economic growth and crises? The second issue is whether particular periods of capitalism, especially the more developed, reinforce or undermine the validity of value theory – as in monopolization, for example, or the growth of unproductive labor in the 'service' and other sectors. Whilst contributors to political economy and the value debate have always confronted each other across these analytical divides, it has meant that value theory has always been on the defensive. On the one hand, it is subject to continuing assaults for what are taken to be its underlying weaknesses. On the other hand, it is perceived to be inflexible in responding to historically new features of capitalism, both analytically and empirically. In short, is value theory, for example, appropriate at all as the basis for a theory of price and, if so, does it remain appropriate for monopoly pricing?

In this chapter, whilst highlighting this dialectic, I intend to put some emphasis on the positive case for the labor theory of value rather than, as is characteristic of most of the favorable literature, seeking to defend the theory against the mountain of criticism to which it has been subjected. Almost inevitably, the positive case for value theory has been overshadowed and influenced by the weight of argument leveled against it. As a result, the basic reasons and methods underlying Marx's value theory become inadvertently set aside or, as is to be suspected for much of the literature, scarcely consulted let alone absorbed and understood. Instead, a parody of Marx's political economy is paraded for ritual attack and defense not least on terms dictated by bourgeois economics – does Marx's value theory provide an adequate theory of equilibrium prices, for example? More constructively than going through a patient and increasingly futile exercise of responding to the idea, correct on its own terms, that Marx's value theory is poor mainstream economics, I intend to demonstrate that there are fundamentals to the labor theory of value which are internally coherent. Further, this coherence provides the basis for unraveling the increasing complexities and specificities of the capitalism mode of production as they have emerged over time – even though these complexities have induced rejection of value theory on the basis of incoherent and inaccurate understandings of it.

At a more mundane level, as a proponent of value theory, the positive account offered here will also be personal to a greater extent than intellectual modesty might otherwise reasonably allow. For I do want to illustrate the arguments offered here by showing how value theory has informed my own work and to reference it accordingly. It might, thereby, help to inform the future work of others. To this end, I have frequently only referred to my own work in the text, although these generally contain useful references to others. Further, I would here suggest some important sources, other than Marx himself, that the reader may also wish to consider.[1]

Smith, Ricardo, Marx

Adam Smith provides an excellent starting point for interrogating the methodological and substantive basis of Marx's value theory. He argues that the labor theory of value would hold but only in that rude society, or primitive communism as Marx called it, in which laborers simply hunted deer and beaver as required for personal consumption. Significantly, in view of the theme laid out above – does complexity undermine the labor theory of value? – as soon as the economy developed to allow for the presence of rents and, ultimately, profits, Smith argued against the labor theory of value. He replaced it with a components theory of price, with the latter naturally made up of the contributions or claims from wages, profits and rents. For Smith, once labor was no longer the sole element in price, the labor theory of value needed to be jettisoned. The addition of the simplest element of economic complexity was sufficient for Smith both to draw this conclusion and to embrace his components theory. This is despite the components approach itself either being tautological (a price, indeed anything, is necessarily made up of its constituent parts) or erroneous (since the three components are not independent of one another as they mutually exhaust net product).[2]

Implicitly, and explicitly from the vantage point of Marx's value theory, Smith's contribution raises two crucial methodological issues. The first concerns the status of the argument in favor of the labor theory of value when Smith deems that it does hold. For, in a rude society, there would be no exchange. Whatever you want, you go out and hunt it. This implies that there are no prices, so there is no need for a value theory at all! Quite clearly, Smith has gone through an inadvertent mental exercise. Suppose the rude society were like a capitalist society, would the labor theory of value hold? It is a totally meaningless question, and this implies there must be considerable doubts about the notion of value that Smith has constructed. Of course, it could be argued that there may be random disposal through exchange of more or less accidental surplus or specialization and skills in one activity rather than another. But this then raises the issue of who appropriates, controls and exchanges the surplus, and who gets to have one skill rather than another. The nature and terms of exchange can be addressed only on the basis of these prior questions – although I am conscious that, by posing them, I am increasingly being drawn into a more complicated version of Smith's imaginary rude society.

There is in this context considerable difference between Smith and one aspect of Marx's own materialist method, one that is highly attractive in terms of its appeal to realism. For Marx depends upon justifying the use of particular concepts by demonstrating their correspondence, even if necessarily within the theory itself, with the realities of the society under consideration. From this perspective, concepts such as value and price are invalid if applied to the rude society since the society does not systematically generate them itself. By whatever intellectual route that value has been derived as a concept, it is merely a general, mental, ahistorical and asocial construct for Smith. On his terms, it may or may not be useful in explaining exchange in the rude society (where the question is irrelevant) or more developed economies where revenues also accrue other than to labor. In short, Smith has ideally constructed a labor theory of value as an instrument for understanding exchange in the (equally constructed) rude society where there is no exchange to explain, and has rejected the theory when it is transposed to societies where there is exchange. In contrast to such instrumentalism in the understanding and use of the labor theory of value, Marx's own approach can be understood by its first establishing whether value exists or not (Pilling 1980). If not, it has no analytical status – as in Smith's rude society. When the answer, however, is in the affirmative, it leads to a number of subsequent questions – which labor counts toward value, by how much does it count and by what (social) mechanisms does it do so, and what are the relations between value and more complex economic and social outcomes?

The second methodological point that arises out of Smith's rejection of the labor theory of value is whether value, however defined and understood, and price should be seen as identical to one another or not. Is value, for example, some sort of center of gravity around which prices fluctuate? If so, certain factors determine value and others determine deviation from value. It is not clear where the boundary should be drawn between them unless some notion of equilibrium is to be deployed. More specifically, for Smith, it is a matter of whether value as labor time is identical to price or not. If not, value has to be amended until it does equal price, as in Smith's components theory. Of course, such natural prices, as they are called, are perceived as the center around which actual price fluctuations occur. This, in itself, involves the arbitrary division between those factors that determine the natural price and those that determine the deviations around it. In some sense, one set of factors is supposedly more fundamental than the other. This opens the way for any number of factors to enter the fundamental set, as is the case for price theory based on generalized theories of supply and demand.

Again, Marx's approach is different and not arbitrary. Value as labor time is understood as an abstract and simple category derived from production. It cannot be directly observed but is the basis on which the more complex exchange categories, such as price, are constructed both in reality and, correspondingly, within theory. In other words, the theory has an analytical structure or structure of abstraction in which more complex categories like price reproduce rather than displace the simpler categories like value. This reflects the previous methodological point in that the existence of value has already been established. It cannot simply be thrown away because of the complex forms that it assumes and which are its effects. If price is seen as the form taken by value in exchange, the value/price nexus forges the relationship between producers as a relationship between buyers and sellers of goods. By analogy with the physical world, the element carbon can assume the form of either coal or diamonds depending upon the way it is structured and worked upon by nature. But carbon does not cease to exist nor to be of analytical relevance simply because it can become a number of different products.

In short, the value relationship is quantitative in terms of the labor time expended by individual workers but, qualitatively, it is much more besides. The existence of complicating factors, some of which are considered fundamental and some not – such as equalized profit and random or unsystematic factors, respectively – is by no means a reason for rejecting value theory but the very basis on which it is constructed. It is perhaps unfortunate that the dialectical elaboration of this perspective in terms of essence and appearance, or substance and form often expresses the second element of each couplet as *mere* phenomenal aspects (or forms and appearances). Whilst, in a sense, appropriate for a grand vision of fundamentals, it can lead to an unwarranted denigration of the importance of critical features of the capitalist economy. If price is the mere form of value, is profit the mere form of surplus value, and the financial system the mere monetary form of capital? On the contrary, these are not symbols of the essence like the monarch on a banknote but material relations with effects even if they are derived from the class relations between capital and labor. But I anticipate. The important point, though, is that value theory does not fall merely by virtue of the complexity through which it moves through the world of capital and otherwise.

Turn now to Ricardo. Even though he shared some of the methodological deficiencies with Smith, he was firmly committed to the labor theory of value. He was determined to explain as many features as possible of the capitalist economy on the basis of value theory as he understood it – which is, as for Smith, the labor time required for production. Ricardo demonstrated that Smith's argument was, at least in part, wrong – that the formation of a separate claim on production other than from labor was not a reason in itself why price should diverge from value. Rather, if profits as an element of price were non-zero or increased, this would be at the expense of wages, and prices could continue to equal value. Unfortunately, for Ricardo, this argument is only correct as far as the mere presence of profits is concerned. Once there are differences in what is now termed the composition of capital, prices do deviate quantitatively from values, with higher prices relative to values for those products that have high capital-intensity, since they are liable to command disproportionately larger amounts of profit relative to labor time of production. Once again, as Ricardo realized giving rise to what is now termed the transformation problem, the labor theory of value appears to falter as it confronts the simple distribution of profit between capitalists.

Setting these difficulties aside, Ricardo attempted to explain rent on the basis of his value theory. He succeeded, by asserting that value should be determined by the labor time of the worst piece of land in use, with rent making up the difference in productivity on better lands. But by attempting to deal with a more complex form, rent, this creates an inconsistency in Ricardo's value theory, one that he never resolves. For, there are now two value theories, one for agriculture on the margin of cultivation, the other for manufacturing that is presumably based on average production conditions. Why should value in industry not also be determined at the margin of the worst producer, other producers reaping profits in the form of what Marshall termed quasi-rents until, at least, they were eroded by the catch-up in technique or whatever by the marginal producers.

The extension of Ricardo's margin to each of the sectors of the economy provided the basis for the marginalist revolution, especially in conjunction with dependence upon other factors of production and the incorporation of the margin on the demand-side in the form of utility maximization by consumers. This neatly put aside the class content of Ricardo's value theory, one that conveyed the idea of a distributional conflict between capital and labor, with landlords as the passive recipients of (rising) rents attached to productivity differences across lands (as the worse lands are brought into use).

For Marx's value theory, these issues have to be treated differently. But first consider some of the methodological issues raised previously. The opening chapters of Volume 1 of *Capital* can be considered to be establishing that value does exist but only in societies dominated by commodity production. The process of exchange necessarily forges an equivalence between the different types of labor that are used in production, although that equivalence is rarely, if ever, direct. Rather, the relation between (the labor of) producers is expressed as a relationship between commodities, as use values, in terms of relative prices. Only, in part, for convenience is it assumed that commodities exchange at their value for, then, the distinction between value and price, as previously discussed, can be made prominent. By contrast, those unaware of this motivation see the abstraction merely as a simplifying assumption, as unjustified and as inconsistent with Marx's treatment of price of production in Volume 3 of *Capital*. Further, it becomes apparent in Volume 1 that value is most extensive, indeed predominant, only under the capitalist mode of production for which, it is not only the proletariat that joins the market, being both able and compelled to sell its capacity to work. Means of production and means of consumption are in general also brought into the orbit of exchange. The value relationship then, as for other modes of production where commodities are less pervasive, is not simply synonymous with the market. For it represents a set of entirely different economic relations between producers and those that command them, as well as differences in other socio-economic relations, such as access to consumption and, hence, social reproduction.

In establishing the nature of the value relation, as a relation between producers and not simply as quanta of labor time, Marx pinpoints the peculiar character of the money commodity. Initially, this is constructed on the basis of a particular use value, gold. But Marx, even at this early stage in his analysis, establishes that gold, as a general equivalent for other commodities, soon takes on a symbolic role – first of all with the debasement of the currency through wear and tear and even clipping and filing, and eventually through paper symbols themselves. What this demonstrates is that the distinction between value and price is such that one can be represented by the other even with the increasing displacement of commodity money from the process of exchange.

In short, Marx's theory of money is in part based upon the notion that commodity money is displaced by symbols of money and, hence, indirectly, symbols of value – although ratification of such symbols ultimately requires intervention by the state. Paradoxically, it is precisely this displacement in its most modern form, in which the functions of commodity money or gold are more or less confined to the reserves of central banks, which leads many to reject Marx's monetary theory where they have genuinely considered it. How can a theory of commodity money, based on value theory, be of relevance when commodity money is no longer in use. In riposte, it can be argued that Marx's monetary theory implies the displacement of commodity money. How this occurs needs to be explored in theoretical and empirical context, moving beyond the mere symbolic circulation of values as commodities to incorporate the symbolic, at times fictitious, circulation of surplus value. But, this is to anticipate, although it does root consideration of the currently evolving financial system within the bounds of the production system on which it depends for its profitability however much it might wish otherwise.

Although the abstraction that value equals price draws the qualitative distinction between the two and establishes value as a social relation between producers specific to a commodity producing society, the importance of this abstraction is arguably more important for another reason – the light that it sheds on class. For, throughout Volume 1, once value is established as a legitimate category, Marx is primarily concerned with exchange only to a limited but crucial extent. His concern is solely with the exchange between capital and labor, treating the economy, as it were, as a single enterprise. On this basis, Marx initially addresses a single question – how is it possible that surplus value can be produced when every commodity exchanges exactly at its value? His answer is remarkably simple; the commodity labor power, the capacity to labor, is what is purchased by the capitalist but at a value that itself bears no necessary quantitative relation as such to the quantity of labor performed by that capacity. Surplus value arises out of the ability of the capitalist to extract more working time, and hence value, than is required to purchase labor power. Interestingly, having answered this question qualitatively, the vast majority of Volume 1 is concerned both theoretically and empirically with how do capitalists extract surplus value quantitatively. By proposing the concepts of absolute and relative surplus value, Marx draws attention to the extensive (longer, harder work) and intensive (productivity increase through mechanization) methods of production by which capital exploits labor. Each generally requires the accumulation of capital to proceed.

Value theory, then, gives rise to and ties political economy to a number of notions: the classes of capital and labor are divided by a fundamental conflict over the production process – this is prior to distributional considerations in contrast to Ricardian-type analyses; accumulation of capital is imperative for the capitalist system; and there are definite methods by which the expansion of surplus value is pursued, with Marx suggesting, to be breathtakingly brief, that productivity is systemically pursued through the relative displacement of workers from the production process as given amounts of raw materials are worked up into final products through the use of machinery, and so on.

Value and capital

However briefly, I have now implicitly covered, and will soon review explicitly in slightly more depth, what I take to be not only five distinguishing features of Marx's value theory but also those which make it stand out most positively. Although the distinctiveness of Marx's value theory in these terms is not so controversial, it is astonishing in this day of scholarship how little even those subscribing to some form of Marxism and especially those who do not, are unaware of, set aside or distort these defining characteristics. Favorable and defining features of Marx's method are readily ignored in dismissing what is presumed to be his faulty economics, with the use of arguments that are not so favorably endowed methodologically.

First, methodologically, Marx's value theory is based on a dialectics in which the concepts employed are shown to have a correspondence to the reality under study both socially and historically (Harvey 1996). Further, abstract concepts are based on simple concepts such as value – itself derived from the notion of the two aspects of the commodity as exchange and use value – which are reproduced and not displaced by the emergence of more complex concepts such as price. This method is illustrated by the passage through the three volumes of *Capital*. In Volume 1, Marx is concerned with establishing the nature of value and, then, how – as a category rooted in capitalist production – (surplus) value is produced. Qualitatively, surplus value depends upon the exchange between capital and labor. Its origins are revealed by stripping away, or abstracting from, all other forms of exchange. Quantitatively, it entails a thorough analysis of how the production process is directed toward both the intensive and extensive exploitation of labor. These are coupled to more or less direct consequences – in the accumulation of capital, the factory system, limits to the length of the working day, the emergence of a credit system, the formation of a reserve army of labor, and so on.

In a sense, then, Volume 1 can be considered as being primarily concerned with the use value of that very unique commodity, labor power. The focus of Volume 2 is upon the exchange value of commodities more generally and how, with the intervention of money, the accumulation and reproduction of the capital–labor relation can be sustained. This is not, however, simply a shift from one sphere of activity, production, to another, exchange, but, rather, a refinement of the concept of value itself. For Volume 2 is concerned to show how economic reproduction is simultaneously a balance between value magnitudes (as in the famous equations) and a balance between use values across the sectors of means of production and means of consumption (with a further analysis, often overlooked, of the different ways in which these values circulate as revenues). This is far from being an analysis of equilibrium – at which word, all genuine Marxist scholars should reach for their critical red pen, ready to strike out.

In short, Volume 2 has nothing to do with equilibrium although it can be interpreted in this way by those seeking analogies with various strands of orthodox theory. Rather, it reconstructs the concept of value, as understood in Volume 1 (and not just a quantum of labor time but the whole capital–labor relation as laid out there) in the more complex form of balance and movement, at whatever quantitative level, between sectors of the economy. Interestingly, there is, of course, the notion that use values are no longer simply defined by their physical properties but that they take on a social content, peculiar to capitalism, of also being defined by their capacity to command money through sale, a point to be taken up later. In addition, the refinement of the concept of value allows a variety of more complex forms to be defined more rigorously and fully. Unproductive labor is that wage labor which is not engaged in the production of surplus value (because used for commerce or non-profit-making services), fixed capital is that part of constant capital which only releases its value into circulation over a number of periods of production, and so on.

Volume 3 of *Capital* is concerned with the distribution of surplus value but not in the simple sense of who gets how much of the surplus value that has been produced. Note, however, that even this superficial interpretation presupposes, correctly in line with Marx's method, that the surplus value has to be produced before it is distributed. If, though, the distribution is simply interpreted as a cake-division exercise, as in the (neo-)Ricardian (or Sraffian) interpretation, then the concepts of surplus value and profit collapse and the former simply serves as a superfluous accounting exercise. In contrast, Marx deals with the distribution of surplus value as a refinement of the concept of value. The results of the previous two volumes are brought together and used to develop more complex and concrete categories in terms of the economic processes by which production and exchange are integrated.

Thus, the so-called transformation problem addresses the formation of prices of production. Whilst this has incorrectly been seen as an equilibrium theory of prices (and the rate of profit), a careful reading, drawing the distinction properly between the value and organic compositions of capital, reveals that Marx's preoccupation is entirely otherwise and remains much more sharply and abstractly focused. It is concerned with the question: How does the inevitable development of productivity at different paces across the different sectors of the economy allow for the tendency for capital to be equally rewarded according to the quantity of capital advanced? For, when the rate of change of productivity differs across sectors, profitability would change in favor of those performing better. Prices have to adjust, and capital move, for profitability to move toward equalization. But the situation is more complex than this in that productivity and corresponding price changes and movements of capital will have knock-on effects on the input costs of means of production and in the price of items of consumption.

This is an appropriate starting point for Marx's law of the tendency of the rate of profit to fall (LTRPF), and counteracting tendencies, although the LTRPF and the transformation problem have traditionally been treated separately – despite sharing in common the capacity to attract target practice for those seeking to reject Marx's value theory. This separation between the two 'problems' – what happens to prices and profits for given values and what happens to them when values are changing – has been almost universal even amongst those sympathetic to, and supportive of, Marx. The approach adopted here is different. The LTRPF is seen as more complex than, and different from, an empirical prediction or mathematical proof of movements in the rate of profit. Rather, it deals at a relatively abstract level with the coexistence of the consequences of accumulation, as laid out in Volume 1, and the need for these is to be coordinated through the mechanisms of exchange as detailed in Volume 2. Quite apart from a host of socio-economic change attached to the accumulation of capital, such as monopolization, urbanization, the reproduction of a reserve army of labor, and so on, the exchange system has to accommodate the shifting rates of productivity and profitability analytically laid out in the treatment of the transformation of values into prices of production. Marx draws the conclusion that this cannot always be done without the accumulation of capital being punctuated with crises from time to time.

Volume 3 does, however, go much further than this by confronting the previously developed categories with capital more generally. Volume 2 has highlighted the need for commodities to be sold; this can itself become a specialized activity within exchange undertaken by merchant capital which tends to earn a rate of profit equal to that of industrial capital but without itself creating any (surplus) value. Volume 2 has also shown how money is continuously entering and leaving the circuits of capital, thereby creating a pool of idle money. Volume 1 suggests that capital prospers to the extent that it can command money-capital through the credit system. Through these insights, Marx forms the notion of interest-bearing capital, the borrowing and lending of money for the purposes of producing surplus value (upon and around which any number of other forms of credit and money-dealing can be incorporated or evolve).

Volume 3 also considers circumstances in which there are potential obstacles to the accumulation of capital in the form of landed property. In contrast to Ricardian and most other rent theory that are its variants, Marx is concerned with how the presence of class relations on the land affects the access of capital to a vital means of production. The result is to modify the pace and nature of accumulation, quite apart from the rent that emerges as a consequence. For this reason, Marx's theory is organized around the potential for a lower organic composition of capital (properly understood) and the necessity for, but the limits that this imposes on, (absolute) rent. Significantly, this yields the result that there is no such thing as no rent land. Whilst a totally common and common-sense experience, Ricardian theory insists otherwise, that the worst land (in use) must pay no rent but for monopoly rent (which would not distinguish the intervention of land from monopoly conditions in other sectors or factors of production).

The immediately preceding discussion is intended to show how the distinctive method of Marx's value theory is embedded in one particular interpretation of the flow of argument through the three volumes of *Capital*. It is perhaps worth reiterating that on every occasion in which Marx introduces a more complex concept, this is often deployed positively by critics (even supporters of Marx) as a means to reject his analysis. Volume 2, for example, has induced theories of underconsumption, as in the work of Baran and Sweezy and many others, for which the notion of (unrealized) potential surplus suffices and value theory as such is no longer necessary. The transformation of value into price of production and surplus value into profit is reconstrued as an equilibrium problem. Merchant capital, and even unproductive labor in the state sector devoted to non-commercial activity such as education, are conceived of as akin to any other sector of activity and equally a source of profitability, possibly indirectly. Interest-bearing capital is indistinguishable from credit in general, to whatever purpose it might be put, and is geared to the exchange process as a whole and is not specific to the accumulation of capital and creation of surplus value. And rent is simply the consequence of a more or less powerful monopoly over a particular factor of production. Paradoxically, in each of these cases, Marx is accused of being insufficiently sophisticated, whereas it is his critics who are generally responsible for collapsing socio-economic structures, process and agencies into an unduly simplistic mould. It is as if, for example, education could produce and appropriate profits in exactly the same way as an industrial sector, the capitalist economy could be in equilibrium, an inability to sell prove an insurmountable and chronic problem, and so on.

I have attempted to deal with many of these issues of method in my writing although others, to whom I refer in these writings to the best of my knowledge, have done so in greater detail and with greater success and insight. Fine (1989) provides an elementary overview. Fine and Harris (1979) provide an early survey of many contributions to Marxist political economy as they emerged in the 1970s. It is based on interpreting the relative emphasis upon, and interaction between, the three *structures* – on which see below – of production, exchange and distribution and also, unfortunately, reflects a heavy Althusserian influence in vogue at the time of writing. Fine (1986) provides readings on the value debate, including those of my own that have addressed both the transformation problem and rent theory, with the latter specifically employed in a historical and empirical account of the British coal industry in Fine (1990), and oil and diamonds in Fine (1994). Fine (1982) develops the interpretation of the LTRPF as an abstract law leading to more complex outcomes and shows how it is the antithesis of alternative accounts based on comparative statics and, hence, equilibrium. Fine (1985/86, 1988), in debate with Panico (1988), argues for the distinctiveness of Marx's theory of interest-bearing capital.

Class, structure, tendency and history

This long account of the first distinctive feature of Marx's value theory will allow most of the others to be handled much more briefly. Second, then, the value theory incorporates a particular understanding of class, one based on the fundamental conflict between capital and labor over production. The increasingly complex way in which (surplus) value is reproduced has its counterpart in an increasingly sophisticated understanding of class and of class relations. For there is an implication of differentiation of the capitalist class – by sector, productivity, by fractions across industrial, merchant and interest-bearing capital – and also of the class of labor by the same factors as well as by skill, employed or not, and so on (Fine 1998a). Once again, greater complexity induces a rejection or refinement of Marx's theory of class for a range of criteria deployed in finer or alternative forms of stratification. This is so even before the social reproduction of the capital–labor relation is considered where political, ideological and other socio-economic relations become involved (as in gender, race, nationality, etc.). Whilst it is essential to avoid economic reductionism (the capital–labor relation as such cannot inform us any more about these issues than it can about the exact outcomes for prices and profits), value as a class relationship is an essential foundation on which to examine other non-economic issues, especially politics, ideology and the state.

Third, Marx's value theory is attached to a particular understanding of socio-economic structures. This is not simply a matter of the basic class relations from which the logical possibility of other classes can also be derived by their divergence from the simple but fundamental dichotomy between capital and labor. The self-employed, for example, constitute a category that is neither proletariat nor bourgeois but is defined relative to them. Such derivation of categories also applies to other socio-economic structures. As is apparent, capital defines a fundamental distinction between production and exchange, and also between economic and social reproduction, the latter comprising those relations that are conditioned by, but which are not incorporated within, the direct orbit of capital – the two most favored examples being the non-economic interventions, nature and determinants of the state and the role of the family system (and domestic labor, for example). These can be identified but not filled out by an abstract analysis of capital alone.

It is important to recognize that these structural divisions can themselves only be identified qualitatively. We know that the freedom of labor implies that it is not reproduced solely by capital, although this by no means implies that economic and non-economic freedoms are either guaranteed or mutually exclusive (consider, for example, the right to demonstrate). Similarly, which particular activities occupy the realm of production, exchange or lie outside the direct control of capital altogether (as in provision by the state or the household on a non-commercial basis) is variable both historically and within and across countries.

Transport and storage, for example, could be incorporated under the control of either industrial or merchant capital. Privatization and commercialization (introduction of user charges) of public utilities illustrate a shifting boundary between productive and unproductive labor either between the public and private sector or even within the public sector itself. And the domestic provision of consumption goods is generally believed to have been undermined by the assault of capitalist mass production. But even here, the shift in structural boundaries has often been in the opposite direction as capitalist production has enhanced the scope for domestic provision, as in home entertainment and a host of consumer durables from building tools through to microwaves. I have attempted to deal with many of these issues both in theoretical and empirical detail in Fine (1990, 1992, 1998a, b, 2002a), and Fine and Leopold (1993). Both in identifying structures and in constructing appropriate theory and construing empirical evidence, value theory has proved invaluable.

Value theory has, however, often been rejected on the basis of structuralist arguments whether the latter are recognized as such. This is especially so in case of what has been termed categoricism, for which a particular inequality or difference is identified empirically and then 'explained' by being referred to as a structure. This can take the form of class analysis, as in the notion of capital and labor in conflict over distribution, or along different lines, as in theories of patriarchy and racism in which these are used as structures to explain disadvantage. Inevitably, categoricism is antagonistic to Marxism. This is not only because it, possibly erroneously, identifies structures that are perceived both analytically and empirically to contradict emphasis on class but also because, methodologically, structures are erroneously interpreted as the most fundamental of categories. To a large extent, such an approach was encouraged for a time by Althusserianism. But it begs the question of where these structures originate and how they are reproduced for, otherwise, how can they ever change or be transformed.

In short, Marxism in general and value theory in particular do not deny the existence and significance of socio-economic and other structures but this is not to embrace a methodology of structuralism, whether categoricism or not. More specifically, structures need to be analytically justified on the basis of class relations and the socio-economic processes to which they are attached. Theory of value is an exemplary illustration as suggested by the ground already covered above, as in the distinctions between production and exchange, and between economic and social reproduction. But structures can also be understood as the consequence of more complex, historically contingent outcomes, as I have tried to demonstrate with the economic history of the South African economy, in Fine and Rustomjee (1997), and the way in which consumption and food systems are constructed and evolved (Fine and Leopold 1993; Fine *et al.* 1996; Fine 1998b, 2002a).

Fourth, an important part of these analyses is to specify the socio-economic processes by which structures are reproduced and transformed. Like class relations these are abstract and are the basis on which the more complex structures are reproduced (or not). Often, the underlying processes are mutually contradictory as in the imperatives toward vertical integration and disintegration, for deskilling and reskilling, and of crucial significance in value theory, how productivity increase via the accumulation of capital is experienced both as a boost to profitability in the form of lower production costs and as a threat to profitability in the form of more intensive competition for markets. For equilibrium analyses, these processes interact harmoniously and, subject to no upward adjustment in wages and rational choice by capitalists of least cost production techniques, must enhance profitability. In contrast to Marx's theory of the tendency of the rate of profit to fall, there is no attempt to understand how the forces generated by the accumulation of capital and productivity increase place enormous strains on the economic structures and processes of the value system, and the social formation within which it is embedded.

In this respect, Marx's value analysis is uniquely successful in the links that it forges between the theory of value and productivity *change*. Orthodox economics does not even address the issue and has always used equilibrium analysis with given technology, although value as price can change from one equilibrium to the next in a comparative statics for one set of given technologies as opposed to another. Ricardo did very little better, with value being determined in a similar way in industry but in a dynamic but relatively trivial way for the distinct theory of value used for agriculture. The value contributed by labor time on better lands increased simply by virtue of the use of other, possibly equivalent, labor on lands of worst quality.

Smith contributed a much more penetrating if chaotic understanding and can even be credited with having first addressed the issue of how to define value as productivity is changing. This was a consequence of his motivation to explain the wealth of nations in which he ultimately gave priority to the growing division of labor as a source of productivity increase. Within the context of his components theory of value, he argued that wages would be higher with the *growing*, and not the level of the, division of labor. It follows that price depends upon the pace of productivity increase. Although not in the context of the labor theory of value, this implies that Smith indirectly establishes an equivalence in the formation of price between technologies of the past and technologies of the present (through the wages, profits and rents that are the components of the raw materials, previously produced, but which are added as indirect costs to the direct cost components that make up current production). In doing so, he made the elementary error of overlooking that he cannot use the same wages, and so on, for the indirect costs as for the direct costs since he has already argued that the latter are amended by the growing division of labor.

In Fine (1982), I discuss these aspects of Smith's value theory in greater detail. What is remarkable is that he unconsciously poses the issue of how do previously produced materials enter into value when conditions of production are themselves changing? To my knowledge, only Marx has answered this question in a non-trivial sense, avoiding both comparative statics (i.e. a sequence of equilibria for each of which technology is given) and a simple neutrality in the improvement in productivity for which all prices decline in proportion. But Marx shifts the analytical terrain on which the issue is addressed. On the one hand, not surprisingly, the labor theory of value displaces the components theory. This, in itself, implies an acknowledgement that different labors, in different sectors, of different skills, exercised at different times with different levels of productivity are all brought into equivalence with one another through the system of commodity exchange (although these differences are often referred to as a rationale for rejecting the labor theory of value). On the other hand, the outcome is not tied to an equilibrium theory of natural prices but to the laws of development of capitalism as they are expressed through its relations, tendencies and structures. On the relatively rare occasion on which mainstream economics does address the sources of productivity increase, in the rapidly expanding and highly fashionable new or endogenous growth theory, it does so without benefit of value theory at all and proceeds as if the longstanding and accepted criticisms attached to the Cambridge Capital Controversy had never existed.[3]

Fifth, there is the historical aspect to Marx's value theory. As already observed, its applicability is limited to those societies in which there is the presence of commodity exchange that only attains its peak with capitalism. This is not only to justify the use of value as labor time on materialist grounds but also an acknowledgement that value is a social relation between producers whose interaction with one another is through the system of exchange in complex and potentially historically variable ways. These elementary historical and social insights should suffice to recognize that the labor theory of value is not adequate if based solely on the idea of value as a quantum of embodied labor. For then, of course, in a sense, we do not need to know anything about social relations at all in understanding value, as in its application to Smith's rude society, just as we do not need to know about other objects or substances if we want to know how much iron is embodied in a particular object. Of course, the notion of the labor theory as labor embodied has been seen by critics from mainstream economics as arbitrary and has led to parodies in terms of iron or energy theories of value.

From the historical to the contemporary

Once, however, value is seen as a relation that is historically and socially specific, then it is possible to recognize that value does itself change with the underlying socio-economic relations by which it is constituted. Interestingly, the historical specificity of value has been the focus of a debate – the so-called historical transformation problem. Here, the issue has been whether there was an early period of capitalism or even simple commodity production, as suggested by Engels, during which commodities exchanged at their values which was then followed by the situation of developed capitalism for which exchange at value no longer obtains. According to the argument offered here, as laid out in Fine (1986), this is an inappropriate way to view the historical transformation (see also Milonakis 1995). For rather than a given value exchanging at price in one historical instance and then at price of production at another instance, the nature of value itself is different according to whether it is attached, for example, to simple commodity as opposed to advanced capitalist production – a rather obvious point if value is seen as a relation of production through which labor time is represented in exchange. Both the nature of production relations themselves as well as the way in which they are integrated through exchange are entirely different.

Whilst such insights are what gives value theory its analytical strength, the issues concerned are otherwise seen as indicative of weakness. How can an economic theory based on labor embodied be appropriate both for simple commodity exchange and for advanced capitalism? And, of course, the answer is that it cannot, as Smith discovered two hundred years previously in erroneously confining his particular understanding of the labor theory of value to the rude society. Today social scientists and commentators tend to be too sophisticated to review Smith's arguments and are bedazzled by the increasingly complex economic and social developments that appear to reinforce the irrelevance of value theory.

In general, this has led to two broad responses. One is to rely upon empirical and descriptive analyses, which are relatively void of theoretical considerations. Where theory is involved, it tends to be simplistic, presuming a correspondence between correlation and causation, however many variables are statistically embroiled together. This implies an absence of relations, structures and tendencies – an analytical structure of concepts and causation – except in the sense of categoricism outlined above.

The other response is to be conceptually inventive but without consciously rooting such innovation within existing theoretical frameworks, and certainly not within that provided by value theory. The most obvious and relevant example of this is provided by the theory of post-Fordism, critically assessed in Fine (1995, 1998a), although it is now being supplemented by the idea of globalization. For each of these, value theory has ultimately been totally discarded although, as post-Fordism was initially given a Marxist gloss by Aglietta (1979), it only took a little time for it to gain its 'freedom' from value theory altogether. Consequently, standard concepts within Marxism, which were rooted theoretically in value theory and historically in the current phase of capitalism, have more or less disappeared without trace – notions such as imperialism and monopoly capitalism (with monopoly being seen as the form in which competition takes place rather than as its antithesis).

Such flights of fancy pale into insignificance when set against many of the offerings associated with post-modernism. Here, the critique of Marx's value theory, especially as it has evolved in the work of Baudrillard, concerns his neglect of the use value aspect of the commodity. It is wrongly argued that this is taken to constitute the physical properties of the commodity by Marx, and it is also suggested that in the social construction of use value, the meaning and significance of the commodity to the consumer is almost limitless. In contrast, it is imperative to recognize that the culture of consumption is a material culture, one that is deeply embedded in the relations and mechanisms through which those commodities are produced and eventually find their way into consumption. Value theory takes as one of its starting points that the commodity must constitute a social use value (otherwise it cannot be sold) and it must also be produced; far from precluding an incorporation of the role of the nature and meaning of the commodity, this is one of its most important determinants without which the role of other factors, including culture and subjectivity, become arbitrary. To put it bluntly for a moment, are we really to believe that the meaning of Coca-Cola, and the way that this meaning is purveyed through massive advertizing campaigns, is independent of the way in which Coca-Cola is itself produced, distributed and sold? In short, as has been argued in Fine and Leopold (1993), and Fine (2002a), an appropriate understanding of modern consumption depends upon developing and not rejecting value theory in the context of the social construction of the use value of the commodity in which this is not artificially detached, as in much post-modernist discourse, from the value relations by which we have commodities at all.

The task we face

The constructive rationale for the labor theory of value that has been outlined is well established through Marx's own work and also, equally, through the value theory debates that have continued. My own views are laid out in Fine (1986). In other publications, I have sought to develop and apply value theory in greater complexity, addressing issues such as privatization, the British coal industry, the British economy, women's employment, labor market structures and dynamics, the political economy and culture of consumption in general and of food in particular, the South African economy, and social capital (the last of these containing references to the other work, Fine 2001a). Throughout analysis has been rooted in fundamental principles derived from the labor theory of value, originality deriving from retaining elements of political economy that enable the reconstruction of value in more complex forms. Yet, at the outset, I suggested that the increasing complexity of capitalism simultaneously strengthens the case for the labor theory of value, to uncover underlying determinants, and strengthens the resolution of opponents in view of the apparent inconsistency of value with those complex outcomes. This means that the intellectual balance for and against is dependent upon the vigor, resolution and skill with which value theory is elaborated by its supporters, quite apart from the economic, political and ideological climate within which the debate is engaged. In the academic world, mainstream economics has rarely been stronger and has never been prepared to confront the labor theory of value on any terms other than as labor embodied in an equilibrium framework, for which rejection of value is the only possible outcome. Many supporters of value theory have been seduced by the associated arguments involved. This is despite ingenious analytical devices that draw piecemeal upon aspects of capitalist reality.

The most prominent in this vein is the new interpretation of the transformation problem. It suggests that the latter's problems can be resolved by treating the value of labor power as the wage revenue (with value equivalent) received *ex post* rather than as a quantity of *ex ante* labor time (attached to a 'subsistence' wage bundle). Without the space to provide details, Fine *et al.* (2001), the new solution suffers from collapsing the complex determinants of the value form (price) into a single step, thereby precluding appropriate consideration of intermediate factors and processes. Accordingly, its theories of money, the value of labor power, and the structures and dynamics of the capitalist economy (especially value formation in the presence of technical change) are both underdeveloped and insecurely founded within the value theory that is purportedly being defended. In effect, the new solution is merely a sociology of exploitation, using the labor theory of value (LTV) to establish that exploitation obtains whenever wages do not exhaust total revenue. This exercise is both limited in importance and scarcely needs value theory in any case – profits as evidence of exploitation is clear to all who care to see.

In light of the new interpretation and the more general commentary above, the prospects for value theory from a radical tradition within economics have rarely seemed bleaker. But, as first argued in Fine (1997), with Fine (2002a) referencing subsequent work, economics is currently going through what might prove to be a change as profound as that of over a century ago, the marginalist revolution, which established the discipline as we know it today. This involved a retreat and separation of economics from the other social sciences because of dependence upon methodological individualism, equilibrium and the isolation of the economy from society more generally. Now, orthodox economics is attempting, on the very same theoretical basis, to colonize the other social sciences suggesting that it can explain institutions, collective agencies, economic development and political outcomes, and so on.

This is a result of its own internal developments, deriving from information-theoretic economics, in which the market and non-market, the individual and the social, are all seen as reducible to optimizing in response to market (informational) imperfections. How the other social sciences respond is vital not only for value theory, possibly the most important element with which to defend properly constituted social theory against the incursions of economics imperialism, but for the very health of those disciplines. These have always been much more open to serious treatment and acceptance of value theory (and Marxism). This is especially so when seeking to cross the artificial boundaries dividing the academic disciplines and confront economic issues in the form of political economy rather than on the basis of the esoteric and blatantly unreasonable assumptions that are so characteristic of orthodox economics. In addition, in complete contrast to mainstream economics, Marxism itself is also treated seriously as an alternative in itself and as a source of insight for non-Marxist analysis. Also currently, the intellectual environment is one of the uneven retreats across the social sciences from the excesses of both neo-liberalism and post-modernism. There is a wish for greater material content to analysis – a return to the real not least in the warmth with which the nebulous notions of 'globalization' and social capital have been embraced (Fine 2002b). The prospect is for social sciences other than economics to prove an intellectual battleground in examining the economics. Given the traditional, and warranted, antipathy of social sciences toward mainstream economics, the potential for reviving commitment to the labor theory of value is strong. But it has to be won and cannot be taken for granted.

Notes

This chapter draws on Fine (1998c, 2001b). It was presented to the Conference of Marxist Economists, Beijing, April 2002, Renmin University. Thanks to Costas

Lapavitsas, Alfredo Saad-Filho and others for extensive comments and suggestions on an earlier draft.

1. Concerning questions of theoretical approach, see for example, among others, Aglietta (1979), Dobb (1940), Elson (1979a), Fine (1986), Fine and Harris (1979), Fine *et al.* (2001), Foley (1986), Lebowitz (1992), Lee (1993), Meek (1956), Rosdolsky (1977), Rubin (1972), Saad-Filho (2002), Steedman (1977), Steedman *et al.* (1981), Sweezy (1970), and Weeks (1981). For discussions focusing on money, see de Brunhoff (1976), Arnon (1984) and Itoh and Lapavitsas (1998). For views on Marx's method, see Colletti (1973), Ilyenkov (1982), Moseley (1993a), Oakley (1983, 1984, 1985), Pilling (1980), Reuten and Williams (1989), and Shamsavari (1991).
2. See Fine (1982).
3. See Fine (1980, 2000), Harcourt (1976), and Hodgson (1997) for critical exposition.

Part II

Money, Finance and Competition

2

The Rationality and Irrationality of Money

Simon Clarke

Money is the supreme social fact of modern society. For good and for ill, money is both the symbol and the substance of wealth and power. The movements of money constrain and undermine national governments and daily determine the fate of billions of people. The privileges of the few and the want of the many are determined by their respective possession and their lack of money. Yet where are we to find the social theory of money? How does money acquire its social power? By what social laws is the exercise of that power determined? Is money a beneficent or a malignant force? It would seem that the anonymity of the power of money has rendered it invisible to social theory.

The theology of money: the classical tradition

The so-called 'primitive' societies attach mystical powers to gifts and tokens. But this is nothing compared to the fantastic powers attributed to money in our own society. While the former have been exhaustively analyzed by anthropologists, social scientists have very largely been content to leave the powers of money unexplained. In the true traditions of a Christian 'civilization,' faith is sufficient ground for attesting that a supernatural power that has created global devastation is, nevertheless, a force for good. The cult of money is truly Dr Pangloss's revenge.

We might expect to find an explanation of the social powers of money in the works of the theologians of the cult – the economists. However, surprizing as it may seem, the economists have almost nothing to tell us on this matter. For the economists money is simply an instrument, a rational means through which the 'hidden hand' realizes its beneficent mission. Economists since Adam Smith have progressively elaborated their systematic models which establish the instrumental rationality of money within the capitalist economic system, insulated from the reality of a world within which money is not merely a means, but has become the central end of social existence.

The dominant conception of money dates back at least to Aristotle, who explained the emergence of money in terms of the inconvenience of barter, defining the primary function of money as its role as *means of exchange*, but recognizing also its derivative functions as the *measure of value* and, at least implicitly, also as a *store of value*. Various theories since Aristotle have differed mainly in the hierarchical relationship they establish between the different functions of money, setting those who follow Aristotle in seeing the function of means of exchange as being primary against those who have attributed primacy to other functions, most notably the function of store of value. This has by no means been a purely academic debate, for the different views have profound political and policy implications: If the primary function of money is means of exchange, an increase in the quantity of money will lead only to rising prices. If the primary function of money is a store of value, an increase in the quantity of money will lead to falling interest rates and increasing economic activity. The orthodox view of money is therefore connected with the quantity theory of money and monetary conservatism. Unorthodox views of money are connected with the various heresies that have littered the pages of monetary history: mercantilism, bullionism, free credit, bimetalism, Keynesianism.

These different views of money have been intimately connected with different views of the relation between money and the state in the regulation of the social reproduction of the system of social labor. Money and the state represent complementary forms of social regulation, but the critical question is, what should be the relation between them? Should state regulation be confined within the limits of money? Or should the rule of money be confined within limits dictated by the state?

These are theoretical questions that have been debated since the dawn of capitalism. The debate between the two positions has ebbed and flowed, and there has even been some theoretical advance in the rigor and sophistication within which the two positions have been formulated, but the debate has never been resolved. The balance between the two positions alters over time in a more or less regular cyclical process. At the peak of the cycle one or the other position is in the ascendant, the alternative being regarded as an untenable heresy which is propounded by cranks and extremists. In periods of transition, there is much talk of a 'third way,' which offers an appropriate balance between the two extremes, and the pendulum begins to swing back.

This is a debate that takes place within theory, but the balance of theoretical forces is not determined by any intellectual considerations but by the development of the class struggle, above all by the extent to which the state is politically compelled to moderate the claims of capital in order to accommodate the aspirations of the mass of the population. This is not to say that the intellectuals engaged in the debate are the self-conscious lackeys of the capitalist (or even the working) class. There will always be true believers on both sides of the debate, but the weight of conviction (and publication and academic appointment) will fall on the side that conforms most closely to the demands of political realism because it conforms to the realm of immediate political possibility. To be a Hayekian in the 1960s was to plow as lonely a furrow as to be a Keynesian in the 1980s. To propose a 'third way' in the 1980s was to make yourself as much the object of ridicule as it is to endorse 'monetarism' today. Although the debate is renewed every decade, the terms, and the limitations, of the debate have not changed for the past two centuries. To identify these terms and limitations it is worth going back to the beginning of the modern debate.

Adam Smith and the modern theory of money

Adam Smith, following his friend David Hume, laid the foundations of modern economics by reasserting the Aristotelian orthodoxy against the mercantilist heresy, which saw the primary function of money in its role as store of value and favored state policies oriented to the accumulation of a monetary hoard. Smith was concerned to demolish the mercantilist myth that money was an end, that the accumulation of wealth could be identified with the accumulation of money, and to establish instead the instrumental rationality of money as a mere means to the superior end of enhancing the material prosperity of the nation. For Smith 'it is not for its own sake that men desire money, but for the sake of what they can purchase with it' (Smith 1976 Vol. 1: 385), so that the accumulation of money, far from contributing to the prosperity of the nation, constitutes a drain on the national revenue. According to Smith, the mercantilist prejudice arose as a sophistical argument devised by the merchants to further their own self-interest by falsely identifying it with the national interest. The system of monopoly that hoisted their profits restrained trade and so limited the development of the productive forces of society.

There are two dimensions to Smith's critique of mercantilism. On the one hand, Smith argued that money had no value in itself: money is just a commodity like any other. The value of money lies in the fact that it is the product of labor and in the fact that, like any other desirable commodity, its possession bestows the power of command over labor. On the other hand, for Smith this implies that the possession and accumulation of money is irrational. The accumulation of money involves the expenditure of a considerable amount of labor in order to acquire a reserve of the money commodity, but the power of command over labor, that is the only reason for acquiring money, can only be realized by disbursing the money that has been acquired. The only purpose of acquiring money is to spend it. Money is therefore only the mediating term in relations of exchange between individual actors, its rationality is purely instrumental.

Smith's argument rested on a proposition that has marked all subsequent economic theory, but that is fundamentally erroneous. It is his assertion that 'consumption is the sole end and purpose of all production,' a maxim that he claimed 'is so perfectly self-evident that it would be absurd to attempt to prove it' (Smith 1976 Vol. 2: 155). Thus the instrumentality of money is simply asserted. Yet the belief that money is an end is not simply a mercantilist prejudice, it is of the very essence of the reality of capitalist society. If money were desired only as a means to the acquisition of consumption goods the appetite of the capitalist for profit would be limited by his consumption needs. Yet the very dynamism of capitalist accumulation, on which the justification of the capitalist system rests, depends precisely on the insatiability of the appetite of the capitalist for money not as a means, but as an end in itself, as the means to, and expression of, social power. The great merit of the mercantile system was that it recognized this uncomfortable fact. Smith can only smuggle in his 'self-evident' maxim by presenting an evaluative proposition as though it were an empirical one. Indeed it is self-evident that economic activity should be subordinated to the consumption needs of society. Yet it is just as self-evident that this proposition is violated not simply by the mercantile system, but by the existence of capitalism itself, with the deleterious consequences of which Smith was well aware.

However, if money is not an end in itself, but is merely a means of exchanging one thing for another, the powers attributed to money are not inherent in money, but derive from its function as a means of exchange. The rationality of money is the rationality of the system of exchange whose development it facilitates. Money is the means by which the hidden hand of the market achieves its ends.

Smith regarded the development of the market as the result of the propensity in human nature 'to truck, barter and exchange one thing for another' (Smith 1976 Vol. 1: 12), a propensity rooted in the faculty of reason. The virtue of exchange was that it made it possible for each producer to specialize according to his or her talents and so stimulated the advance of the division of labor, of productivity, and so of economic prosperity. As far as the individual economic actor was concerned, each could make free judgments of the gains to be made from any particular exchange, gains rooted in the increased productivity permitted by specialization, and so could decide whether or not to exchange accordingly. So long as the market is free, and property and the person are secure, each individual exchange that takes place will contribute to an increase in individual and social prosperity. On the other hand, any political or institutional barriers to the freedom of exchange will prevent advantageous exchanges from taking place, and so will reduce the national wealth, even if they work to the advantage of particular individuals. These are the general principles according to which economists have justified the rule of the market ever since the days of

Smith. The general conclusion is that free competition allows the individual to be the best judge of his or her own economic interests and provides the opportunity to each to act accordingly. Since every agent is free to decide whether or not to make an exchange, and will choose not to do so if he or she judges the exchange disadvantageous, nobody can suffer loss as a result of exchange. Since both parties gain from each and every exchange, the system of exchange must work to the benefit of all.

Smith established the self-evident rationality of exchange on the basis of a parable concerning barter in a simple hunter–gatherer society. If Smith's little parable is to have any relevance to a capitalist society, it is necessary to establish that the introduction of money and of capital does not affect the results of the analysis, so that a capitalist society can be understood on the basis of this simple model of a barter economy. This Smith achieved, firstly, by arguing that money is simply an instrument of accounting and exchange that has no substantive economic significance. Smith's argument again has provided the essential framework within which economists have discussed money ever since. The form of his argument is equally paradigmatic: he devised a homely parable within which the instrumental rationality of money is established as self-evident, and rests his case on the extension of the argument by analogy to the capitalist system.

With the development of exchange the inherent limitations of barter meant that 'this power of exchanging must frequently have been very much clogged and embarrassed in its operations... In order to avoid the inconveniency of such situations, every prudent man in every period of society, after the first establishment of the division of labour, must naturally have endeavoured to manage his affairs in such a manner as to have at all times by him, besides the peculiar produce of his own industry, a certain quantity of some one commodity or another, such as he imagined few people would be likely to refuse in exchange for the produce of their own industry' (Smith 1976 Vol. 1: 20). We can all appreciate the inconvenience of barter, so the rationality of money is clear to all of us. Money simply provides a means of exchange that enables the barter economy to work more efficiently. We can now sell our bows and arrows for money, and use the money to buy venison, rather than having to find a venison-owner who happens to need a new bow and arrow. The introduction of money makes no difference to our simple barter model.

But what happens if we cannot find a buyer for our product? Perhaps nobody wants a bow and arrow? Then we have simply misjudged the needs of others, and misread the market. We will have to find some other specialization that meets others' needs. Perhaps somebody else is better than us at making bows and arrows, so that we have to demand less venison in return? Then our reduced reward simply corresponds to our own incompetence and if we are dissatisfied we should improve our skills, find a new vocation, or hunt our own venison. We cannot blame the market for our own failings.

But perhaps we are highly skilled, and our bows and arrows are much needed, but nobody has any money to buy them? Would this surely indicate a failure of the market economy to meet human needs? It would indeed, but in Smith's ideal world it could not happen. This becomes clear once we examine the implications of Smith's conception of money as serving merely as a means of exchange.

For Adam Smith, there is no reason for wanting to hold money in itself since 'it is not for its own sake that men desire money, but for the sake of what they can purchase with it' (Smith 1976 Vol. 1: 385). This proposition rests on Smith's 'self-evident' but absurd claim that 'consumption is the sole end and purpose of all production.'

The implication of this 'self-evident' maxim, which was drawn out by Smith's French popularizer J.-B. Say, is that the money economy continues to work just like a barter economy. Since nobody has any reason to hold money, but merely seeks money in order to purchase some other commodity, every sale will be matched by a corresponding purchase as the seller immediately disposes of the money acquired in the sale by buying some other commodity. Thus the introduction of money cannot introduce any barriers to exchange, it simply avoids the inconvenience of barter. If a seller is unable to find a buyer it can only be because he or she is asking too high a price. The commodity is not sold simply because the buyer chooses not to sell it at a price which reflects the evaluation of its worth by potential buyers. So long as buyers and sellers are prepared to adjust their prices in response to changing market conditions, reflecting changes in the conditions of production and in the needs of consumers, the action of supply and demand insures that full employment will be maintained. The operation of the market insures that the system is self-regulating.

Smith, as later economists, was well aware that money did not always function as effectively as he might have hoped. However, the limitations of money are in no way inherent in money itself as a social phenomenon. They arise from human venality and human ignorance that prevent us from living up to the standards set by this apotheosis of rationality. Thus for Smith, it is the greed of the merchants, the ignorance of the laboring classes, and the indolence of the landed class that gives rise to the abuses that make money into an end of state policy that restricts the growth of the wealth of the nation.

The classical theory of the market describes a world of freedom of choice and equality of opportunity, marred only by the attempts of the rich and powerful to abuse their command of the power of the state to secure their own gain. Money is the rational instrument by which the hidden hand of the market asserts itself, and so provides the adequate means of social regulation of economic activity. The proper role of the state is to preserve the freedom and security of property and to defend the integrity of the currency on which the smooth functioning of the market depends.

Money and manufacture: money, capital and the state

We should not forget that Smith wrote as a radical critic of the *ancien régime*, the target of his attack being the apparently monolithic configuration of the absolutist state that united the power of the sovereign, the privilege of the landed aristocracy and the wealth of the great merchants. Smith was the model of a disinterested intellectual, although in his work he appealed to the interests of an emerging class, represented by tenant farmers, small merchants, manufacturers and artisans, which was developing a consciousness of its own independent interest, in opposition to the system of privilege and monopoly that Smith condemned. However, Smith had no expectation that his views would have any political impact because he believed that the weight of vested interest that he confronted was so strong while the class to which he appealed had insufficient understanding of its own interest.

Yet Smith had overestimated the strength of the system. While it may have appeared invincible in the metropolitan heartland, it was a global system and it was on the periphery that its fate was sealed. Ironically, the turning point was the rebellion of the American colonists in 1776, the year that Smith's *Wealth of Nations* was published, followed by the French Revolution thirteen years later. These two revolutions in turn precipitated the disintegration of the established political order in England. It was trade and money that had eroded the old order, and money and trade were the pillars on which the new order was constructed. This dramatic political reconfiguration had equally dramatic intellectual consequences. Within two decades, Smith's theories had been transformed from a radical critique of an old regime that had confined money and trade within the limits of political power into the defense of a new regime that sought to confine political power within the limits of money and trade, the apostle of the new system being the stockbroker, David Ricardo.

The collapse of the old regime, and the freeing of trade and banking from political restraint was associated with a succession of economic booms, but each boom was soon followed by a destructive slump. Moreover, while merchants and bankers profited in the booms, it tended to be the workers and the manufacturers who were the principal victims of the slumps. These fluctuations, therefore, precipitated conflict between the manufacturing and banking interests, each appealing to the state to regulate the issue of money in accordance with the interests of its own estate, which, of course, each represented as the general interest. It should not be surprising to find, therefore, that the theory of money was once again the focus of the class struggle in social theory. The outcome of this struggle over the theory of money defined the contours of modern social theory, yet it is another blind spot in social theory's consciousness of its own foundations.

The currency issue was the central focus of the class struggle in social theory throughout the first half of the nineteenth century. The key issue in this phase of the struggle was that of the relation between money, capital and the state, and the struggle focused on the question of control of the quantity of money. The bankers accumulated great fortunes by lending money at interest and by speculating in commercial and financial ventures. The manufacturers depended directly and indirectly on the bankers to provide them with the credit they needed to carry on their business, particularly when they were buying and selling on distant markets. When trade was flourishing, the bankers would make credit freely available and manufacture could expand in the wake of, and even in anticipation of, the expansion of demand. The growth of manufacture led to a growing demand for hands, so that both waged workers and independent artisans could prosper. At such times it appeared that all the promise of Smith's vision was being realized. However, such booms were never sustained for long. At a certain point there would be a series of commercial and financial failures, as a result of which stocks of unsold goods would accumulate.

Just at the point at which the resumption of normal trade called for an easing of the terms of credit to enable manufactures to maintain production and their buyers to buy their products, the bankers would turn on the screws, restrict the supply of money and raise the rate of interest. To the manufacturers it was evident that their misfortune was the direct result of the bankers' abuse of their monopolistic control of money and the solution for the banks was to provide enough money to meet the legitimate needs of trade. The currency reformers therefore came forward with various schemes that would insure that money was always put at the service of production and of trade. Such schemes ranged from demands for free banking, through bimetalism and land banks to labor currencies. What all of these schemes had in common was that their viability depended on the state taking control, directly or indirectly, of the issue of money in order to insure that the quantity of money was regulated in accordance with the general interest of society. Against such schemes, liberal orthodoxy came to be represented by the currency theorists, who argued that it was precisely money, not the state, that embodied the general interest of society, so that the economic activity of society and of the state should equally be subordinated to the constraints imposed by the natural limitation of the supply of money. Just what was this natural limitation was a rather more complicated question, the simplest answer (politically at least) being that it was the supply of gold, so the 1844 Bank Act in England supposedly restricted the issue of the currency in accordance with the reserves of gold held at the Bank. This meant that the terms of credit throughout the economy were determined neither by the political decisions of government nor by the self-interested decisions of bankers but in accordance with the inflow and outflow of bullion to and from the reserves.

The currency theorists won the battle hands down. However, although their opponents are remembered nowadays only as monetary cranks, the battle was not won in social theory but by the outcome of the class struggle in the real world as both manufacture and banking came to be subordinated to the expanded reproduction of capital, the manufacturers settled their differences with their bankers and new lines of class division emerged, between the employers and their employees. In England the victory of the currency theorists was associated not only with the 1844 Bank Act, but also with the repeal of the Corn Laws, the passage of the Factory Acts and the defeat of Chartism, which were followed by the mid-Victorian boom. More equivocal victories were achieved in Continental Europe and the United States with the political settlements following the revolutions of 1848, the American Civil War and the Franco–Prussian War, which similarly laid the foundations for the relatively sustained growth of prosperity of the turn of the century. Divisions within the capitalist class were no longer between its financial and industrial wings but were increasingly drawn along national lines, with manufacturers seeking to articulate a common interest with 'their' workers not on the line of opposition to the bankers but on a national basis. The power of the state was not to be directed to the control of money but to the aggrandizement of national capital by traditional mercantilist means. The wheel had come full circle.

The critique of money and the challenge of the working class

The liberal theory of money emerged triumphant within the realm of economic theory as an expression of the triumph of capital over its concrete forms of existence, as finance and manufacture were subordinated to the expanded reproduction of capital. The political opposition to liberal orthodoxy no longer came from dissident elements within the capitalist camp, but increasingly from those whose labor-power was commanded by the power of capital. The various schemes of utopian co-operativism began as schemes to contest the power of bankers, but soon developed into schemes to contest the power of capital. It was not the bankers who were extorting profit from the honest manufacturer by imposing unnatural rates of interest on their loans; it was the manufacturer who was exploiting his laborers by paying them less than the value of their labor-power. The labor theory of value, which had been developed within economic theory to articulate the interests of the manufacturers against the parasitic commercial, landowning and banking interests, was now given a radical twist, expressing the interests of labor in opposition to capital as a whole.

The focus of this new radicalism was, of course, the theory of money. All of the evils to which modern society was subject were evils that derived from the unfettered tyranny of money. The early utopians took many of their ideas from currency cranks and from romantic conservative critics of capitalism, but they soon came to develop specifically socialist perspectives which drew on the experience of the workers who were being herded into the new factories, schemes which drew on the contrast between the co-operation that was a feature of socialized production and the anarchy that was the distinguishing characteristic of the market, their proposed solutions moving on from currency reform to schemes for the centralized regulation of production and trade. This critique came to focus on the relation between money and the state in the regulation of social production, so its realization required access to political power. Thus it was closely associated with the democratic political struggles that reached their peak in the 1840s. It was through these struggles, and particularly through the defeat of Chartism and then of the revolutions of 1848, that the class character of the opposition to capitalism became more clearly defined.

At this stage in the development of the class struggle, of course, a clarification of the lines of class division implied the marginalization of the industrial working class, which even in England still comprised only a minority of the population. Moreover, most of the working class was unorganized, so the social base of the radical critique of capitalism developed in the 1840s was not so much the factory operatives as the skilled workers seeking to defend the integrity of their trades, many of whose skills were being displaced by the advance of the factory system. The defeat of Chartism and of the Revolutions of 1848, therefore, marked the end of this phase of the class struggle in social theory and the apparently definitive triumph of the capitalist class, which could turn its attention to extending the intellectual and material rule of capital across the face of the globe.

However, the struggles of the 1840s left a theoretical legacy in revealing the need for a critique of money that saw money not just as a means by which the bankers exploited the manufacturers, but as an articulation of the social power of capital. This critique had been developed in the 1840s in fragmentary form, particularly by the Owenites in England, the Proudhonists in France and the True Socialists in Germany. The three rather different versions of the critique were synthesized and advanced by Dr Karl Marx, of Trier, and his friend Dr Friedrich Engels, a Manchester cotton manufacturer. Marx, in particular, devoted most of his life to developing the critique of money and of liberal monetary theory, which he eventually published in his *Critique of Political Economy*, a text which he rewrote half a dozen times but never completed. I will just draw out the main points of this critique.

The focus of Marx's critique was Smith's simple model of a barter economy within which independent petty producers exchange their own products and in which money is a pure instrument, with no substantive effects. Marx argued that Smith's account ignores the social relations within which production takes place and which are the presupposition of any individual act of exchange. Even Smith's simple model rests on the existence of particular social relations that limit the freedom of choice of those involved in the system of exchange, even before they enter any particular exchange relations. Once committed to the division of labor, the petty producers are already committed to producing not for their own needs, but for the needs of others, expressed to them through the market in the form of the money that they obtain in exchange for their product. They can command the labor of others in order to meet their own needs and satisfy their own desires only to the extent that they can sell their products in the market in order to secure the money to buy their own means of consumption, and the raw materials and tools required for further production. They no longer have any choice about whether or not to engage in exchange, but merely as to the terms on which they exchange their products. The propensity to 'truck, barter and exchange' is no longer a natural propensity, but one imposed by the social relations of production. Money is now a social power that defines both the opportunities and the limits that confront every member of a commodity-producing society. Before I have sold my product, I can dream of unlimited possibilities. Once I confront the harsh reality of the market, I may find myself fearing for my very survival.

The specialist in making bows and arrows cannot eat those bows and arrows if they cannot be sold. While conditions are favorable, the market appears to the bow and arrow maker as a munificent opportunity. But, if conditions change for the worse, the market appears as a coercive force, appearing in the form of the pressing need for money. Thus money is no longer simply a means of exchange, it has become a social power which regulates social production, rewarding those who can meet its demands, but penalizing those who do not live up to its standards. Production is no longer oriented to need, but to money, and so is regulated according to the imperatives of the market imposed by money.

With the development of the market, not merely as the forum in which occasional surpluses are exchanged, but as the framework within which the interdependence of producers within a division of labor is regulated, the market becomes not merely a convenience, but a system of social relations. Producers can only survive by submitting themselves regularly to the judgment of the market, which evaluates the social worth of their labors. The market thus becomes both a material and a moral force, imposing its own morality through its system of punishment and reward. It is this morality that is expressed through the social power of money, which is the form in which the social evaluation of the market is expressed and in which its rewards are distributed.

In a capitalist society exchange no longer relates petty producers to one another. Rather it expresses the social relations of production within and between the capitalist class and the working class. But the division of labor between capitalists and workers cannot be assimilated to the division of labor between different talents. What distinguishes capitalist and worker is not a distinction of talent but a distinction of means. Those petty producers who are successful may be able to accumulate money wealth beyond their immediate consumption needs, but those who fail have a pressing demand for money to subsist. Smith regards this polarization as a reflection of the moral differentiation of humanity between the frugal and hard working, who are able to save, and the idle and dissolute, who fall into dependence. However, the success of one and the failure of the other is not an expression of a moral distinction, it is inscribed in the monetary regulation of their co-operation: success and failure may not be due to any fault or virtue of either party, nor to any circumstance that either could have foreseen. But, having failed, the loser falls under the sway of the more fortunate, mortgaging their possessions, falling into debt, and, losing their own means of production, being forced to work for someone who has the money to provide for their subsistence in exchange for the application of their labor-power. Money, from being a means of exchange and an immobile store of value, has imperceptibly turned into capital: value in motion, money with the miraculous power of expanding its own value.

As capital, money provides not only command over the products of the labor of others, it provides command over their labor, or, more precisely, their labor-power. The exchange economy is no longer based on free and equal petty producers, it is based on a fundamental inequality, on a class division between those who have nothing left to sell but their labor-power and those who have the money to command that labor-power. Since the latter have no interest in buying labor-power unless they can profit by it, the price paid for labor-power must be less than the price the capitalist anticipates receiving for its product, the difference constituting the profit of the capitalist, a profit which constantly provides him with the means to expand the capital at his disposal. A growing capital enables the capitalist to enlarge the scale of production, to revolutionize the methods of production, to increase his profit, and to drive out all the inefficient petty producers who remain. The capitalist has no choice in this, for the need constantly to expand his capital and to transform the methods of production is imposed on him by the forces of competition. Thus the system is marked by a growth of capital, on the one side, and a growth of the working class on the other.

None of this development is the result of free choice, it represents the working out of the logic of the market economy as money becomes capital, a logic imposed on capitalist and worker alike through the pressure of competition expressed in the power of money. Those who enter exchange do not do so of their own free will; they are compelled to exchange in order to survive, as capitalist or as worker. Once the fateful decision is made to enter the market economy, a decision that is not, as Smith shows, necessarily an irrational one (though, as Marx showed, it is most often initiated by the forcible expropriation of the mass of the population), the logic of the market and the power of money takes over. The market is no longer simply a means and money simply an instrument of exchange. The market and money become the means by which particular social relations are reproduced and developed. Thus the rationality of the market cannot be divorced from the rationality of those social relations.

Once money exists as capital, as we have seen, it ceases to be primarily a means of exchange, and the circulation of money is dominated by its circulation as capital. While in Smith's model there appears no reason to hold money in an idle hoard, since money is acquired only to secure the means of consumption, this ceases to be the case once money serves as capital. The capitalist is seeking not means of consumption, but opportunities for profit so as to enlarge his capital. His aim is to accumulate an ever-greater hoard of money wealth, and he throws his money into circulation only in order to enlarge that hoard. If for any reason the opportunities for profit are closed off, the capitalist will not throw his money into circulation, but will accumulate it in an idle hoard, so interrupting circulation and precipitating a crisis as stocks of goods are unsold and the circulation of capital is further restricted. Thus, with the rise of capital, a commercial crisis ceases to be an impossibility and becomes the normal reaction to any threat to prospects of profitable investment: Say's law of markets ceases to hold. With the rise of capital the circulation of money is not subordinated to the requirements of exchange, rather the possibility of exchange is subordinated to the demands of the expansion of money as capital. The rise of capital is the culmination of the inversion from money being a rational means to satisfying social needs to the satisfaction of social need being subordinated to the power of money. The rule of the market, the power of money, is the power of money as capital. Far from being the beneficent means to the realization of human ends, money is an autonomous social power, the expression, and means of realization, of the subordination of all human needs to the needs of capital, to the capitalist thirst for profit.

Marx's critique of political economy showed that the evils of capitalism are inseparable from its benefits. The polarization of wealth and poverty, overabundance and want, overwork and unemployment, boom and slump, freedom and tyranny are all inherent in the contradictory dynamics of capital accumulation expressed in the subordination of social production to the power of money. In particular, and this was the principal political focus of Marx's critique, it showed that the schemes of the various currency reformers, foremost amongst whom were the Proudhonists, could not overcome the contradictions of capitalism but would only displace them into the political sphere. The contradictions of capitalism could only be overcome by overthrowing capitalism and, in particular, the subordination of social labor to the rule of capital in the form of money.

Money and the state in the world economy today

I will not follow the twists and turns of liberal monetary theory over the past two centuries, which have added technical sophistication but nothing of substance to Smith's account, nor will I discuss the neutralization of the implications of the 'Keynesian Revolution' by the 'neo-classical synthesis' (for a detailed discussion see Clarke 1988), but Marx's critique of liberal monetary theory is as valid today as it was when it was first written. Although capitalism long left the gold standard behind, and the dollar has lost its pre-eminence, the state today is as effectively confined within the limits of capital by the movements of world money as it has ever been. The renewed integration of the world capitalist economy in the past fifty years, after its fragmentation through revolutions, wars and depression in the first half of the twentieth century, has led to the close integration of all but a handful of national economies into the circulation of global capital, and so confined their governments within limits set by that circulation.

On the one hand, governments are subject to political and electoral pressures to maintain the growth of incomes and employment, which can only be achieved by fostering the expansion of the activity of capital on the national territory. This implies in turn the provision of a secure and favorable social, labor, legal, fiscal and monetary environment for capitalist activity on that territory and the freedom of capital, whether in the form of money or commodities, to cross the national frontiers. On the other hand, the state's own activity is directly subordinated to the expanded reproduction of capital, since its income and expenditure are only moments within that reproduction. These latter pressures are imposed on the state economically in the form of the requirement that it finances its expenditure by means that are, or at least are perceived as being, relatively non-inflationary, and politically through the reluctance of the majority of the employed population to pay increased taxes.

These constraints on national governments are by no means absolute. They are determined by and they express the accumulation of capital and the development of the class struggle on a global scale. In the middle of the last century, postwar reconstruction was boosted by the Korean War and the boom was sustained through the 1950s by the liberalization of international trade and payments as national government sought to benefit from the boom by securing the closer integration of their national economies into the circulation of global capital. In this period, global capital presented national governments with opportunities rather than constraints. As the momentum of the postwar boom began to falter and class struggle intensified in the metropolitan capitalist centers, the emphasis in the 1960s at the national level moved toward Keynesian interventionism, increasing state expenditure in the attempt to maintain full-employment. Although such measures tended to stimulate inflation, while having a limited impact on the real economy, individual states retained a considerable degree of latitude during the late 1960s and early 1970s, because the global economic climate, stimulated by US expenditure on the Vietnam War, was inflationary. The aftermath of the 1974 oil price shock marked the turning point of the class struggle on a global scale. National governments sought to reverse the gains made by labor in the postwar decades, reinforcing the attempts of capital to confine labor within the limits of the valorization of capital by pursuing deflationary policies. Moreover, where capital had confronted the organized working class through the immediate postwar decades, from the 1970s it increasingly sought to by-pass the organized working class, fragmenting the labor force by transferring production facilities and employing unorganized workers. As a result, the balance of political, financial and fiscal pressures on the state shifted quite radically in favor of a reduction of state expenditure and an increasingly strict subordination of state intervention to the power of capital in its money form.

Accumulation on a world scale was sustained through the last two decades of the century not by government expenditure and military escapades but by the mobilization of the reserve army of labor on a global scale and the inflation of private credit, which stimulated the increasingly speculative over-accumulation of capital toward the end of the century. The collapse of a succession of speculative bubbles at the end of the century generalized and intensified the deflationary pressures in the world economy, imposing renewed pressure on individual capitals to reduce wages and intensify labor, while further restricting the freedom of maneuver of national governments that sought to restore the conditions of accumulation within their national economies. Capital and the state continued to seek to resolve their crises at the expense of the working class, removing restrictions on the freedom of capital to fragment the labor force, intensify labor and reduce wages in the name of a more 'flexible' labor market.

Through the 1960s to the 1980s the organized working class had largely sought to use its existing strength in the vain attempt to retain its relatively privileged position in national and global labor markets. However, such a narrow strategy merely weakened and divided the organized working class at national and international levels. As Marx had anticipated in the *Communist Manifesto,* this experience brought home to the leadership of the labor movement the need to adopt broader organizing strategies and to bring the unorganized into the national and international labor movements to build the basis on which the working class could pursue solidaristic rather than exclusionary strategies in the face of capital. Of course, this rebuilding of the labor movement is a long-drawn-out and uneven process, but every small step forward, however partial and localized, contributes to the strengthening of organized labor on a global scale and so to the capacity of labor to constitute itself as the subject, and not merely the object, of social regulation.

3
Value, Finance and Social Classes

Suzanne de Brunhoff

In the period from 1980 to 2000, it was finance, not productive capital and labor, that appeared all-powerful in the capitalist world. However, in order to analyze the role finance really plays in capitalism, we have to study its economic roots. How is it that people can make money from money? Which social groups are becoming wealthy in this manner? We need a theory of value not only to formulate proper answers to these questions, but even to ask them without falling prey to ideological traps.

This chapter therefore begins by focusing on the way in which different theories of value introduce the concept of money into the study of capitalism (see section 'Value, monetary prices and money-capital'). It illustrates how the labor value theory paves the way for analyses of capital materialized in a monetary form (hereafter referred to as money-capital) and of capitalist finance. This is a necessary albeit insufficient precondition for studying the relationships between the two main categories of capitalists involved in accumulation: financiers and entrepreneurs (see section 'Entrepreneurs and financiers'). We then demonstrate the way in which monetary policy since the 1980s has impacted the changing balance of power between capital and labor (see section 'Monetary policy'). Finally, the effects of these changes on the position of the working class will be examined (see section 'Inequalities and social classes').

Value, monetary prices and money-capital

Regardless of whether a given economic theory focuses on utility or on labor (or has transcended this conundrum in one way or the other), all theories find that their particular conception of value struggles to account for the phenomenon of monetary pricing. To demonstrate this, we will first look at neo-classical theory, and then at Keynesian theory, before ultimately showing how a Marxian conception has made it possible to establish a link between money-capital and productive capital.

Neo-classical theory

Neo-classical theory offers no theory of money or nominal prices. As K.J. Arrow writes, according to this theory, 'rational individuals are interested in the commodities they can exchange and produce. The motives are measured in "real" terms (in terms of goods), not in "nominal" terms (values expressed in money)' (Arrow 1981: 139). What is important here is the market price equilibrium for 'real' transactions of goods and services, regardless of the variation in monetary prices and/or economic imbalances that can result.

The theory of utility-value makes no provision whatsoever for decentralized market transactions of goods and services carried out with money that has been 'properly' centralized. Instead it resorts to a substitute for one of the functions of money, that is, it apprehends money in its 'numeraire' form (as Walras calls it). In this conception, one of the n goods that are traded in a given economy is simply chosen to be a unit of accounting for all of the $n-1$ other goods. However, this 'numeraire' cannot be used concretely in decentralized exchanges between individuals.

One way out of this dead end would appear to be a quantitative theory of the supply of money, that is, a theory that refers to the centralized issuance of fiduciary money by the State. To preserve the primacy of utility-value as well as rational individual choices in such a theory, individual demand for cash holdings (as opposed to an exogenous supply of money) is introduced. This is another dead end, however, since we end up with the truism that if the State issues twice as much money, monetary prices will be multiplied by a factor of two. Individual demands will adjust and the increase in nominal prices will be 'neutralized,' meaning that it will not have any economic effect on 'real' relative prices.

Yet there is no indication that this is what actually happens. For example, as Arrow (1981: 147) reminds us, when the supply of State money increases we do not know 'if this increase will take the form of an increase in prices or in real national income.' Either money is neutral, lacking in internal consistency and constituting 'a veil for the real factors which remain dominant,' or else it has specific effects, notably in those markets where transactions 'do not occur instantaneously or simultaneously. Therefore money becomes valuable as such.' Furthermore, if investment and savings activities whose ultimate outcomes are marked by a 'future orientation' have the effect of changing the conditions in which money is to be used, what is the value of money? The dominant model according to which 'prices clear markets at every instant' does not help us to establish, within an overall conception of money, any general relationship between 'monetary magnitudes' and 'real quantities.'

Nor has the considerable development of mathematical models of finance (and of forward markets) helped us to resolve problems relating to the relationships between the 'real economy' and the financial markets. This failure has thwarted the ambitions of those theoreticians who have chosen to analyze the financial markets' rising power as a decisive step toward the determination of 'complete markets.' The conception of trade amongst economic agents that dominates neo-classical models is thus incapable of incorporating money. Consequently it cannot guide the study of the economic role played by finance in the current period.

Keynesian theory

These issues have already been the subject of numerous discussions over the years, specifically since the latter half of the nineteenth century when the first price indexes were being calculated. Keynes touched upon these questions in his book (1930), *A Treatise on Money*, in which he situated conceptions of money in a newly dominant theoretical framework, which included a rejection of classical political economists' (and Marx's) conception of labor value; a replacement of these views with marginalist and Walrasian theories; and a shift in focus from the objective value of money to its 'purchasing power,' whose annual variations were to be calculated through a statistical construction of price indexes for goods and services.

Keynes kept the marginalist conception of value, but rejected the notion of a general equilibrium of relative 'real' prices. He also introduced distinct categories of economic agents, and in doing so paved the way for studies of the different financial behaviors of employees, entrepreneurs and rentiers.

For Keynes, once money has been conceived as a State institution, hence defined in a centralized manner as a unit of accounting that applies to all transactions, the construction of a suitable price index becomes a central theoretical challenge. The only thing that has changed is the historical form of money. For instance, the credit money that banks create, and which by Keynes' time had already become the most important factor in the facilitation of transactions, is linked through the Central Bank and its monetary policy to modern Fiat Money. What is important in Keynes's *Treatise* is the way in which the purchasing power of 'Current Money' is calculated and managed with a view toward the spending, saving and investment behavior of different categories of economic agents.

Private monetary behaviors vary depending on whether the agents involved are employees, entrepreneurs or financiers. Hence the many different price indexes that Keynes proposed before beginning his search for which type of monetary behavior has the most crucial macroeconomic effects. This is a pragmatic conception of the role of money. Constructing his theory in this way, Keynes avoided a challenge set by Jevons and Edgeworth, concerning the origins of price fluctuations. According to these authors, 'there are two distinct sets of influences (one due to "changes on the side of money," the other due to "changes on the side of things") which affect prices relatively to one another' (Keynes 1930: 81–88). According to Keynes, this question is impossible to solve because it has been formulated incorrectly. He refuses any reference to a 'real price' equilibrium in the market for goods and services. From the beginning, Keynes argues that prices are monetary in nature. To build price indexes corresponding to the different types of transactions, the benchmarks chosen have to be the right ones, that is, based on economic magnitudes that are significant.

The two main standards the Treatise proposes are the 'Consumption Standard' for retail prices and the 'Labor Power of Money or Earnings Standard' (Keynes 1930: 57–64) for wages. 'In practice, the best we can achieve is to take as our index of the Labor Power of Money ... the average hourly money-earnings of the whole body of workers of every grade' (1930: 63). These are the standards 'in terms of which the monetary unit should be stabilized.' Moreover, the Earnings standard can indicate how 'changes in the efficiency of human effort should be reflected in changed money-earnings or in changed money-prices.' These ideas can be used to steer monetary policies to stabilize prices.

Keynes criticized Irving Fisher's quantitative conception of money which he called a 'truism.' At the international level, he rejected Cassel's exchange rate theory of money, as it was based on the notion of Purchasing Power Parity. In these conceptions, monetary prices are linked to fundamental prices and to magnitudes that supposedly constitute the 'real economy,' this being an underlying reference to national and international monetary transactions. This dichotomy does not help us understand the economic status of money.

Here the issue of the value of money itself is replaced by issues concerning the rules for building relevant kinds of monetary price indexes, that is, indexes that display variations in the purchasing power of money. Keynes does not break with marginalist conceptions of utility-value, but he does transform their field of application and alter the nature of the relationship between monetary and economic disequilibrium. Money is the central institution of all transactions, but all the various categories of economic agents do not have the same access to money, nor do they have the same relationship to it. This approach was subsequently developed in *The General Theory of Employment, Interest and Money* (1936).

Here Keynes introduces money as a liquid asset, something that distinguishes it from all other forms of goods and wealth (tangible and intangible assets). This is the basis of a monetary interest rate's uniqueness. It is also the basis of the particular influence of the 'preference for liquidity' as opposed to capital spending or financial investment. The demand for money has two separate aspects: one which is transactional and precautionary (L1); and the other which is speculative and varies with interest rates L2(i) and asset prices. It is this second form that explains the arbitrage between investment and liquidity – in this conception, money, as the only asset that is perfectly liquid, is distinct from other tangible and intangible assets. This is what makes the preference for liquidity so dangerous when it materializes to the detriment of the real funding needs of an economy.

This analysis highlights the effects of the private appropriation of money as a financial asset. Keynes indicates that most available money belongs to the rich rentiers, people who are concerned with their own needs and not with economic growth or employment. He contrasts such agents with others who are economically active, such as wage-earning workers and entrepreneurs whose expenditures underpin economic growth.

This conception, together with studies of the irrational nature of stock market behavior, continues to have considerable influence even today. The excessive power of international private finance in economic decision-making, the destabilizing role of speculation, the parasitic behavior of rich rentiers – all of these are criticized by opponents of current capitalist globalization who call for new policies to regulate financial flows.

Nevertheless, if we really want to understand the structures of capital and the relationship between private finance and capitalist accumulation, we need to undertake a broader range of analyses. Keynes's approach does not explain the complex role that money-capital performs with respect to the production-capital that entrepreneurs use. It does not further our understanding of the nature of the various oppositions between capital and labor. For this, we should look at another conception of money and money-capital – the approach that Marx introduced and was based on a labor value theory.

Labor value theory

The labor value of money refers to the view that classical economists and Marx shared, before and after the establishment of the gold standard in the nineteenth century, of gold as a commodity (i.e. as a product of labor). Today, capitalism operates with a Fiat Money regime, but this is not a good reason to avoid discussing the relationship between money and the labor value. On the contrary, the gold standard was operative at a time (in the latter half of the nineteenth century) when theories of utility-value and neo-classical equilibrium focused on money's status out of 'real' goods and services. More generally, the rejection of the labor value of money has left us with unanswered questions about the economic roots of monetary prices and money-capital.

Marx's theory suggests, first of all, that money usage is not the result of choices made by individuals to use money because it is useful as a means of exchange in a decentralized economy operating according to 'real' relative prices. When Marx analyzes circulation of commodities at the beginning of *Capital*, he shows that money is an objective central constraint in commodity trading. It is an expression of a social division of labor in which the products of decentralized individual labor are validated socially in the form of commodities that are bought and/or sold for money. Sales and purchases of commodities, C, are made through money, M. This means that commodities circulate with monetary prices, and that the money that is circulating has a value. This value comprises an omnipresent core benchmark in the circulation of commodities, for which money constitutes a 'general equivalent.' Money becomes the general form of wealth.

State intervention attributes a unit of accounting function to this monetary standard, turning money into a mandatory currency benchmark for all transactions taking place within a national territory. Here the monetary constraint is also an international foreign exchange constraint between different currencies.

The domination of credit-money in capitalism has modified these monetary constraints without eliminating them. This applies not only when accounts are being settled, but also when purchase/sales prices are being set. All contracts for commercial transactions are based on monetary prices. This includes wages and the buying and selling of labor power. Money wages are set with reference to the prices of commodities that the workforce needs to reproduce itself.

On the other hand, Marx criticized the different utopias of 'labor-money,' that is, the possibility of distributing product purchase vouchers to workers depending on the number of hours of work they supplied. For Marx, labor has no inherent value. Instead, it is the commodity that the worker produces through his/her 'socially necessary' labor that has a value. Here the 'workforce' is also seen as a commodity, one that is a basic given of the capitalist system and whose value depends on the commodities required for its production and reproduction. So you cannot suppress money and keep commodities in circulation.

Now that gold, which Marx had once deemed to be the 'general equivalent,' has been taken out of the money-prices equation, various Marxian authors have tried to come up with new and different definitions of the objective value of money. They continue to grant a key role to Marx's monetary constraint (i.e. the relationship between money and the value that is produced through labor). And the money form of capital remains vital to the circulation process of capital: $M-C-M'$, where the capitalist has money-capital (M, that she/he owns or has borrowed); production of commodities by means of purchased commodities, C (including the labor force); and gets M' ($M+m$) at the end of the production process, *when the new commodities are sold* (*if there is no crisis*). It is out of the surplus labor that employees provide, above and beyond the labor cost for which they are remunerated, that surplus value m is born, this being a source of capitalist profit that is split amongst entrepreneurs and providers of money-capital.

How can this simplified presentation of the relationship between money, capital and labor elucidate the connections between finance and capitalist production? This is the subject of the next section.

Entrepreneurs and financiers

We have seen that according to Keynes, the relationship that an economic agent has with money depends on the category to which she/he belongs (wage-earning employees, entrepreneurs, rentiers/financiers). The preference for liquidity will have a given economic effect (i.e. speculative financial behavior, which is related to variations in the interest rate of money). Asset prices fluctuate irrationally under the influence of contagious psychological factors. Despite the usefulness of this conception at a descriptive level, it does not help us to analyze the relationships between the 'real' capitalist economy and finance.

The connection that Marx makes between the creation of value through labor, money and the different forms of capital is a better way of analyzing capitalist structures. Money-capital can be the property of a capitalist entrepreneur, or else it can be borrowed. In the latter case, the profits derived from employees' surplus work are split between the entrepreneur and the creditor. Here Marx has reproduced the classical concept of interest as a secondary type of income, one that is derived from profit. The financial sector is not a producer of value. Marx often refers to its parasitical nature, and to the way in which the particularities of credit crises influence general trading conditions.

However, both capital in its money form and finance play a specific role in the modalities of capital accumulation. Marx demonstrates this by introducing the 'credit system' that he considers typical of developed capitalism. He also discusses its effects on the changes in inter-firm relationships (Marx 1967a: 626–28). The money-capital centralization and distribution system has become 'a terrible weapon in the battle of competition and is finally transformed into an enormous social mechanism for the centralization of capital.' Marx includes several institutions in this account, notably the banking system and the stock exchange. It is the existence of a stock market that enables mergers and acquisitions to occur. In this way finance has its own type of circulation, one that lends it its functional nature within capitalism. Marx gives as an example the building of the railways, heavy investments that could only be achieved via a concentration of funds by means of joint-stock companies.

The 'credit system' is an ambiguous notion. Though it is a functional structure, it is at the same time a parasite of the money form of capital (as opposed to its commodity-form and wage-form). Unlike productive equipment and other commodities that wage-earning workers put to use, money-capital is somewhat abstract and mobile. For a creditor lending the funds that are needed to launch a productive process, the returns on the circulation of capital $M-C-M'$ are in fact derived from $M-M'$, even if this ultimately depends on the actual production of surplus value. The diverse nature of the capitalist 'credit system' contributes to the relative autonomy of money-capital, which seems to be able to create profits without production and surplus labor.

This illusion sometimes extends to the valuation of all individually owned assets, including 'human capital.' Here these assets are capitalized using a monetary interest rate. This leads to pseudo-capitalization, which, when applied to money-capital, is what Marx calls 'Fictitious Capital' (Marx 1967b: 466–70).

It is the relative autonomy of the financial markets (where rights to real products circulate without any direct relationship to the creation of value) that underpins the general ignorance as to how essential the labor value theory really is in helping us to understand how revenues can be fashioned out of capital. The fundamental nature of the relationship between capital and productive labor seems to have become secondary to that of the relationship between finance and economy.

In modern capitalism, the enormous success of private finance between 1980 and 2000 has been accompanied by a massive centralization of money-capital in large institutions such as Anglo-American pension funds and mutual funds. Stock market investments and sharply rising share prices have become the symbols of social wealth, especially in the United States. Yet the relationship between American economic growth during the latter half of the 1990s and the sheer amplitude of share price rises, especially when compared with variations in corporate profit,[1] remains unexplained.

Expert analyses are torn between two contradictory ideas: rational financial markets that allocate capital efficiently; and the irrational fluctuations (be it 'irrational exuberance' or else defiance) that cause price variations in these markets and bear no direct relationship to fluctuations in the economic cycle.

The notion of the financial markets' rationality has served as a means of justifying the considerable success of deregulated international finance. The idea that this constitutes a positive economic driver has been encapsulated in notions of 'good corporate governance' and 'the creation of shareholder value.' Shareholders have been appointed the true owners of companies and the high returns they demand have come to be seen as profit norms that must be satisfied. Many pundits construe this capitalist stimulant as a fundamental factor in the growth of the 'new economy' (even though the financial market's economic rationality has been disproved in 1996, with the observation of an 'irrational exuberance' manifested in the gap between rising share prices and corporate profits). Nor has a recurrence of monetary and financial crises, notably in 1997/98, been enough to quell the ideology which holds that financial markets are rational.

The continuous drop in share prices in May and June 2002 was widely attributed to a loss of confidence in the Stock Exchange itself, the result of a series of financial scandals. Fraudulent accounting practices and the concealment of losses by top managers of several large firms (such as Enron in the United States) certainly played a role in the weakening of the market. However, this explanation did not take note that securities were already 'overvalued,' indicative of a speculative bubble driven by the market's 'irrational exuberance.' Some, reminded of the 1929 Wall Street Crash and its fallout in the 1930s, called for a restoration of confidence via greater transparency, regulatory compliance and closer monitoring of the 'real owners' of capital, that is, large institutions such as pension funds (*Economist* 2002: 63–66).

In the 1990s complementarities between top managers and financiers increased. Both required high profits and the creation of value for shareholders. Finance-linked standards helped reinforce the power of capital versus labor. However at the end of the decade, when profits began to fall, the decline of high and quick profitability affected the capitalist coalition of entrepreneurs and financiers. Scandals were attributed to the greed of top executives, which deflected responsibility away from owners of money-capital.

The complex relationship between corporate profits and financial returns cannot be analyzed properly with hypotheses based on the simple opposition between rational/irrational financial markets and the 'real' productive economy. The links between entrepreneurs and financiers must be understood in the light of their respective roles in the accumulation of capital. These two categories of actors are complementary, inasmuch as productive capital needs money-capital, which then creams off part of the profits that are generated in production. This is the basis of capitalist solidarity vis-à-vis workers. On the other hand, the distribution between entrepreneurs and financiers of the gains that are derived from the use of capital does not result from some calculation regarding the equilibrium of a balance of power between these two groups. The history of capitalism shows that there have been phases during which the influence of financial capital was on the rise, and others during which corporate executives were in command. However, a mixture of complementarities and tensions between productive and financial capital (the composite that Marx suggested) has been a constant in both of these situations.

Thus the private centralization of money in capitalism's own 'credit system' relies on the specific attributes that money assumes within the process of capitalist circulation. There is a specific need for money to be relatively stable, inasmuch as it is a unit of accounting as well as a means of making payments. The private financial centralization of funds cannot in and of itself guarantee this stability at a general level of circulation. Rather, this depends on the State's mode of intervention and on its central monetary role (which is qualitative and not quantitative) as a public expression of the monetary constraint. The same has been true with the gold standard regime, with money minting rules and the international circulation of currencies. The modern Fiat Money regime has reinforced this need whilst complicating the conditions in which it can be satisfied. The considerable success of private finance in the capitalist world today has been promoted by policies of monetary disinflation and financial deregulation.

Monetary policy is situated at the very limit of the private centralization of funds (and of the stabilizing monetary influence of state-run Central Banks). With respect to international financial circulation, the absence of a single global currency raises doubts over the role of monetary policy in terms of currency exchange rates. This issue has become particularly poignant since the advent of the floating exchange rate regime that has turned currencies into financial market assets lacking any benchmark in an objective international standard.

Monetary policy

It is crucial to understand how the State intervenes in today's so-called globalized economy. Capitalism has always had an international dimension but in the world economy today, because of the position that the multinational companies fulfill and due to the free movement of capital, the role of the State seems to have been considerably reduced. In terms of monetary policy, this weakening of the State has raised doubts over public policies aimed at price stabilization.

State intervention is still symbolized today by the influence of monetary policies. This was not the case in the aftermath of the 1930s and the World War II, a period marked by major public spending and extensive regulations covering some of the modalities of capitalist accumulation (specifically finance and wages). Back then, international monetary policy was dependent on the relaunching of commercial trade with mutual convertibility of currencies, and domestic monetary policy on the needs of public finance. Central Bank demands for independence, tied to the primary objective of protecting one's currency against inflation, began to meet with a favorable reception. In the developed capitalist world, the official monetary benchmark after 1945 was the US dollar, convertible into gold at an official rate of $35 per ounce. Other currencies' exchange parities were supposed to be pegged to the gold-dollar, and supervised by the International Monetary Fund (IMF). Born out of the 1944 Bretton Woods Agreements, this public financial institution's mission at the time was to make short-term loans to member countries experiencing provisional balance of payment and exchange rate difficulties. This system changed following the dollar crises of the late 1960s and early 1970s. Currency speculation compounded the effects of rising international commercial trade, an outflow of US capital and a re-opening of the private gold market. The major capitalist currencies started to function via floating exchange rates and became dependent on the financial markets.

The dollar has been the international benchmark currency since the 1980s, even though its exchange rate is no longer tied to an objective monetary standard. At the international economic level, the dollar's monetary domination is based on the United States' hegemony as a global power. The United States is the world's biggest commercial trader, main financial market and a principal source of technological innovation. Moreover, it is home to most, as well as the largest, multinational firms. At the same time, the chronic deficit in the American balance of payments is funded by inflows of private foreign capital, predominately from Europe and Japan. To a certain extent, these flows are what underpin the dollar's relative strength.

At an institutional level, the American Central Bank (the Federal Reserve, or Fed) is supposed to insure price stability and full employment, whereas the only mission of the new European Central Bank (ECB) is to intervene against inflation, which is not supposed to rise above 2 percent annually. The Fed does not set any reference rates, although in practice it would appear that its threshold for current or anticipated price increases from 3 to 3.5 percent. The ECB has been intensely criticized for an anti-inflationist rigidity deemed to be anti-growth, although it did not raise interest rates in 2002, even when the 2 percent inflation threshold was crossed. Conversely, few commented upon the Fed's forecasting error in 2000, when it raised interest rates sharply even though a recession was just starting to break out in the American manufacturing industry. Even so, the Fed only changed its posture in January 2001.

The main instrument of the Central Bank is the manipulation of the interest rate at which it lends reserve money to banks in the banking system. There has been much discussion regarding the Central Bank's role in economic growth. We agree they do impact upon the general conditions of credit required by an economy; conditions that are transmitted via banks. Utilization of another mode of Central Bank intervention, that is, a direct restriction of the quantity of money in circulation, is rare. This would be the product of a quantitativist or monetarist conception of monetary policy, and it was applied in the United States and Great Britain between 1979 and the early 1980s, against a specific backdrop of economic and monetary crisis. This was altered by the political 'counter-revolution' of Thatcher in Britain and Reagan in the United States, before diffusing internationally.

The social aspect of this counter-revolution consisted of changes in the compromise between capital and labor, to the detriment of the latter. We will return to this point below. For now we restrict ourselves to the role that US monetary policy has played, led by the Federal Reserve Bank.

During the 1970s, the dollar crisis reflected both an inflation of domestic US prices and a weakness in the dollar's exchange rate versus the Japanese yen and the German mark. These events were supported by the latter two countries' commercial surpluses. An analogous crisis affected the British pound and other, less important European currencies such as the French franc. In some capitalist countries, monetary crisis came along with an economic crisis that stemmed from lower profit rates – a condition known as stagflation.

In 1979 and until mid-1982 Paul Volcker (Chairman of the Fed at the time) implemented an extremely restrictive monetary policy that was quantitativist in nature. The purpose was to revive the dollar's strength. The effects of this disinflation policy were sudden and severe, as it restricted the supply of central money to members of the banking system. Interest rates skyrocketed, thereby suffocating credit and triggering a recession despite an increased public deficit as a result of the policies of the Reagan Administration. This deficit was not a Keynesian measure. The tax cuts it involved benefited the rich and welfare spending came under a great deal of pressure. Labor unrest was brutally confronted, the purpose being to restore the confidence and profits of capitalists. In this new environment, once monetary policy had refocused on interest rates in mid-1982, financial markets which had regained confidence in the strength of money and capital could begin their march upward.

Analogous policies (albeit in different forms) were also practiced in other major capitalist countries, and forced upon those countries whose currencies were dependent on the key currencies. One example was France in 1983, with the measures taken against domestic inflation and the franc's depreciation. To stay in the European Monetary System that had been built around the Deutsche mark in 1979, French Socialists (in power at the time) pushed through a 'competitive disinflation' monetary policy along with a policy of budgetary and wage-related 'austerity.' The IMF often forces these kinds of policies (albeit with the approval of local leadership) on emerging countries whose currencies are highly dependent on the majors. Thatcher and Reagan's 'counter-revolution,' notably the new power of money and of money-capital, crystallized the elements of what came to be known as neo-liberalism.

At the international level, the foreign exchange relationships between the major capitalist currencies did not really reflect the Central Banks' actual monetary policies. In a floating rate system, exchange rates are managed by the financial markets. Speculation on the relative prices of currencies can provoke large fluctuations that have nothing to do with the so-called 'economic fundamentals.' Neither the reference to 'interest rate parity' nor the doctrine of 'purchasing power parity' can explain such variations. When the outcomes that derive from these ideas lead people to say that the dollar is 'over-valued' against the Euro, such affirmations are not based on an objective criterion of value. The main practical issue is to insure that the major currencies' exchange rates are kept relatively stable through the application of *ad hoc* Central Bank policies. This is what happened in 1985 when the Reagan Administration officially asked its G7 allies to help the United States reduce the 'value' of the dollar, when its excessive strength was harming American exports. Since then there have been similar *ad hoc* interventions involving currency purchases/sales by Central Banks, but these one-off actions have been of a consensual variety. In a deregulated free floating system, there is no institutional benchmark to define acceptable variations between the major currencies' exchange rates.

Financial market-friendly monetary policies have had to contend with other contradictions as well. Reference lending rate manipulations have been undermined to a certain extent by the further development of the financial markets – something that these very same policies had encouraged. The question is not only how such Central Bank policies affect non-inflationary growth, but also which policy levers are at their disposal (i.e. the reference lending rate, or, where quantitative restrictions apply, the amount of money being supplied to the banks). This question is not addressed here through the notion of 'free banking,' a conception that is generally rejected as impracticable, notably because it eliminates a central unit of account. Other variants of the thesis of the decline of Central Banks are based on changes in money forms, like the new electronic form. Still, in both cases, money is primarily seen as an individual asset rather than a definite condition imposed on all capitalist transactions.[2]

Discussions of Central Bank capacity for action focus on the new financial landscape at the end of the 1990s. Some American analysts (Woodford 2002) claim that a powerful private centralization of financial assets has taken place. This modifies bank practices as well as the conditions in which these are provided with available liquidities. So the volume of banking reserves in the Federal Funds system has declined although the market for these reserves of Fiat Money remains the Central Banks' primary theater of intervention. Banking system practices have changed. They are now more oriented toward the management of all sorts of financial assets, with one pre-condition that allowed this to happen – the deregulation of their activities. Furthermore, transactional liquidities for all economic agents seem to be increasingly predicated on the new conditions for accessing money (i.e. bank-managed credit cards, the constant shift from current accounts to interest-bearing term accounts, etc.). This would appear to have created a new type of individual liquidity management behavior.

All of these changes have raised questions about how important Fed Fund rate manipulations really are. It looks possible that the role of monetary policy will be increasingly limited to massive but temporary interventions during major liquidity crises or, to the contrary, the daily management of interbank operational balances.

A more detailed analysis of these new types of financial behavior is clearly indispensable, but it would have to stay connected to the fundamental elements discussed above, with their affirmation of the central role that money plays in all capitalist commercial transactions, including those that are financial in nature (i.e. private financial accumulation of the $M-M'$ variety, regardless of its specific centralizing effects on liquid funds). Secondly, changes in individual monetary behavior should be analyzed in the light of the fundamental disparities between the different social classes' access to money and to money-capital.

Inequalities and social classes

The connection between labor value theory and the class oppositions between workers and capitalists was well established in classical political economics. Marx modified this with his conception of the exploitation of industrial wage labor, this being the basic producer of value and of surplus value. By so doing, he situated working classes in the capitalist countries at the very heart of anti-capitalist social struggle. We should examine to what extent this conception remains valid today.

Income and wealth inequalities have been rising in the developed capitalist countries since the 1980s. The increased wealth of these countries, in contrast to the countries of the South, has not benefited all Northern workers equally. Even so, this situation has not exacerbated class conflict. On the contrary, the working class seems to have become all but invisible: the labor unions have weakened considerably, there have been fewer conflicts over wages, and European communist parties have shrunk and/or disappeared. Paradoxically, all of these changes have coincided with an increase in social inequalities. Whereas the balance of power between capital and labor has changed to the detriment of the latter, under the aegis of money-capital and finance, the working classes in the developed capitalist countries have endured this situation without mobilizing themselves on a mass scale in order to resist it. We will point to a few elements necessary for an analysis of this situation.

It was indicated above that monetary disinflation policies have had a selective class effect. Of course, their overall objective has been to stabilize monetary prices, and this impacts the whole of the economy. However, these policies are part of a worldview oriented to the restoration of profits – a perspective based on the notion that money-capital and finance should have a pre-eminent role in the accumulation of capital. They have helped to facilitate corporate restructurings, the new 'corporate governance' that has fed off of changing forms of labor exploitation, and the moderation of workers' wage demands. This has transformed the entire value creation and distribution chain, including employees involved in the provision of peripheral services, even though it is mostly industrial workers who are evoked here.

The monetarist policies of 1979 and the early 1980s were accompanied by attacks on wage-earners and their social rights. More generally, the inverse relationship between higher wages and higher employment has been an underlying assumption of monetary policies. First there was the statistical relationship between these 'variables' represented in the Phillips Curve. Then, in the 1960s, came the calculation of the 'Non-Accelerating Inflation Rate of Unemployment' (NAIRU), formulated by post-Keynesian economists.

Here wages and jobs should be thought of as dependent variables of non-inflationary growth, that is, price rises were to stay below a given threshold. Productivity gains were supposed to nurture profits instead of wages.

A problem was posed when the United States experienced inflation-free quasi-full employment, starting in 1996. According to some analysts, this situation stemmed from the fact that American workers have been the ones to enjoy the fruits of growth, to the detriment of companies and shareholders. Wages have risen and wage-earners (as consumers) have been able to benefit from lower prices, something that firms have been forced to accept due to competition. Yet, this is an erroneous interpretation. In reality, the analysts' own figures show that workers on the whole have needed 15 years to make up for the drop in their wages since the 1980s. Furthermore, only skilled workers in open-ended contracts had actually succeeded in catching up, unlike temporary workers, despite the higher official minimum wage.

This working class division does not have its origins in the 1990s, nor has it only taken place in the United States. In the early twentieth century, Lenin was already calling the stratum of best-paid skilled workers a 'labor aristocracy.' What should now be discussed are the new forms taken by this division, and their new effects.

We also have to account for capitalist globalization, that is, when capital mobility translates into an industrial relocation to the so-called 'emerging' and 'transition' countries. Even if this relocation primarily affects those jobs that are relatively less skilled, it also touches upon sectors of activity (i.e. steel or automobile) in which skilled workers are employed. In the developed capitalist countries these changes provoke sector-specific or nationalist reactions rather than any unitary and internationalist mobilization. While the new 'balance of power' between capital and labor has been detrimental to the latter, workers' class solidarity has been seriously eroded.

There is another aspect of this division between workers that is just as paradoxical – the access of certain workers to company shares. In the opinion of some, this access modifies workers' class position in relation to the ownership of capital. On this note, some observers have even started to talk about a 'worker capitalism' that workers' pension funds have specifically fostered. In fact, when Wall Street was in its growth phase, and in the context of the increasing wealth of corporate executives supplementing their pay through stock options, American unions were asking that stock options be allocated to all workers. Access to financial wealth was seen as one way of offsetting wage moderation.

Yet, data on household financial wealth has revealed a highly unequal distribution. Access to individual financial ownership has escaped the grasp of most workers and employees. Inversely, when combined with the new forms of credit (discussed above), access to finance (even where this has been modest and indirect) has probably increased wealth-related individualism to the detriment of anti-capitalist worker solidarity. Referring to worker deposits at savings institutions, Marx spoke of a new link in the golden chain that ties workers to capital. However this was never a basis for class compromises.

The contrast between workers' class position and their class-related demands is then analyzed differently, in the light of the world restructuring of production (relocation, development of subcontracting and externalization, etc.). Industrial employment has diminished in relative terms in developed countries, with some analysts suggesting that the trend points in the direction of its disappearance. If this were the case, profits from international capital would mainly stem from an over-exploitation of labor in 'developing countries,' feeding the rent revenues paid to the populations in the developed capitalist countries where money-capital and the main financial markets are found. The labor value theory would not be disproved by such capitalist globalization, but it would be modified by it.

For example, it is said that industry in France (as in the United States and Britain) is now less important than services today when the economy is considered as a whole. And within factories themselves, about half of the workers have 'tertiary' tasks (handling, maintenance, transportation, etc.). In some accounts, the productive working class has thus been disappearing from the developed capitalist countries at the same time as it has been participating in the extraction of rents from the Third World.

It would certainly be necessary to analyze how social classes (and their relationships to the modern capitalist world) have changed with respect to the creation of value by labor. However, the idea that the working class has had a tendency to disappear from the developed capitalist countries, along with other ideas relating to the rent-receiving status of those skilled workers who still have a job, remain highly questionable. In these views there appears to be some confusion regarding workers' reduced visibility as union members and political activists, and their class-related economic position, which has been maintained.

As indicated above, one form of the compromise between labor and capital was torn asunder by the changes that took place during the 1980s. Central Banks took part in this, with their monetary policies that were so beneficial to money-capital. Public finances were also involved, with fiscal reforms that benefited the rich and the corporate sector, and through the restrictions on the Welfare State. The various deregulations and privatizations of public services also worked in the same direction. All of this means that we still have to ascertain the contours of the new social compromise that has yet to be established.

In reality, despite the relocation of some jobs to the 'emerging' or 'transition' economies, a national manufacturing sector will have to be maintained in the developed capitalist countries if they want to maintain their dominant position in the international economy, particularly with respect to technology and the new goods they must diffuse to preserve their wealth (notably military equipment). The neo-liberal policies that encourage the globalization of capital are not incompatible with nationalism – quite the contrary.

One new element of compromise between capital and labor has been witnessed in the financial compensation of wage moderation, that is, through access to finance. However, in addition to the aforementioned structural class limitations of this phenomenon, there is also the risk that the financial markets may decline and share prices drop. If this is accompanied by a recession, the working class will be weakened by a wave of dismissals, at the same time that aggravated pressure from the capital side will put further pressure on whatever remains of the previous social compromise. For example, in 2002 the unemployment benefit reforms that were being prepared in Europe, whether they involve lower payments or tighter restrictions on eligibility, were intended to make workers even more dependent on the needs of capital. Curiously, this has been the straw that broke the camel's back: in Italy and Spain, such reforms have led to general strikes being organized by unions that have protested very little about everything else until now.

While the economic position of the working class has been altered in the big capitalist countries, what changed the most during the 1980s and 1990s was the weakening of the economic and political expression of 'class consciousness.' Such expressions typically emanated from organized workers who rallied others to the struggle against the excesses of capitalist domination. For 20 years these have been symbolized by the vagaries of deregulated finance, which all across the world have reinforced the power of money versus labor. It is yet unclear how this will change after 2000.

The reforms demanded by the various opponents of 'neo-liberal globalization' in their efforts to limit the excesses of finance also vitally concern the balance of power between capital and labor. The political outcome of these struggles will depend on the participation of workers, who remain at the heart of the contradictions of modern capitalism.

Notes

1. The most common method for evaluating this is the price-earnings ratio, which compares share prices and company profits. Since the 1980s this indicator has risen considerably on Wall Street, the world's leading financial market, reaching levels of 30/1. Another evaluation, according to the Tobin Q (that is the ratio of share prices to the physical replacement of physical capital such as factories, machineries, etc.) also indicates that financial assets are 'over-valued.'
2. See the section above outlining the labor value theory of money.

4

Bridging Differences: Value Theory, International Finance and the Construction of Global Capital

Dick Bryan

In the now vast literature about globalization, there is little engagement from within Marxian economic theory. The *Communist Manifesto* has been widely cited, even by conservatives, for its perspicacity in depicting capitalism as a system that expands across the globe. But few look to Marxian economic analysis to explain the process of that expansion.

Marxian categories are not ready-made for the depiction of global integration in the twenty-first century, but the categories do expose neatly some key tensions that drive current accumulation. This chapter uses Marx's circuit of capital and his conception of money to explore some such tensions. The circuit of capital and money is not an obvious combination. Money appears in the circuit as a unit of measure (means of exchange and store of value), but its intrinsic value is not called into question. On the other hand, Marx's theory of money addresses directly (though imprecisely) the ways the monetary unit and commodity values are related.

This chapter uses the tension between these two dimensions of money (unit of measure and produced commodity) to explore the ways in which modern forms of international finance, financial derivatives, have transformed the role of 'money' and given new meaning to the circuit of capital as a way of depicting the economic contradictions of globally integrated accumulation.

The circuit of capital and globalization

The circuit of capital, presented by Marx in Volume 2 of *Capital*, is a simple but elegant device for depicting accumulation. As a circuit, its starting and end points are arbitrary, although each different starting point exposes a different facet of the circuit. Marx presented the general form of the circuit as $C' - P - C'' - M'' - C''$.

Commodity inputs (C') are converted via production (P) into commodity outputs of expanded value (C'') which are then sold ($M'' - C''$), to be converted back into a new, expanded value of inputs. Marx saw $C' - C''$ as the general form of the circuit because it shows capitalism in general as a system of 'the immense collection of commodities,' as he put it in the very first paragraph of *Capital*. Note also that Marx's depiction starts with C' – indicating that surplus value is already presumed at the 'start' of the circuit. This is what characterizes it as the general form of the circuit – it already presumes a developed capitalist economy.

Marx described the circuit $M-C-P-C'-M'$ as the circuit of the individual capitalist. A capitalist starts with a store of money and, via production, converts it into a larger store of money. The individual capitalist pursues monetary profit and the circuit illustrates the process by which surplus value is converted into money profit.

The circuit, in either representation, is a visual characterization of accumulation as a process of (expanded) reproduction. It could easily be read as a mechanical statement of perpetual growth. Yet the 'dashes' that link the circuit are each points of negotiated settlement – there is nothing predetermined about any of the rates of conversion around the circuit. Nor is there any guarantee that the circuit will keep going at its current rate – hence each point of conversion on the circuit is also a point of potential crisis.

In these ways the circuit is an implicit depiction of capitalist competition – who (which part of capital) can get their hands on the surplus value created by labor in the process of production, and what do they do with it? The circuit shows that competition is not just a market relationship between producers in the same industry, but between all capitals. Each point of negotiated settlement in the conversion of capital from M to C to P is determining the distribution of total surplus value among the constituent components of the circuit – money lenders, suppliers of commodity inputs (including labor power), industrialists and merchants. Who gets what is expressed by terms of exchange within the circuit, and we understand these terms of exchange as complex political as well as formal market processes.

But this circuit has been of limited use in the analysis of concrete historical processes of accumulation because it has been understood at a level of abstraction that presumed a competitive (perfectly competitive) framework. There is always the presumption that as capital moves around the circuit, the value of capital is maintained – that the value of capital in the money form (M) is equal to the value of capital in the commodity form (C).[1] The point here is not that monopoly rents are thought impossible ($M-C-M$ and $C-M-C$ are readily understood as processes that involve monopoly rents) but the underlying notion is that monopoly 'distorts' the price rate of exchange.

The identification of historical processes as a theoretical distortion is always analytically dubious, and we should not lose sight of the fact that Marx developed the circuit as an abstraction, not intended to be directly applicable to concrete analysis. But *if* the circuit *is* to be utilized as a way of interpreting concrete accumulation, there is an outstanding need to theorize the movements in the circuit in a way that does not simply presume that value is sustained as it moves between the forms of *M*, *C* and *P*. This issue will be addressed shortly.

Nonetheless, the circuit has been put to work effectively in identifying spatial (especially cross-territorial) tensions in the movement of capital. Writing over 30 years ago, Palloix (1971, 1973) presented a seminal work showing the circuit in a spatial dimension, and used it to depict the 'internationalization' of capital. Palloix argued how the circuit could be used to understand multinational firms (the dominant conception of global integration in the 1970s), and extended it to a framework for understanding the internationalization of capital as a social relation.

As Marxist theory fell from grace in the 1980s, Palloix's work failed to receive the recognition it deserved. His framework provided a simple but elegant approach to analyzing the spatial transformation of capital in the 1980s and beyond. But in an untimely theoretical rupture, the political scientists discovered 'international political economy' and the rest, as they say, was history. Palloix's framework was pushed aside and a discourse of 'international regimes' and debates between 'realists' and 'constructivists' took over. Palloix's work remains implicitly utilized in economic geography (though with the Marxism of the original source often diluted by several generations of re-telling) and Marx's original circuit appears occasionally in Marxist essays; notably in John Weeks' writing on competition.[2]

Time and space in the circuit of capital

This essay applies Palloix's spatial development of the circuit of capital and adds the dimension of time to consider globally integrated finance. In the process, I hope to show how developments in finance actually bring the circuit to life by addressing the presumption that the value of capital is preserved (and inherently expanded) as it moves around the circuit through space and over time. To clarify, let me repeat the above presumption in a spatial and temporal framework.

Spatial and temporal expansion of capital in the forms of money and commodities depicts globalization as a 'logic of capital.' Competition between and within different forms of capital (money, production and commodities), in playing out this 'logic,' signals the question of the commensuration of capital as it expands across space and through time. We are inclined to simply assume that the value of capital is spontaneously preserved as it changes form, time and location: that the circuit 'tracks' the movement of capital of unquestioned stable value.

But there are potential problems. Capital, we know, has different values in different times. A stock of money decreases in value at the rate of inflation. Capital equipment will both deteriorate over time, and its replacement cost will change with innovation in its method of production. Innovation in production technology also means that commodities produced at different times embody different socially necessary labor times.

The same concern applies to space. Space is not uniform, and the commensuration of capital in different sites and forms is a moot point. Does a machine in Paris have the same value as that of a machine in Hanoi, where notions of socially necessary labor time are different from those in Paris? In the context of globalization, there is an additional question of how we know that the value of capital is preserved in an $M-C-M$ transaction when the two '*M*s' may be different currencies.

In general, my concern is how we understand value on a global scale outside of assumptions (abstractions) which insure that *M*s and *C*s and *P*s are themselves of consistent value. I want to stay with the space dimension to explore some issues related to how space is segmented and will return to the time dimension shortly.

In addressing the spatial expansion of capital, Marx and Engels wrote extensively and dramatically in the *Communist Manifesto* of the spread of capital both physically and as a system of calculation. For example, they contended that 'old established national industries [are dislodged by] new industries that no longer work up indigenous raw material but raw material drawn from the remotest zones [and] whose products are consumed... in every quarter of the globe,' and that the bourgeoisie uses cheap prices as 'the heavy artillery with which it batters down all Chinese walls.' Such phrases we could readily understand as a depiction of capitalism incorporating the whole world into an integrated circuit of capital.[3] While it was a perspicacious depiction of capitalism's expansion 150 years on, there is a danger of Marxism sliding into a 'borderless globe' vision of a closed value system. This would see China simply 'entering' the circuit, with value moving freely in, out and around China and individual capitalists expanding their individual circuits to include China in various ways.

But the problem made stark is that we know that 'globalization' is not about the construction of a 'borderless globe' or a 'global level playing field': it remains constructed by spatial 'differences' of all sorts; the most conspicuous being nationality or regionality. Business in China is done 'differently' from that in the United States. Japanese capital markets operate 'differently' from European ones.

Conversely, we are not just talking about interacting national circuits of capital, as if globalization were simply an arms-length transaction between discrete national units. Global integration both transcends and at the same time reproduces (national) difference: it breaks down the legal and technological barriers between Japanese and European capital markets, yet these markets display clear differences in stock prices and interest rates. Indeed, national (and other) differences are thereby accentuated precisely because they cannot be attributed simply to 'artificial barriers' in international capital markets. But how are we to comprehend this ambiguity within a single, integrated theory of value?

Note that the word 'difference,' in relation to the process of accumulation being 'different' in different countries, is conspicuously vague in its use above – of course there is difference around the world. The critical question is 'difference' with respect to what? There is no immediate, absolute answer here; indeed, I want to hold off a direct answer to that question and consider the analytical object of constituting 'difference,' for Marxism has to construct a distinct, Marxist notion of 'difference' that is specific to its theory of value.

Difference: defining what needs to be commensurated

In explaining 'difference,' the temptation is to talk of the world as 'fractured' or 'divided' by political (and cultural) space. The problem with those conceptions is that they start from the notion that the world is, in the first instance, a unified, seamless totality (there is a single unit of value; a uniform process of accumulation), and 'then' segmented (fractured/divided) by the intrusion of territory. They conflate the process of abstraction (an integrated world) with a historical process (the conflicts and contradictions by which capital expanded across the globe).[4] The notion of the world fractured or divided by political space is, therefore, both predicated on an ideal type (uniform, apolitical, non-territorial space: the borderless globe), and limited in its depiction of the possible significant sources of 'difference.'

This ideal type appears conspicuously in the way neo-classical economists constitute 'difference' (especially nationality) as economic distortion, and Marxian value theory is in danger of the same slide. For the neo-classicals, nationality may be understood economically in terms of immobile factors (products of nature, immobile labor) yet capital is excluded from being classified by this spatial fixity. Hence when capital retains characteristics of nationality, a series of neo-classical riddles arise that have no analytical answer, for example:

- why does arbitrage not eradicate mutually profitable financial swaps contracts?
- why does share ownership stay based in 'local' companies?
- why do exchange rates not gravitate to purchasing power parity (PPP)?

These questions have a common premise: that for capital the globe is integrated as a single economic entity, in which difference is either eradicated by cross national movement or arbitraged into insignificance. Hence the conventional neo-classical answer to these riddles is that time will solve them: the market will overcome difference. Difference is eradicated by efficiency; ongoing difference is a market distortion.[5]

The issue Marxism needs to address is quite distinct from this neo-classical framing. The 'differences' that matter are not those that are (or could potentially be) eradicated by increased market efficiency: they are the differences that are integral to accumulation. Our object, therefore, is not to constitute an equilibrium that eradicates difference, but to identify the irreducible differences that must be bridged in the process of globally integrated accumulation. These irreducible differences then set the problem for a theory of value: how to systematically cross those bridges in a way that shows that difference is both mediated and reproduced at the same time. In the process, we also come closer to explaining why mutual benefit in swaps contracts is not arbitraged away, why share portfolios remain locally focused, and why exchange rates do not gravitate to PPP.

So how is this 'difference' crossed concretely, such that we can talk about capital (and class) as a global phenomenon despite the reproduction of spatial (and temporal) difference? My proposition is that it is through the operation of globally integrated financial markets. The huge growth in volumes in these markets in the last 20 years is, I suggest, driven almost entirely by capital's need for mechanisms that will bridge differences. While finance is not the sole mechanism of global integration and commensuration, it will here be the focus of analysis both as illustrative of a general answer, and as the key to a general answer.

Finance and derivatives

A radical response to this question of why arbitrage does not generate a borderless globe will invoke the power of a small number of large international financial houses. It will point out that these institutions allocate funds around the world according to a global profit maximizing agenda, in which they use 'hot money' for short-term speculative gain and manipulation of national government policy for securing long-term concessions, generating a 'casino capitalism.' It is a story of the capacity of big capitals to play on 'difference' of all sorts for their own advantage. Mounting evidence of this style of analysis is not difficult, but, as with all explanations based on monopoly power, the underlying process of accumulation is downplayed in favor of a radical spin that focuses on the anti-social nature of large corporations.

Marxian value theory needs an explanation on its own terms. Reversion to the monopolistic side of capitalism does not sit with a theory that focuses on the competitive momentum that drives capitalism. Indeed, the emphasis in institutional power is directly compatible with the neo-classical preoccupation with distortions, sharing the premise that if it were it not for monopolies, there would indeed be a global level playing field, with arbitrage eradicating 'differences.'

An alternative explanation can be found in looking in practice at the way non-equivalence in value is being bridged in global capital markets. I use the term 'bridging' because it is a continual process: 'difference' is not eradicated (as in an arbitrage model), for difference is being continually reproduced, but it needs to be mediated on an ongoing, though variable, basis.

Let me be more specific, though at the danger of being too narrow. When we think of global money we immediately hit the problem that money (more generally a financial asset) is always denominated in a particular national currency: there is no universal, singular monetary unit. We use exchange rates to 'convert' between currencies. For the neo-classicals, the original vision was that exchange rates would gravitate to PPP – the law of one price – by arbitrage in foreign exchange markets. Different national forms of money would not be an issue because their rate of conversion would always be at a rate that guaranteed the perpetuation of 'real' value (purchasing power). Marxism is in danger of the same presumption, and there are plenty of times when Marx simply assumed that exchange rates would spontaneously 'convert' one national value unit to another. For example, in discussing national differences in wages (*Capital* I, Chapter 22), Marx concluded the following in relation to the national differences in the productivity and intensity of labor:

> The different quantities of commodities of the same kind, produced in different countries in the same working time, have, therefore, unequal international values, which are expressed in different prices, i.e. in sums of money according to international values. The relative value of money will therefore be less in the nation with a more developed capitalist mode of production than in the nation with a less developed capitalism (Marx 1867: 702).

What is meant in a global setting by 'unequal international values' is quite a matter of concern, but our central focus is in the international role of money. Here, the exchange rate is presumed to reconcile these two 'national values' with international values.[6]

But we know that exchange rates do not adhere to this calculation: All differences are not eradicated by the global integration of financial markets. So how are different 'national values' reconciled, and how are different currencies commensurated, such that we can consider the global profit calculations of an individual company? In a globalized circuit of capital, how do we reconcile the value of '*C*' produced in different countries with labor power of different values? And how do we know that the value of '*M*' (money capital) is sustained around the circuit as it crosses exchange rates? Conversely, what becomes of the concept of money *capital* (*M*) if its value is continually changing between currencies?

The answer to these 'problems' is found empirically, for individual capitalists confront it daily: they do not want the value of their assets to vary at the whim of foreign exchange rates, so they hedge in derivatives markets: they use a vast array of financial instruments such as swaps, options and futures contracts to cover the risks of exchange rate volatility and to secure the value of financial and commodity assets. These derivatives do not eradicate exchange rate volatility and they do not establish PPP, but they bridge the discontinuities in the international money system that arise from different national currencies being 'generated' and 'sustained' in different national localities.

The raison d'etre of derivatives is the management of financial risk associated with borrowing, lending and owning. They are instruments to hedge against uncertain movements in interest rates, exchange rates, commodity prices and the future price of financial instruments themselves. Derivatives are not new – futures contracts on commodities have a more than two thousand year history. But derivatives markets shot to prominence in the 1980s associated with 'globalization': in particular the ongoing existence of different national currencies circulating globally, and each currency accompanied by a different set of determinants of its short- and long-term rates of interest. In a global context of the free flow of finance, these national monetary 'systems' generate discontinuities in a global financial system. A globally integrated financial system requires that these currencies and interest rate discontinuities be bridged. Accordingly, in the context of the last 20 years of globalization, interest rate and currency swaps, options and forward rate agreements (FRAs) have dominated derivatives trading, for these are designed specifically to bridge the nationally derived differences in global finance. Indeed, in 2001 in over-the-counter (OTC) derivative markets, foreign exchange and interest rate instruments had a daily turnover of around $US575 billion (BIS 2001: 1).[7]

When these derivative markets started to emerge in the early 1980s, the arbitrage theorists suggested that they would soon reduce to small proportions – markets would comprehensively integrate, 'difference' would be eradicated, and swaps contracts would become largely redundant. But history shows the opposite: turnover on swaps markets grows exponentially, and the capacity for two parties in a swaps contract to share a mutual gain has not been arbitrated away. Between 1995 and 2001 OTC derivative turnover increased by 180 percent (BIS 2001 Table 6). Differences in national monies (and their associated interest rate regimes) are not being eradicated: on the contrary they manifest as essential components of globalized accumulation, for nation states remain the incubators of global capital.

But derivatives are not restricted to reconciling different national monetary units: our illustration of exchange rates is too restricted, and our notion of 'difference' that needs to be mediated in international financial markets should not be determined by this one conspicuous 'difference' of national currencies. So although recent history has seen derivatives focused on bridging national currency and national interest rate differences, there remains the underlying role of derivatives in bridging differences of all sorts, not just between nationally denominated monies. And here time re-enters the analysis, for derivatives simultaneously address the bridging of temporal and spatial difference.

This general role for derivatives requires nothing more than that there are differences in capital that need to be compared and reconciled. These differences may be in space, in form (money capital in different currencies, different commodity assets, etc.) or in time (money today compared with money in the future; coffee today compared with coffee in the future).

Combined, they present some quite complex combinations of bridges to cross. For example, floating rate of Japanese yen today compared with Brazilian coffee beans in 6 months time depends on: interest rates on the yen today compared with interest rate on yen in 6 months time; the yen/peso exchange rate in 6 months time compared with today's exchange rate, and the price of coffee today compared with price of coffee in 6 months time. Derivatives are designed to bridge each (all) of these unknowns so that assets in floating rate yen today can be *directly* compared with the price for Brazilian coffee in 6 months time. And the way in which these two financial assets are commensurated may involve hundreds of different sorts of derivative contracts that disperse exposure to risk in a range of different spatial and temporal directions.

Derivatives, then, bridge discontinuities in the value of capital. They do not eradicate the differences that are the source of discontinuity (they do not turn the present into the future, money into coffee, or yen into pesos). But they provide a means to commensurate different forms and temporalities of capital.

Derivatives and the circuit of capital

I want to take this proposition back to the circuit of capital, for it is in this process that we can define what Marxism means by 'difference.' In the circuit $M-C..P..C'-M'$ we conventionally assume that the value of capital is sustained as it moves perpetually round the circuit, and that there is a simply measurable addition to surplus value in production. But why do we assume this? The answer is standardly in terms of the level of abstraction at which the circuit is presented: at the 'right' level of abstraction, there is no reason *not* to presume that there is equivalence in each point of the circuit! But if the circuit is to be used to inform the understanding of real accumulation, in a world structured by difference and discontinuities, the explanation of equivalence in terms of abstraction is inadequate. Moreover, it obstructs opportunities for Marxism to explain coherently the actual process of capitalist competition within the circuit.

The problem, stated simply, is that there is no unique '*M*' and no unique '*C*' in the circuit: the value of '*M*' and '*C*' is always contingent, and always in need of mediation. I will break this down to its constituent parts.

Explaining commodity capital '*C*'

Marxist value theory focuses on explaining the values of different '*C*s' but only in the present, at a particular site. The explanation is in terms of socially necessary labor time. But how do we deal with space and time? Marx was clear that transportation across space is productive labor (but only if it is socially necessary transportation), so that commodities have different values in different locations. How we compare those different values – at what spatial point – is a difficulty. For example, if the well-head value of (identical) oil in Indonesia and Kuwait were the same, the transportation of Kuwaiti oil to Indonesia would not see the value of the Kuwaiti oil higher than the value of the Indonesian oil because the transportation did not constitute socially necessary labor. On the other hand, if there were a shortage of oil in Indonesia, and oil had to be shipped in from Kuwait to Indonesia, the value of the *Indonesian*-produced oil would have to be recalculated to include the labor time taken to ship Kuwaiti oil to Indonesia, for the latter process is part of *socially necessary* labor time in the provision of commodity oil in Indonesia. Hence the problem: in which location is the value of commodity oil being measured?

Transportation over time poses an identical problem. Storage, says Marx, constitutes socially necessary labor time. But it does so only when the stored commodity meets the norms of socially necessary labor time in the future. In our oil case, technological change in exploration and drilling may (and indeed has) reduce the socially necessary labor time required for the production of a barrel of oil. Oil stored from the past, being identical to oil produced in the present, has a value equal only to the socially necessary labor time required to produce oil in the present, even if that barrel was produced in an era of higher socially necessary labor time. But if we do not know the value of oil in the future, what is the value now of oil being stored for the future? Hence the problem: what is the time at which the value of commodity oil is being measured?

Explaining money capital '*M*'

Marx grappled hard with this question, and it was more out of frustration than conviction that he embraced the gold standard, and the notion that the value of money is determined by gold. Yet (and Marx was well aware of this) the concerns raised above about '*C*' applied directly to gold. How (where) was socially necessary labor time in gold production determined? Is the value of gold (and money) devalued by technological innovation in the gold mining industry?

It is important to not be diverted by the gold question, however, for while it was the basis of money in Marx's time, it does not warrant contemporary concern. Our more general question has already been exposed in the above discussion of exchange rates. If exchange rates do not adhere to the law of one price, there is a discontinuity in the value of '*M*.' If different currencies have different interest rates, the future value of '*M*' has a double discontinuity. There is, essentially, the same space and time problem as there is for '*C*,' but with extra layers. Indeed, the dominant form of swaps contract is not between commodities and money but between different forms of money, and this is some signal that reconciling different forms of money is more complex than reconciling the value of different physical assets.

In summary, these discontinuities between different sorts of money and different sorts of commodities at different localities and in different times are an irresolvable problem for a purely abstract labor conception of value, yet they are resolved explicitly in practice by derivatives contracts. For Marxian analysis, derivatives secure commensuration of value across time and space. The huge growth in derivative products over the past decade is a reflection of just how many bridges there are to cross in mediating the complex representations of value.

I will not be diverted here by the question of how derivatives themselves may be theorized as commodities within Marxian value theory.[8] The simple point to be made is that derivatives provide a means for the value of '*M*s' and '*C*s' to be compared wherever they are in the circuit, wherever they are in space and wherever they are in time. This is the process by which our abstracted assumption of the equivalence of value around the circuit is empirically verified.

To be sure, these bridges are crossed in the form of money (the equivalent form of value), not in the form of embodied labor time, and hence there is only a price process of commensuration. But there are direct implications for labor and production, which draw our bridging process into the issues of abstract labor and class.

Rethinking competition

The abstract version of the circuit of capital, which assumed an equivalence of value as capital moved round the circuit, can now be thought of as an empirical reality but not, as in the abstracted version, because of the assumption of a seamless globe and uniform time. Rather, it is an empirical reality because there are systematic mechanisms, in the forms of derivatives contracts, to bridge discontinuities in space and time.

This process leads us to reconsider the process of competition. We know that, for Marx, competition is the central driving force of accumulation. We know also that for Marx, unlike the later neo-classicals, competition is not an idealized process contingent on strict assumptions about market structure and behavior (perfect competition). Competition is simply the way in which every individual capitalist maneuvers to increase its share of total surplus value – it knows no behavioral rules or rules of market structure. Competition drives each individual capital to secure a monopoly over something – a technology, a product, space, an image – and what we observe of the competitive process in our daily lives is indeed the many and diverse manifestations of monopoly. But this monopoly is the expression of a competitive process, not its negation.

The propensity of capital to expand globally is driven by this same momentum: the competitive search for monopoly (a niche). But which side of this dialectical relationship between monopoly and competition is most prominent? Look at almost any literature on globalization, and it will have monopoly at its centerpiece: the role of transnational corporations, including financial institutions, and the enormous power wielded by the world's largest companies over smaller corporations, over nation states and over workers.

But derivatives cause us to re-think this focus, for they cause us to re-think the nature of monopoly power. Derivatives permit any form of capital at any place and time to be compared in value with any other form of capital at any place and at any time. They show 'at a glance' when any form of capital in any place at any time is over or under-valued (generating a monopolistic or less-than-competitive rate of return). Derivatives represent the competitive momentum within an increasingly monopolized process of globally integrated accumulation, for they re-focus the process of competition on all capital (and the circuit of capital) rather than just on transnational corporations. Following Clifton's (1977) proposition that the competitive process is as much intra-capital (for the allocation of investment between options) as inter-capital, even the largest transnational corporations have to hedge on derivatives markets and, as such, they subject their own capital in its various forms and locations to market evaluation in that same way as do all other capitals.

So what manifests as short-term movements of capital is often called speculation; hot money, and so on, may indeed be just that. But more likely (as a proportion of market transaction) is that these movements involve the largest companies repositioning themselves in asset markets, systematically seeking to avoid holding assets in under-valued or excessive risk-exposed forms.

Posed this way, the growth of international finance is not explained by the power of large companies and banks, but by the intensely competitive process of hedging risk in a market where other capitals are trying to do the same. 'Difference' as it has been characterized above, ceases to be a safe haven for the accumulation of monopoly profits (a company's control of some facet of a market in time or space), for differences are being actively bridged. The result is that many of the traditional sources of monopoly profits are being traded away in derivatives markets: the profits of circulation are being undercut. The focus on profit-making thereby reverts squarely to the appropriation of surplus value from labor, only now the focus on surplus value appropriation is made within a global calculation.[9]

Let me put this in simple, though potentially trivial, terms. Think of a circuit of individual capital for a large corporation. There are lots of interconnecting

'*C*s' and '*P*s' and '*M*s' depicting this corporation going about its global transactions and production. By hedging in futures, options, swaps, and so on, this corporation can assess the current and future value of any of its '*C*s' and '*M*s' anywhere in the world – they can be compared with each other and assessed against 'the market' generally. Corporate strategy follows directly. Underperforming assets are readily identified and transformed or sold. Competition between capitals thereby intensifies – it ceases to be an annual profit and loss statement calculation; it is a daily exercise of verifying the value of every form of asset against every other form of asset through time and across the globe.

As importantly, in this intense global market for the value of '*C*' and '*M*,' the focus shifts back to the process of production as the only site in the accumulation process where corporations can go about it their own way. But this site is also caught up in the process if instantaneous comparison is facilitated by derivatives markets. Each corporation, in each of its own sites of production, is under global pressure to intensify the conversion of commodity inputs into commodity outputs ($C-P-C'$) as its one discretionary source of profitability. Moreover, because the value of commodity inputs and commodity outputs can themselves be commensurated on a global scale against the value of all other forms of capital, here too, in the site of production, the global pressure to secure an internationally competitive rate of surplus value has intensified.

For Marxists, this focus on production (the generation of surplus value) has always been the centerpiece of accumulation. But in recent debates about globalization, this issue has been largely lost in a focus on the profits of trading and the profits of lending and financial services. Finance and class relations in production have appeared analytically separated – 'casino capitalism' and 'the working poor' have become distinct issues. This chapter has sought to show how finance and financial markets are not only providing the means for commensuration across the differences that define the global economy but, in this process, they are minimizing 'difference' (defined in circulation) not in itself, but as a source of profitability. The strategic focus then shifts back to 'difference' in production, and innovation in the intensification of the labor process.

It is surely no surprise that we see the globalization of finance and the intensification of the extraction of surplus value as part of the same process.

Notes

This chapter is part of a research project with Michael Rafferty, Department of Finance, University of Western Sydney, on a Marxian analysis of international finance.

1. Of course, surplus value created in production expands the value of capital, but the point here relates to the process of circulation and the exchange of equivalents.

2. I have also used it extensively to differentiate forms of internationalization of capital (e.g. Bryan 1987).
3. Marx planned a volume of *Capital* on the world economy, but it was never written. Indeed, it remains an area of debate as to how he might have extended the framework of the three published volumes into that arena. I have elsewhere suggested that there are quite different conceptions of internationalization in each of the volumes of *Capital* (Bryan 1995b).
4. Marx emphasized a difference between social capital and total capital. Total capital is the aggregation of individual capitals, and as an aggregation it remains characterized by all the diversities and divisions that exist between individual capitals. Social capital, on the other hand Marx depicted, at a higher level of abstraction, as the underlying shared characteristic that defined all capital. Globalization as a depiction of a seamless globe is conceived at the level of abstraction of social capital, but slides into the category of total capital. In the concept of social capital there are no seams; in the concept of total capital, seams are everywhere.
5. We can see Marxists and, indeed, Marx adopting the same sort of framework in the context of reconciling the global and the national in a unified theory of value. For Marx, the problem originates with the value of labor power having national (local) determination but the value produced by labor having a globally determined value. At what point these spatial inconsistencies get resolved is a matter Marx did not address in much detail and when he did, the answer was not well considered.
6. I have suggested elsewhere (Bryan 1995b) that this proposition is conceived by Marx in a national economy framework – i.e. without values being transformed into international prices of production.
7. This figure comes from the Bank of International Settlements, three yearly global surveys, the most recent results coming from April 2001.
8. This is a project of current research with Michael Rafferty. See also Kay (1999).
9. Note here the importance of avoiding confusion on the difference between production and circulation. All individual capitals, even those in circulation industries such as finance and wholesale retail, undertake a circuit of capital – they use inputs (labor power and the means of production) to produce an output. Marx (1885: 133) emphasized that money capital, commodity capital and productive capital are not 'branches of business that are independent and separate from one another. They are simply particular functional forms of industrial capital, which takes on all three forms in turn.' The point here is that for all capital, the labor process becomes the focus of profit-making (turning inputs into outputs more cheaply) in an environment when mark-ups in circulation are less available as a source of profitability.

Part III

Production, Crisis and Globalization

5

Globalization: The Retreat of Capital to the 'Interstices' of the World?

Richard Westra

Introduction

Despite extensive treatment in a burgeoning literature, the world economic phenomenon dubbed 'globalization' is not well understood. The position taken in this chapter is that the fault resides with a gapping lacuna in the research agendas of globalization: that is, as we shall see, while current analysis of globalization has been deeply fixated upon questions of the relative force of states and world 'markets' in shaping the economic future, it has failed in a rather studied fashion to problematize *capitalism* in this effort. In other words, there exists a universal assumption in the literature, often implicit, though in some cases quite explicit, that the *market* being referred to is in fact the *capitalist* market and that the *state*, the potency and potential scope of action of which is placed at the center of the debate, remains a capitalist state. From this follows another assumption, that whatever political position one takes, one can comfortably rely upon received theories purporting to explain the workings of capitalist markets as the basis for making claims about market-state dynamics with respect to future political and social policy outcomes. To be sure, the foregoing afflicts most severely those perspectives on globalization animated by neo-classical economics, given how the latter completely evades the question of capitalism. However, it also impacts deleteriously upon Marxist scholarship that blithely accepts that the universe of state and class action continues to operate according to the principles of capitalist economy.

Problematizing capitalism as a prelude to addressing the transformations of the world economy confronting us is, however, not a simple task. For Marxian economics, with its *value theory*, which lays claim to best capture the workings of capital, is also steeped in internal turmoil with no competing conception of value theory achieving anywhere near paradigmatic status. The purpose of this chapter then, is to defend a particular version of Marxian value theory as optimally achieving the goals of Marx's *Capital* (which Marx unfortunately never survived to complete), and then to apply this theory as the touchstone for making a judgment on the capitalist substance of the contemporary global economy. This work, which will also include a brief discussion of the role of the capitalist state in supporting capital accumulation, is designed as a formative attempt to explore new avenues in a complex area of political economy study. The chapter will therefore adopt the following procedure: First, the debate over globalization will be briefly reviewed with the focus placed upon the way perspectives deal (or, more appropriately stated, do not deal) with the question of capitalism. Second, I intend to introduce the approach to value theory and discuss how it can be utilized to make claims about the world economy today. Third, I will offer some tentative assessments on the capitalist substance of the contemporary economy and suggest directions for further analysis. The chapter will then be concluded.

Specifying globalization

For expository purposes this section will commence its engagement with the debate over globalization through the prism of a discussion of the three representative positions on the subject outlined in the work of Held *et al.* (1999). To begin, on the market side of the debate, is what the authors refer to as the 'hyperglobalist thesis.' This perspective, in both its neo-liberal and 'postmodernist'/neo-Marxist representations adverts quite simply to the view that the multiplication and cross-cutting of cross-border transnational production, financial and trading linkages and networks has ushered in a new historical epoch in which the notions of a *national* economy and the *Westphalia* nation-state system itself have been rendered obsolete. Neo-liberal contributions, it may be noted, resurrect the core tenets of the old *modernization theory*; that globalization realizes world economic neo-classical 'perfect' market integration as well as a *convergence* of market systems and, of course, manifests an inexorable telos.[1] Radical hyperglobalist approaches, on the other hand, emphasize the ascendancy and triumph of a 'global capitalism' and the 'powerlessness' of the state and its policy arsenal in the face of it.

On the state side, according to Held *et al.*, is the 'skeptical thesis,' which strives to counter the hyperglobalist position at every turn through extensive empirical evidentialization. Skeptics, for example, hold that the realities of the world economy, far from constituting a monolithic global capitalism or perfect market integration, in fact involve extreme asymmetries. They cite the growing disparities of wealth including the absolute impoverishment and marginalizing of whole regions despite world economic interpenetration – including the waves of 'liberalization' and 'openings' enforced by international institutions such as the IMF and World Bank (Weeks 2001). Skeptics also demonstrate that strategic patterning of transnational corporate (TNC) production, finance and trade, if remarkable in any novel way in the latter quarter of the past century, reflects 'regionalization' rather than globalization (Hirst and Thompson 1996; Mittelman 2000; Larner and Walters 2002).

That is, varying forms of capitalist investment tend to both emanate from and concentrate in a *triad* of capitalist blocs – North America, the European Union (EU) and Japan/Northeast Asia – and if there exists any significant extra-triad investment flow it has been into the wider area of East Asia.

The skeptical thesis interrogates hyperglobalist claims through comparative studies of levels of internationalization of trade, foreign direct investment (FDI) flows and internationalization of finance across capitalist history, though particularly in comparisons of the periods of the first quarter and last quarter of the past century, only to discover much 'hot air' (Giussani 1996; Hirst and Thompson 1996). That is, in aggregate terms, so the argument goes, the former period was significantly more 'global.' However, it is accepted that if there exists one component of the hyperglobalist package that should be taken into account in differentiating the internationalization of the current conjuncture, it is the revolutionary mechanisms of globalized *finance* – information technology, novel financial instruments such as 'derivatives' and so on.[2] Though it has been suggested in this regard, that from a world-historic perspective, the hypertrophy of finance constitutes evidence of crises of capital accumulation and, while appearing in differing guises across capitalist history, exists as something endemic to capitalism *per se* (Arrighi 1994). In fact, it is important to comment here on the hyperglobalist/skeptic standoff, that discussion of the extent of capitals internationalization across capitalist history along with the arguments over the changing shape of this internationalization (such as its possible current regional thrust) underscores the necessity of studying the *different forms* assumed by the global dimension of capital rather than simply counter-posing a global capitalism to a purportedly *non-* or *less*-global capitalism, or for that matter a *regionalized* capitalism. This sort of analysis forms part of the research territory of the *periodization* of capitalism or study of phases of capitalist development (Westra 1996, 2002b; Albritton *et al.* 2001), ongoing debates within which have unfortunately proceeded apart from much of the globalization debate *per se* (though, because the periodizing of capitalism itself is dependent upon our deeper understanding of what precisely capitalism *is*, and is something that I have treated at length elsewhere, it will also not constitute the primary focus of what follows in this chapter).

Moving from criticism to a more positive statement of their position, the skeptics arguing for the salience and efficacy of the state maintain that notions of expected global market convergence, particularly given the demise of soviet style socialism, are belied by the persistence of varying 'models' or institutional configurations of capitalism marking developed capitalist states (Berger and Dore 1996; Kitschelt *et al.* 1999; Coates 2000). And not only does the empirical evidence point to the TNC continuing do the bulk of its business – sales, high value added production and R&D – in its 'home' national economy, but the foregoing variant institutional matrix's underpin the formation of the so-called 'competition states' acting through policy initiatives appropriate to the capitalist model they represent in order to further the interest of *their* TNCs (Zysman 1996; Dicken 1998: Chapters 3 and 4). This sort of analysis then underpins the skeptics' position that, not only are states empowered in different ways and armored with varying 'capacities' for maneuvering in the world economy, but globalization itself represents strategies of internationalization of the capital of particular states, supported in turn by those states' international policy initiatives (Weiss 1997).[3] Globalization, therefore, it has been suggested (McMichael 2000), may be best conceptualized as a 'political project,' though cloaked in the ideological garb of neo-liberalism with its touting of the necessity of unimpeded markets. And, a strong case has been made in this regard, that much of what masquerades as globalization – international de-regulation of finance, liberalization of trade and so on – has been uniquely engineered to address the economic predicament of the United States and US capital, and the so-called 'Wall Street-dollar regime' (Gowan 1999).

The third representative position in the work of Held *et al.* dubbed the 'transformationalist thesis,' maintains that while current globalization is characterized by significant and unprecedented change in both the structure of national economies and the international order, as well as in the fundamental mechanisms of state/world economy interrelations, its future trajectory and ultimate contours remain unresolved. Transformationalists recognize the sorts of asymmetries and re-configuring of the world order (such as the thrust toward regionalization) remarked upon in the skeptical thesis, but view the emergence of such new 'patterns of global stratification' as part of the establishment of alternative 'sovereignty regimes.' At its most radical pole, the transformationalist perspective believes the foregoing constitutes the harbinger of a world where the very geo-spatial categories that marked modernity (such as national and international) are becoming irrelevant; and that new categories must be deployed appropriate to analyzing patterns of politico-economic interaction of a sprouting 'neo-medievalism' (Kobrin 1999). Hence, in accepting hyperglobalist-type claims of systemic world economic change as well as points made by skeptics on the continued policy efficacy of the state, the transformationalist position has set its intellectual sights on issues of the so-called *governance* in and across both spheres (Prakash 2001). On the one hand, problems of *global* governance, for example, are said to involve shifts in 'jurisdictions' of international organizations as in what Held *et al.* view as the changes forced upon the Westphalia state system by the 'UN model' and the pressures that purportedly now exist for 'cosmopolitan democracy' (1999: 444–50). On the other hand, governance within the context of the state entails what has been dubbed the 'rearticulation' of the state (Prakash 2001), where states reinvent themselves and adopt new functions to better operate in their transformed global milieu.

Let us now, on the basis of this outlining of positions, revisit the issue alluded to in the Introduction, of the failure of the globalization debate to problematize capitalism, and make some preliminary assessments of the implications of that. We can see immediately in the sharp dichotomizing of the hyperglobalists and skeptics that the state and market (or the *political* and *economic*) appear as exceedingly reified concepts with scant attention paid to the historicity or materiality of their analytical separation. One approach, which follows in the spirit of the work of the economic historian Karl Polanyi (McMichael 2000:103–104),[4] seeks to smooth over the problem with the view that markets are from the outset 'political institutions' and are always embedded in differing socio-institutional settings the origins of which reflect the varying geo-spatial conditions of the mutual emergence of market and state. However, while insightful and instructive for some aspects of the political economic study of capitalism, uncritical acceptance of this stance as the final word forestalls investigation into other research domains such as the study of what makes capitalism distinctive as a form of organizing economic life (that is, what distinguishes the principles of operation of the capitalist commodity economy from the general norms of economic life), and the theorizing of the deep economic structure or logic of capital, both of which I believe were at the forefront of Marx's own research agenda. And it is precisely this latter sort of analysis that allows us to judge if an economic order is capitalist or not. For surely, at some point, it has to be asked with regard to the foregoing debate, whether politics or the state interferes with the market to such a degree and in various concrete ways so as to signify a movement away from capitalism? Or, whether the states' neglecting to perform specific functions required of it in its historic role as a capitalist state contributes to the unraveling of the rule of capital?

Even more importantly, though, the problematizing of capitalism must confront the issue of whether it is even possible in the first place to conceptualize a global capitalism as a distinct entity and *form* of capitalism in the same way as a national, geo-spatially determined capitalism – of whatever institutional configuration or model, degree of internationalization, and so on – has been conceptualized. The hyperglobalist/skeptic confrontation proceeds as if such things as a global capitalist economy or global market are in themselves unproblematic notions, and that one can simply counter-pose or juxtapose these to a state and *its* economy/market. Paradoxically, then, while the so-called transformationalist thesis appears on the surface as the most provocative – tackling the difficult issue of the possibility that the whole universe of political and social action and the very meaning of categories such as world economy and state has changed – it is also the approach which has been least explicit in discussion of the economics of such. On the other hand, the problem of the so-called governance (with a broadly conceived understanding of the concept as the concern over world-historic political outcomes) constitutes an important focus, though I believe that sort of research initiative would be far more fruitful once the question of capitalist substance is clarified.

Specifying capitalism

In an important contribution to the ongoing discussion of the power and relevance of Marxian value theory, Foley (2000a: 3) suggests that assessments of the multifarious contributions to value theory debates should manifest an express concern with the varying proponents position on the problem of what precise questions value theory is intended to answer. As I have consistently argued (Westra 1999, 2000, 2001, 2002a), discussion of value theory and Marxian economics *per se* has largely unfolded with the understanding that the latter constitutes a *sub-theory* of an over-arching Marxian project of historical materialism. Thus, the radical pedigree of different approaches to value theory has tended to be appraised on the basis of the extent to which they interface with historical materialism and its perspective on human history and historical transformation. This has embroiled value theory in debates over 'exploitation,' class struggle, historical outcomes of 'tendencies' such as that of the 'falling rate of profit,' and the 'socializing' of production *en route* to socialism. While I would agree that such research initiatives possibly add to the development of Marxist theory as a whole, there exists a far more important question that I believe value theory is required to answer; a question that establishes Marxian economics as a project distinct from historical materialism.

The approach to value theory that animates this chapter emanates from Japan and is rooted in the groundbreaking work of Japanese economists Kozo Uno and Thomas Sekine.[5] What the specific problematic that value theory is set upon to solve, according to the Uno approach, is the unraveling of the mystery of how the capitalist commodity economy is able to pursue its abstract goal of augmenting value while simultaneously meeting the requirement of reproducing human material life as demanded of any viable socio-economic order. Put differently, the question is: How is it possible for an 'upside-down' reified economy, where socio-material relations between people are effaced, and replaced by quantitative 'relations between things,' to organize the economic life of an entire human society in the first place? Through the clear fashion in which this question delimits its subject focus then – to capitalism, a historically peculiar and transient economic order – Marxian economics and the political economic study of capitalism[6] is established as a discrete research domain within Marxist theory.

To answer the question as posed above saddles Marxian economics with a unique epistemological dilemma the full extent of which has rarely been appreciated. At the root of capitalist reification is a process of self-synthesis or self-abstraction whereby capital tends to purge or purify its environment of all non-economic, non-capitalist encumbrances, commodify all use-value life including its wellspring of human labor power, and manage human material existence through impersonal society-wide integrated systems of self-regulating markets. The challenge for Marxian economics is to capture this reificatory logic of capital under conditions where in actual capitalist history the logic of capital is resisted in a myriad of ways. Unoists affirm Marx's adoption of a dialectical procedure to meet that challenge but emphasize that Marx never satisfactorily completed his project of economics in *Capital*. And, Marx compromised his own method of dialectical exposition at key junctures. For Uno, to fully and robustly capture the abstract logic and inner workings of capital required that its tendency to reify socio-material existence be hypothetically consummated in a dialectical reconstruction of *Capital* as the *theory of a purely capitalist society* (TPCS). The dialectical mode of analysis is vital to the study of capital because its procedure of conceptual self-synthesis and elaboration of economic categories parallels capital's own *modus operandi* in which the material force of value subsumes or synthesizes use-value life.[7] Extrapolating the tendencies of capital to a hypothetical conclusion, though one of the more controversial tenets of the Uno approach to value theory, follows from the fact that while a purely capitalist society is never materialized in history,[8] to fully grasp the logical inner workings of *capital* – the *constant* in all historical capitalism – demands that its logic be studied free from all interferences.

Driving the dialectic, as in Marx's *Capital*, is the fundamental contradiction of capital – that between value and use-value – discovered first in the commodity, the most elemental representation of capital. The TPCS then traces this contradiction through three 'doctrines.'[9] In the *doctrine of circulation*, the logic of the phenomenal forms of capitalist exchange relations – the generating of the commodity form, the money form and the capital form – is unraveled. The *doctrine of production* explores the subsumption by capital of the labor and production process through which capital secures the conditions of its self-expansion. Capital is further examined here in its circulation and reproduction processes. Finally, the *doctrine of distribution* exposes the modalities of the division of surplus value in the capitalist market. And it is therein that the logic of capital is consummated, and the dialectic attains closure, when capital itself becomes a commodity as expressed in the category of interest. To sum up, the TPCS constitutes an economic theory of an 'economic' society, a generalized commodity-economy featuring only three social classes – workers, capitalists and landlords that personify respectively the economic categories of wages, profit and ground rent – where all production is commodity production, all labor power is commodified, and the economy is managed entirely by an integrated system of self-regulating markets under the abstract dictatorship of the impersonal *law of value*.

Keeping this caricature of the dialectic of capital in the TPCS in mind let us return to the matter of the material reproductive viability of capitalism. Interestingly, in the afore-cited article on current value theory debates, Foley (2000a) zeroes in on two of the signal puzzles that have dogged the fruitful development of Marxian value theory: One is the introduction of the labor theory of value within the context of discussion of the exchange of commodities in Chapter 1 of Volume 1 of *Capital*. The other surrounds the later analysis in the third volume of that work where Marx grapples with questions of the formation of prices on the capitalist market under varying conditions of capitalist production, though leaves underdeveloped and obscure the connection with such and the labor theory of value; a question which has come to be known, rather infamously, as the *transformation problem*. However, in an otherwise discerning work, Foley does not draw out the vital and intimate connection between the two. Yet, it has been a hallmark of the Uno approach to value theory to view those problems as intimately intertwined with the ultimate resolution impinging upon what I have already suggested is the key question of Marxian economics. To be sure, an exhaustive treatment of the above, by far, outstrips the bounds of this chapter, but in what follows I intend to schematically review the steps in the Unoist argument.

Unoists argue that the problems for Marxian value theory in *Capital* began precisely, when in introducing the labor theory of value in the discussion of the circulation or value forms of capital, Marx vitiated his own methodological procedure which required the immanence and logical interrelation of all the categories of capital be demonstrated. That is, in the ascending of the dialectic into the inner sanctum of capital, the formative elaboration upon the social commensurability of commodities or their 'moneyness'[10] requires only the initial demonstration of the possible *expression* of value in the use-value of another commodity, and then the eventual *measuring* of the value of a commodity in terms of money with the establishment of a 'normal price' for it. Of course, the presupposition of the theory remains that the object of study is the capitalist commodity economy, only at this point in the theory the dialectic must necessarily hold implicit both the modalities and conditions through which such a normal price is actually arrived at in the market and the specific *determination* or *substance* of the value of a commodity.

Following the specification of the *general formula* for capital, $M-C-M'$ which characterizes the *arbitrage* operations of merchant capital (though is itself predicated upon the understanding that material existence in capitalist society is reproduced for the abstract purpose of augmenting value), the dialectic is driven to the question of the substance of value and the potential of capital for *self*-augmentation; a question at the heart of the doctrine of production, which finally demands the introduction of the labor theory of value and its conceptual accouterment (abstract labor, socially necessary labor, surplus value and etc.). The unfurling of the labor theory or law of value here does not mean, of course, that there actually exists a separate value 'system' as distinct from a price system the operation of which can be verified empirically in capitalist society. Rather, the dialectic continues to hold implicit the aforementioned modalities and conditions under which the law of value holds in the operation of the capitalist market. It is only within the context of the doctrine of distribution, which roughly corresponds to the material of

Volume 3 of Marx's *Capital*, that the above, and the question of *price*, can be made explicit. But, it is because scant attention has been paid to the dialectical architecture of *Capital* that what has emerged as the so-called transformation problem persists at all.

A major contribution to Marxian economics by Sekine (1997 Vol. 2: 12ff.), then, has been his elaboration upon the 'twofold' character of the notion of transformation in Marx's *Capital*. That is, Marx used the term in a *qualitative* sense to illustrate a further specification of concepts – the transformation of the commodity form into the money form, the transformation of money into capital, and so on – where there is certainly no requirement for support from a mathematical operation. Understood in this light, there should be no 'transformation problem' with regard to the transformation of value into price, or surplus value into profit, and so on. On the other hand, transformation has a mathematical denotation as the plotting of coordinates across two differing spaces or 'systems.' In the context of Volume 3 of *Capital* or the doctrine of distribution in the TPCS, questions of capitals heterogeneity and the impact of market forces of supply and demand – which underpin the divergence of prices from value – confront the dialectic. What Sekine demonstrates, is that the specification of the 'technology complex' permits the simultaneous *quantitative* elucidation of prices and values. And, through the provision of specific information on the organic composition of capital it is possible to produce the bedeviling 'inverse' calculations or movements between rates of profit and prices *and* surplus value and values (and vice versa).

The upshot of all this is that while on a day-to-day basis our eyes may be transfixed by the movement of market prices or the quantitative dimension of capital that does not mean the concept of value can be dispensed with as prices, though diverging from values, are necessarily always 'tethered' to such. For in the capitalist market, under conditions of capitalist competition, as the economy tends toward a general equilibrium where all commodities are traded at their normal or 'equilibrium' prices and social resources are 'optimally' allocated, what is being confirmed is the economic governance of the law of value. In other words, no human society could survive for long in the absence of some central organizing principle to insure that basic goods are neither over-produced nor under-produced relative to the existing pattern of social demand (and that the direct producers received, at minimum, the product of their necessary labor). Such equilibrating of supply and demand is uniquely guaranteed in capitalist society when all production is carried out by commodified labor power and the commodity, with which the dialectic began, is produced strictly as a value object, with complete indifference to its use-value and finally that this commodity produced as a value object embodies only socially necessary labor. As Sekine (1999: 36–37) puts it, value 'mediates' between that which is specifically capitalist and – material existence itself – something that is supra-historic and without which human society could not exist. In this sense, the viability of capitalism captured in the 'surface' tendency toward a general equilibrium in the market exists in embryo, as Marx intimated, in the commodity. But this cannot be asserted. Rather, it must be painstakingly established through the unfolding of all the categories of capital as the dialectic accomplishes in the TPCS.[11]

Capital and globalization: retreating to the 'interstices' of the world?

Before proceeding to the substantive question of this section and for that matter, the chapter, let us briefly turn our attention back to some crucial aspects of the preceding discussion on the important question of what precise problematic Marxian value theory is intended to provide a solution for. My argument is that capitalism, like any human society in history, requires at its core some principle insuring its material reproductive viability; guaranteeing that under the constraints of a given set of social relations the demand for basic goods is met in a way that does not squander social resources, and the TPCS exposes this – the gravitation of the economy toward a general equilibrium under the dictates of the impersonal law of value – robustly and concisely for capitalist society. And, while it is true that no actually existing capitalism has materialized as stark a society as depicted in the TPCS, I believe the TPCS offers a solid touchstone for carrying out any adjudication over capitalist substance in the current world economy. In short, determinations should be based upon the approximation to the modalities of commodity economic material reproductive viability as captured in the TPCS.[12] However, given the concentration upon the deep structure and logical inner workings of capital in the TPCS, both the *geo-spatial* dimension of capital and the state were necessarily held implicit. Yet, to operationalize the above test for capitalist substance in actually existing capitalism requires that the foregoing be factored into the discussion.

To focus upon the geo-spatial dimension of capital, first, it is possible to imagine the materialization of the *purely* capitalist society of the TPCS as a *global commodity economy*. And in fact, to create the frictionless space for capital to expose itself for what it is, one of the assumptions of the TPCS was precisely that the world of capital was borderless or 'global.' However, at this point, even accepting the most sanguine accounts of the hyperglobalists, we would have to admit that the regularizing or harmonizing of economic life, as required in the specifically capitalist self-regulating market, is not even in the remotest fashion being approximated across the world economy today. And, besides the question of vast and widening world economic asymmetries touched on above, it has been pointed out by even those working within the tradition of mainstream economics that the very 'strategic' international investment behavior of the generally agreed upon prime agents of globalization – the TNC's – is predicated upon the fact that markets are *not* perfect (Ietto-Gilles 2002: 115).

But what about the possibility of a historically existing global capitalism as the outcome of current world economic processes; one that we could then counter-pose to past existent national capitalisms? The fact is, in geo-spatial terms, capitalist development proceeded extremely unevenly and the birth of capital within the relatively narrow geographical bounds of England and Western Europe was, to paraphrase Marx, stamped in distinct ways by conditions inherited from the past. As argued by Anderson (1979), the initial fashioning of the instruments of a 'national' economy occurred within the cocoon of the Absolutist state, an institution that arose in history to manage the contradictions of a weakening feudalism. And following the bourgeois revolutions, it would then be the 'concentrated power' of this state, as Marx put it, that would champion the enveloping of the economic life of the social community by the society-wide integrated system of capitalist markets. It was in this sense, that in contrasting the operation of markets since the dawn of time with the specifically capitalist market, Marx referred to the former case in terms of markets functioning at the 'interstices' or edges of community life and the latter as the subsumption of community material life itself by the commodity economy. The point to be emphasized here is that in human history, the social community the material reproductive viability of which capital is charged with insuring is the national community or nation state.

As the TPCS makes abundantly clear, the *sine qua non* of capitalism is the commodification of labor power, for only with such labor power, rendered wholly *indifferent* to use-value, is capital able to shift production toward *any* good according to the changing pattern of social demand (and thus reproduce the economic life of the community through the chrematistic operation of the self-regulating market). But, what has often been neglected in the focus upon this condition of emergence of capital and that which remains highly consequential for the globalization debate is the question of the relationship between capital and *land*. As elaborated upon by Nagahara (2000), Uno's contribution to Marxian economics involves not only the clarification of how through the category of ground rent capital negotiates with something the fundamental nature and products of which have none of the uniformity of capitalistically produced means of production and commodities, but also the drawing out of the implications of the *modus vivendi* capital develops with that essentially 'external' to it. That is, though not in a capitalist form, landed property pre-dates capital, and following the expulsion of the direct producers from that land (the commodification of labor power), capital finds itself in the position where it must deal with the owner. The relation that evolves then entails the recognition by capital of the *legal title* to the land as private property and while in the TPCS the state is only implicit what is suggested for the development of capitalism in history is that at the most fundamental level capital is bound to the state form and its legal system. And, this tenet carries even greater weight as illustrated when the TPCS turns to the category of interest, the most fetishized mode of existence of capital. For here capital applies the same principle it had contrived to deal with landed property, 'internally' to itself; the principle, that is, of 'property' yielding an income.[13] What Nagahara suggests is that even the 'fictitious capital' of world economic financialization (accepted as paradigmatic of the purported tendencies toward 'de-territorialization' or 'dematerialization' marking globalization) nevertheless requires the state for its capitalist appropriation.[14]

Now the point has been reached where it is possible to attempt an answer to the key question animating this chapter. Authoritative reviews of state theory (Carnoy 1984; Jessop 1990) generally agree that Marxist theories of the state fit into three broad categories of theory: 'class centric'; 'state centric'; and, 'capital centric.' While I will offer a fuller and specifically Unoist account of the capitalist state in a later work this much can be said here: Both class and state centric perspectives reflect an unacceptable level of generality in approach to the capitalist state deriving from the aforementioned problematic view of the political economic study of capitalism as a sub-theory of an overarching historical materialism. Capital centric approaches held out the greatest promise but their development has been compromised both by difficulties related to the above quandary as well as a lack of clarity over the precise theorizing of capital upon which their theory of the state was to be based.[15] My position is that the theorizing of the capitalist state must commence with the TPCS. Of course, a purely capitalist society as captured in the TPCS is an economic society *par excellence* in which no state exists. And it is the TPCS that provides the material foundation for the very notion of base/superstructure or the analytical separation of the economic and political in Marxist theory. But it is precisely the necessary assumption of the theory that all use-value life is sufficiently docile and amenable to complete subsumption according to the principles of the commodity economy that foregrounds the theorizing of the capitalist state. For in actually existing capitalism not only have significant areas of economic life remained external to capital but across capitalist history the commodity economy has required various degrees and types of extra-economic support. And it is the recognition that such 'externalities' must be managed for capital to viably reproduce human material existence upon which the theorizing of the state is predicated.

As noted above (see note 6), the Uno approach to Marxian political economy claims that the study of capitalism as a whole requires three levels of analysis – the TPCS, stage theory and the historical study of capitalism. The role of stage theory is to capture the concretizing of the inner logic of capital in terms of the demands placed upon capital by the production of use values characteristic of its world historic stages of development. The theorizing of the capitalist state here, revolves around the stage specific policies supporting capital accumulation (and the stages of capitalism in Uno theory are in fact named according to those policies). Thus, if we examine capital accumulation through the prism of the paradigmatic eighteenth century *mercantilist* use-value, *wool*,[16] it becomes clear that in this formative period of capitalism where markets, particularly for labor power, are not self-regulating and involve forms of monopoly pricing and so on, the extent of externalities to be met by the state is vast. And given how under such conditions the viability of community material life necessarily involved governance by other material reproductive principles than that of capital, it is only because mercantilist policy was supportive of capitalist development that this period qualifies for theorization as a stage of capitalism.

On the other hand, if there ever existed a historical period in which actually existing capitalism embodied the market equilibrating material reproductive properties of capital depicted in the TPCS – where labor power was largely commodified (labor was unorganized and received a subsistence wage), businesses managed by principals or owners conducted operations through arms length *external* market transactions based on signals furnished by equilibrium prices and satisfied capitalization requirements through re-invested profits, and where the state did little more in the domestic arena than print currency and provide accumulation with an enforceable legal framework – it was the stage of *liberalism* characterized by *cotton* industry in the mid-nineteenth-century England. However, the shaping of capitalist development first by *steel* production typical of early twentieth-century *imperialism* and following the World War II by *automobile* and consumer durable production of the capitalist stage of *consumerism* clearly involved a progression away from the modalities of material reproductive viability of capital captured in the theorizing of the economic tendency toward a general equilibrium. Obvious examples of this transformation are the rise of the joint-stock and corporate forms of capital and the issues of economic agency that such create, the increasing *internalizing* of business transactions, greater reliance upon monopoly and 'transfer' pricing, massive capitalization commitments necessitating the 'socializing' of investment and guarantee of product markets, the unionizing and hence partial de-commodifying of labor power, and so on. My position (Westra 2002b), in fact, is that the very problem of variant models of capitalism referred to above can best be unpacked in terms of institutional responses to precisely these *stage specific* demands of capital accumulation in the stage of consumerism.

As with the stage of mercantilism then, so for the stage of consumerism, which certainly constitutes a huge step away from the principles of self-regulating markets of the commodity economy, the extent of externalities heaped upon the state to manage is vast and in fact dictated that other operative principles of economy such as planning and economic programming be enlisted to insure the viable reproduction of the economic life of the social community. The policy arsenal of the consumerist state in this regard – the management of effective demand, enormous investment in infrastructure (social, business or warfare depending on the institutional model), provision of social wages and insurances, monetary and fiscal policy, to name a few – has been well documented. And to this point I have left to one side the question of the international dimension of capital in stage theory. For the stage of consumerism, with international capital characterized by TNC internationalization of production and finance – including FDI, international licensing, patenting and subcontracting (fostering the emergence of a truly international division of labor for the first time in history), the internationalization of banking and financial intermediation, and so on – the problems that called forth economic planning by the state to support capital accumulation in the national economic context were only compounded. And the international institutional edifice of consumerism – including the Bretton Woods monetary system with its exchange rate adjustment mechanisms and capital controls – is testimony to this.

Referring back to the globalization debate with which the chapter began, it should be clear that the stage specific structures of consumerist capital accumulation, as I have schematically outlined them, constitute conditions of possibility for much of what falls within the ambit of the concept of globalization.[17] Hence, when we consider the momentous policy shift captured under the rubric neo-liberalism – the processes of de-regulation, liberalization, de-unionization, clawing back of social wages and insurances, and so on – what is evident is that whether we conceive of this in the terms of the skeptics, as a political project predicated upon the capacities of particular states (purportedly in support of 'their' capital and capitalist models), or accept the more politically benign view of the transformationalists that globalization is simply the progressive emergence of new sovereignties and forms of governance, the fact remains that the trend is toward the state abdicating its responsibility for managing the externalities required by capital to viably manage the material reproduction of the social community. For, as things stand, the economic structures of consumerism that had necessitated massive state support for their capitalist operation persist in many ways. For example, the productive core of the economies of advanced industrial states continues to revolve around the complex use-value cluster of consumer durables. As well, despite the chants of enthusiasts of 'flexible production,' the economic landscape is still dominated by the TNC the above-cited practices of which have only been further solidified.[18] Further, while the claw-backs of social entitlements and employee benefit packages point toward the re-commodifying of labor power, this is counteracted by structural unemployment and 'third-worldization' of work where wages fall below what is required for the reproduction of that labor power in the advanced industrial states. Such (and the list can be extended *ad infinitum*) only confirms the absurdity of neo-liberal claims that current practices herald a return to a *laissez faire* economy akin to the capitalism of the stage of liberalism. Even internationally the economy is a peculiar amalgam of rule governed trading 'regimes' (with increasing proportions of what appears in world trade statistics composed of the movement of goods between branches of a given TNC), and titanic loosely regulated flows of capital offering little positive fallout for the on-ground economy.

Therefore, as capital has increasingly sought to 'free' itself through globalization from the instruments of planning and programming, that though supporting it also appeared to constrain it, and even enlisted the concentrated power of existing states in this endeavor,[19] it has embarked upon a contradictory process undermining the very conditions of its existence. For if current states abdicate the responsibility for managing the ever-widening field of externalities of capital, the only option for the survival of a specifically capitalist economy in the world economy today would be the rise of a single world capitalist or bourgeois state. This would also satisfy the demand for the legal foundations of capitalist appropriation adverted to by Nagahara. But, given the massive extent of the world economic asymmetries that the critical globalization literature has so aptly drawn our attention to, the rise of a world bourgeois state is pure fantasy. In short, Marx had recognized how categories such as wages and money and the activity of profit-making long antedated capitalism. But their economic force was never central to the material reproduction of social communities until that ontologically unique and transient epoch in human history when they were melded together as part of the logical inner workings of the capitalist commodity economy that would reproduce the economic life of an entire society for the abstract purpose of augmenting value. Of course, this capitalist aberration would last far longer than Marx envisioned as its mounting externalities were adequately contained through the recruitment by capital of support from an increasingly visible and heavy-hand of the state. The liberating of capital from its obligations in this regard also signifies the freeing of capital to retreat to the realm of operation from whence it originated – the interstices of the world. And in this flight, capital is vacating the economic space of historically constituted social communities for the emergence of the other principles of material reproduction.

It is in relation to the aforementioned that I will suggest directions for further research. The first question that arises is why capital is loosening its grip on our economic lives in the current conjuncture? The short answer here is that under the advancing conditions of internationalization of production, capital is able to produce key commodities in selected locales across the globe where labor power is more easily commodified. Hence, capital has tended to divest itself of the cumbersome institutional arrangements that had enabled it to maintain the commodification of labor power in its production heartlands and has taken little responsibility for managing economic externalities elsewhere. The second question involves the sorts of principles of economic reproduction replacing capital. While the contours of the future are undeveloped, our current world economic life is characterized by increasingly ominous extensions of TNC economic programming, 'statist' militarized economies (the US), and the surfacing of new authoritarian forms of labor control. On the other hand, we have witnessed the gestation of potentially progressive principles of material reproduction such as 'local exchange and trading systems,' community barter, and other types of the so-called 'anti-economy.'

Conclusion

This chapter commenced with a cautionary word that the work herein was formative and exploratory. The argument then proceeded with the claim that a lacuna in the burgeoning literature on globalization with disabling explanatory consequences was its failure to problematize capitalism. My position was that 'bringing capitalism back in' to the debate necessitated that capital be adequately defined. It was subsequently maintained that the optimal vehicle for that task was Marxian value theory as embodied in the TPCS of the Japanese Uno approach. The TPCS defines capital through a dialectical exposition of all its categories, which demonstrates how it is possible for capital to simultaneously fulfill its abstract mission of value augmentation while viably reproducing the material life of an entire society. What the TPCS confirms is the law of value as the central organizing principle of capital insuring that basic goods are neither over-produced nor under-produced relative to the existing pattern of social demand. And such is captured in the tending of the economy toward a general equilibrium. It was then argued that the touchstone for detecting capitalist substance in actually existing economies was the approximation of their concrete modalities of material reproductive viability to those embodied in the TPCS. But, given the marking of the reproductive mechanisms of capital in actually existing capitalist economies by an ever-enlarging field of externalities, it was contended that to operationalize the test for capitalist substance required the factoring in to the discussion of geo-spatial questions of capitalist development and the state. On that basis I suggested that faced with the externalities inherent in the capitalist management of the production of the use-value cluster of consumer durables characteristic of consumerism, the final stage of capitalism, capital was pushed to rely further on the support of the state and other principles of material reproduction. However, as revealed in the policy thrust of neo-liberalism, capital also experienced the measures it adopted for managing its externalities as constraints. Yet, in throwing off that apparent yoke to free itself, as depicted in the world economic phenomena of globalization, capital tends to undermine its very conditions of existence. And in this sense, as capital escapes to the interstices of the world, it leaves the social community to adopt other principles of material reproduction. Here, as I noted above, the transformationalist camp is prescient with its notion of an impending new feudalism. For as Marx himself suggested capitalism would be followed either by socialism or forms of 'barbarism.'

Notes

1. Though not discussed in this chapter, it may be noted that current debates also resurrect, in altered guise, the all-familiar 'end-of-ideology' mantra.
2. See for example Strange (1998).
3. This line of argument has also assumed a 'class' dimension in some writing (Moran 1998) in that it is argued that the states' national and international policies reflect dilemmas of its internal class conflicts though the hyperglobalist counter argument would be that there exists a 'transnational capitalist class' (Sklair 2001) with class conflict increasingly assuming a global scope.
4. See also many of the selections in Hollingsworth and Boyer (1998).
5. The key English language monographs of the approach are Uno (1980), Sekine (1997), and Albritton (1991).
6. The Uno approach claims that though Marxian economics is most fundamental, the political economic study of capitalism as a whole must be undertaken at three *levels of analysis* where the movement in theory from the analysis of the inner logic and deep structure of capital to the study of capitalist history is mediated by a *stage theory* of capitalist development. See for example Albritton (1991), Westra (1996).
7. To defend this position requires complex philosophical argumentation the extent of which would outstrip the bounds of this chapter. See, in this regard, Sekine (1997, 1998, 2002). And for the situating of the argument within current debates in the theory of knowledge, see Albritton (1999).
8. The materializing of a purely capitalist society in history as a *bourgeois utopia* would amount to a confirmation of bourgeois ideology that capitalism was the 'natural' mode of organizing human material reproductive affairs.
9. The division of the TPCS into three doctrines mirrors the structure of G.W.F. Hegel's *Logic*. See note 7.
10. What follows draws upon Sekine (1997 Vol. 1).
11. As I have explained elsewhere (Westra 1999, 2000), the relationship between the project of Marxian economics and historical materialism involves a cognitive sequence in which the well-known categories utilized in the latter are grounded as *economic* concepts in the former, rather than the other way around as most conventional Marxism – which reads historical materialism as the master theory and the political economic study of capitalism as the sub-theory – believes. And in this fashion, as well, the very *materialist* research program of Marxism, which is directed toward probing the material anatomy of past historical societies and assessing the potential material reproductive viability of future ones, necessarily germinates in the TPCS where such is undertaken in *pure* economic terms; terms, to be sure, of the capitalist *commodity economy*, but which nevertheless expose economic life *transparently* for first time in human history.
12. Previously, Albritton (2001) has attempted to ground such a judgment in the degree of commodification of the key capitalist commodities of labor, land and money with the TPCS as the template. Sekine (this volume) bases his judgment on the nature of the business cycle and its role in regulating the commodification of labor power as captured in the TPCS and, in this way, produces a far more restrictive view of the existence of capitalism proper in history than does this chapter. However, whatever the perspective on theorizing capitalism one adopts, ultimately, determinations on the coming into being and passing of capitalism in history will involve a subjective judgment. My position here is simply that we

will be in a far better position to make such judgments based on the TPCS than otherwise.

13. Sekine (1997 Vol. 2: 134ff.) constitutes the optimal resource to-date for accessing the Marxian theory of interest. The important notion here, as touched upon above, is that in the closing of the 'dialectical circle' capital returns to where it originated, assuming the form of a commodity in the sphere of circulation. And, appearing as such, as a mere 'asset' the ownership of which demands remuneration, capital expunges all traces of its fundamental determination in the labor and production process.
14. The way in which this delicate 'dance' between footloose capital and the state has unfolded in the world economy today is addressed in part by the interesting study of Palan (1998) on the phenomena of 'offshore.'
15. I have argued elsewhere (Westra 2000: Chapter 2), that the 'strategic relational' theory of the state of Jessop (1990) would constitute a valuable contribution to an Unoist theory of the state if placed within the context of the mid-range level of analysis of stage theory.
16. What follows draws upon Albritton (1991).
17. I have touched upon this in a preliminary fashion in Westra (2002b).
18. Ietto-Gilles (2002) provides an up-to-date overview here.
19. Again, I am leaving to one side the potential *class* dimensions of this. See note 3.

6
When Things Go Wrong: The Political Economy of Market Breakdown

Alan Freeman

> Political Economy is when people ask themselves why they have no money
>
> – Kurt Tucholsky

Why things go wrong: the need for a theory of market breakdown

In this chapter, I ask what happens when markets break down. I aim to show that the answer which any theory gives to this question depends on its implicit, or explicit, concept of value.

I begin with arguably the most basic question in economics: Are breakdown and recovery endogenous or exogenous? Do markets fall or are they pushed? Conversely, do they mend themselves, or does someone have to stick them back together?

If markets can in fact go wrong of their own accord, and if there are circumstances in which they cannot correct themselves, then most modern policy nostrums are open to question: for example, that deregulation improves efficiency, that no one loses from free trade, or that optimal growth depends on the free movement of capital. And since modern globalization is virtually identical to the extension of the market, it leads one legitimately to ask whether globalization itself has intrinsic limits.

The primary 'finding' of all dominant economic theories is that the market works. This rarely appears so crudely as the statement that it is infallible. Instead, such theories predict that it fails only when not permitted to work properly, and that it will always correct itself, left to its own devices: that is, breakdown is exogenous and recovery is endogenous.

I will show that this finding arises from the shared starting point of these theories, the *equilibrium* or comparative static paradigm.[1] The variables of which they speak are assumed, for the purpose of calculating them, to be constant. This is only possible if, and is equivalent to assuming that, the market works so perfectly that nothing needs to change.

This is not a neutral assumption. I will show that it makes it impossible to deduce endogenous market failure. To put it another way: if in fact, markets do fail of their own accord, equilibrium theories are intrinsically incapable of knowing because they will always attribute the failure to something outside the market. Hence, their primary finding tells us nothing about reality because it is the only finding they can produce.

How do we know it went wrong?

Perhaps endogenous breakdown never happens. Perhaps the market really is perfect. How would we know? The problem is that equilibrium theories cannot tell the difference. In the language of Popper (1968), they are unfalsifiable. They cannot test for endogenous breakdown because they cannot demarcate it from exogenous breakdown.

Scientifically, they must therefore be tested against independent evidence. For this reason, I will single out what I term the four 'big' facts of modern capitalism which are the most universally recognized, the most persistent and regular, and the clearest expressions of endogenous market failure:

1. recurrent structural crisis – prolonged 30–50 year periods of falling profits and low growth, such as the one we are now living through;
2. the growth without limit of inequality between nations;
3. the regularity of cyclical crisis;
4. the persistence of class struggle.

Each of these either directly prevents the market regulating the social and political relations required for its survival, or brings into being forces that so act. Each occurs persistently or recurs regularly, under a wide variety of circumstances. And each is more persistent, and more marked, the greater the extent of the market.

History matters. When an event happens once, surrounded by a maze of complex circumstances, a case can be made for any theory relating it to any of these circumstances. But when something happens repeatedly, or persists for a very long time, under circumstances that vary very widely, we must discard any theory that relies on any circumstance not always present. The only circumstance persistently present, through 200 years of the capitalist market, is the capitalist market itself. It is scientifically highly questionable to treat its repeated and persistent failures as produced by anything other than itself.

Is there a theory that can account for this? Yes – but it is treated as heresy. The equilibrium paradigm finds that the principal theory of endogenous breakdown, that of Marx, is incoherent. However this 'finding' itself rests on the same paradigmatic principle: it rests on the supposition that Marx himself was an equilibrium theorist.

I will show that an alternative, *Temporal Single System Interpretation* (TSSI), of Marx's value theory offers a coherent explanation of the major observable manifestations of market breakdown. This capacity resides in two features of the interpretation:

1. Values and prices are non-equilibrium magnitudes, defined without presupposing the market keeps them constant.
2. The magnitude of value of every commodity is given by the total labor time spent producing it.

The evidence that this was Marx's theory will not be restated here and the reader is referred to the copious literature. She should note that whereas the standard interpretation is attributed to Marx on the basis of simple assertion, the attributions in this article are supported by evidence which she may accept or reject.

When things go right: the need for political economy

The converse view, that breakdown is inevitable, is equally questionable. Market breakdown does not happen all the time and is not a simple descent into the void but a definite dynamic process from which recovery is sometimes automatic, seldom impossible, and always costs lives. When the market fails, it does not collapse but brings politics into play. It makes the invisible hand visible, and summons conscious forces to action as governments, peoples, and classes intervene to restore the means to reproduce themselves which the market now fails to deliver.

I seek to transcend the crude polarization between infallible market success, and inevitable market breakdown, by establishing a proper boundary between what is actually endogenous and what is actually exogenous; between automatic processes of which individuals are only indirectly conscious and exogenous acts which they know about, initiate, and take part in.

The requirement of a valid value theory is, thus, that it should be able to explain, and quantitatively account for, *the relation between the market and the society*: specifically, its relation to the social forces summoned to existence by the regular and persistent failures which are intrinsic to it.

Breakdown as the consequence of motion

The essential starting point is a paradigm which is absolutely independent of the assumption of market perfection: the *temporal*, or non-equilibrium paradigm, which this article will explain. Its magnitudes are determinate whether or not the market is static.

This starting point is required because breakdown is produced by motion. All theories that begin by suppressing this motion end up attributing its effects to something external to the market: be it government, monetary regulation, trade unions, communism, terrorism, war, historical backwardness, exhaustion of the entrepreneurial spirit or, in left versions, a special régime of accumulation, anomalous business behavior, the course of technological progress... in this way, breakdown is produced by anything and everything except the economy itself.

Only a concept that permits the market to move can account for the effects of its movement. To put it another way, stasis is a special case of motion, and not the other way around. A waterfall is not a curved lake: a lake is a flat waterfall. The waterfall's curvature is caused by the motion; if we construct a theory of water from which motion was suppressed, we would conclude that all bodies of water are necessarily flat and that waterfalls must be a supernatural creation. This is, effectively, the position in which the equilibrium paradigm places those economic theories unfortunate enough to adopt it.

Rational ethics require that the actual motion is laid bare. Consequently two things are required. The analysis of the economy has to be conducted in terms of quantitatively determinate and measurable variables, and the definition of these variables must be independent, without qualification, of the assumption that the market is functioning while they are determined. It requires, in short, a theory of value.

Motion of what?

The peculiarity of the capitalist mode of production is that its social outcomes are the consequence of private actions. This is the reason, specific to capitalism, that its agents are not directly conscious of the results of what they do. This is also the reason that they become conscious when the results fail them.

The traditional distinction between the 'micro' world of price and value and the 'macro' world of investment, distribution and growth, is therefore artificial: prices are the means by which the market effects social change. The market is the organizer of competition, a struggle for a *share* of something. When oil doubles in price, it does not just modify the relation between one car and one pump; it reallocates access to the whole of a key world resource, on which depends everything in the world economy from the power and wealth of nations to the progress of the business cycle. It takes resources from those who purchase oil and gives it to those who sell it. This is why people go to war about it.

In order to understand how the market interacts with society, it must first therefore be understood as a part of it, as a mode of social organization which allocates definite resources to definite functions on which its existence depends. Breakdown occurs when one of these functions is threatened with non-existence.

The visible expression of this mode of organization is money, to be precise, the money price of commodities. The idea of value arises because although money organizes things other than itself – above all, production – and although it provides a quantitative measure of the results, it does not do so directly. Money price can be increased by fiat or a printing press, regardless of the resources which gave rise to it or the results which it pays for. We cannot therefore know, when prices or profits rise or fall, what produced the change. The decisive requirement of a value theory is to distinguish those variations in money output which arise from production, from those variations that do not.

At least two aspects of production affect the money price of its results, namely the physical size or use-value of the produced commodities, and the social resources that produced them. There is therefore a choice of value concepts. Can we better explain the market's insertion into society by conceiving of money as representing physical, or social, resources?

I will show that the equilibrium paradigm is indissociable from one particular concept of value, which TSSI scholars term the use-value or *physicalist* concept. According to this the value of output is in some sense defined by its quantity. Equilibrium can produce no other value concept, and physicalism is most coherent in an equilibrium paradigm.

Temporalism is however compatible with a wide variety of value concepts – including less coherent variants of physicalism; the Kaleckian concept which is, in essence, that money is value directly; and Marx's concept that the substance of value is labor time. Which of these is conceptually preferable cannot be deduced from temporalism but must be established independently.

The limits to growth – social or physical?

The market achieves the organization of society through competition. Competition arises because the resources allocated by the market are limited; what one person gains, another loses. The question is, from where do the limits come: from things, or people? Money organizes society, not nature, and mediates between producers, not products. A theory that makes it appear as if the market mediates between things will make heavy weather of explaining its insertion into society.

Furthermore if capitalism's limits are imposed by physical resources, it is hard to see where the present phase of market breakdown comes from. Physical limits may well be important in the future, but right now physical output is around $5000 per person at 1995, prices having doubled in the last 30 years. This is absolutely enough for food, clothing, education, health care, a dignified old age, and quite a lot of fun, for everyone on the planet. The fact that these are denied to over three-quarters of the planet can only be possible if these physical resources are distributed by a social and not a natural law.

This law can be understood only through a value concept that recognizes output as it really is, as a magnitude fixed by the human resources actually at society's disposal – its labor time.

This explains why there are winners and losers, why whenever one social function is augmented and one social class, class fraction, or nation is rewarded with additional value, another social function is threatened and another nation, class or class fraction loses out. It explains why growth sets limits on itself, by reducing the profit rate and hence the investment in production. It explains why the diversion of investment capital to financial and speculative ends is an alternative to, and not a complement of, productive investment. It explains why when one nation gets richer, others get poorer.

It also explains class struggle, which is by no means the same thing as exploitation. Marxists spend a disproportionate time accounting for the obvious fact that workers do not receive everything they produce. The real question is: why fight it? Why is their wage not regulated like other prices by market forces but by organized bodies of people, by laws, by strikes, and by force? Throughout most history and in all nations, capitalist accumulation generates opposition to itself. It is hundreds of times higher in some countries than others and varies enormously over history. It is determined as Marx puts it 'morally and historically,' in short, exogenously.

At the end of the day, the argument for a labor value concept is that there is no other basis on which these regularly and persistently observed phenomena can be explained. If every price rise is simultaneously an increase in output, why has no nation ever discovered the means both to accumulate and speculate, simply allocating the extra output as required? If profit is reducible to physical output, why does it fall most persistently during protracted periods of accelerated growth? If either monetary or physical growth can genuinely raise social output without limit, then why do not the rich nations simply raise the poor ones up to their standard? And if there really is no intrinsic social limit on output, it is an impenetrable mystery why wage-workers and property-owners cannot live in harmony. Over two hundred years of the capitalist market, no one found a means to distribute the extra output peaceably. Either class struggle is the most phenomenal worldwide stupidity, or it is time to question any theory which predicts that the market can create value without work.

Equilibrium, physicalism and dogmatism

Use-value: a disguised concept of value

Two excuses are offered for not treating value as quantified productive activity. The first is that price and quantity (use-value), being visible on the surface, are the only magnitudes economics need to deal with. Value is 'not necessary.' The second is that productive activity cannot be independently quantified because Marx's attempt to do so ended up in incoherence.

The claim that 'quantity' of output is visible on the surface is, however, trivially fraudulent. How much 'food' does a restaurant sell? Where is it measured? Where is it recorded? A unique quantitative measure of a collection of heterogeneous goods, as is well known, does not exist.

Even more problematic is the entire idea of physical surplus or net output, which is, according to the use-value concept, the actual result of production. With technical progress, there is a negative net product of almost everything because like is not replaced with like. Old goods are not reproduced but phased out and replaced with new ones. Without a positive net product, most physicalist results are false or even meaningless. Not least, an economy can have surplus labor but a negative physical profit rate.[2]

These inconsistencies do not stop people who should know better arguing that they work with quantities because a labor time value concept is logically inconsistent. The real attitude of equilibrium economics is thus not that physical quantity is perfect, but that there is no other. It may be bad, but there is nothing else.

Conceptually, however, it is perfectly reasonable to suppose that 'behind' price lies not the produced thing but the process that produced it. The issue is whether this concept is consistently quantifiable. What has to be proved, therefore, is not that value is a necessary category but that production can in fact be quantified and that no contradiction arises. Once this is achieved then value can legitimately be conceived as the amount of 'production' contained in a commodity, and a straightforward scientific test between competing concepts of commodity value can be applied: namely, to see which best explains reality.

Equilibrium: necessary foundation of physicalism

There are reasons to think that an independent concept of production is not merely empirically required, but logically superior. The fundamental issue is that things are produced before they are consumed. If the value of output is in any meaningful sense caused by something, it is hard to avoid the conclusion that this 'something' is located in production. This point is clearly recognized by the marginal school, and was the reason the general equilibrium approach of Walras and Marshall triumphed over the Austrian school of Böhm-Bawerk and Hayek.[3]

The equilibrium paradigm brushes this efficiently under the table. If nothing changes, causation becomes timeless. It is equally coherent to argue that the inputs determine the output to which they give rise or that the output 'determines' the inputs required to produce it. The chicken determines the egg, and the egg determines the chicken. The question 'which came first' becomes meaningless because the egg that hatched the chicken and the egg the chicken lays are now the same egg.

The equilibrium paradigm, and the physical concept of value, are thus mutually interdependent both logically and in the history of thought.[4]

An illustration helps understand the issues at stake. Suppose at a given point in time which we will call *t*, a capitalist buys 100 units of some use-value and, during production, creates 160 of the same use-value.

$$100 \to 160 \tag{6.1}$$

Two issues arise. First, what relation is there between this fact and the price of the product? Second, what implication does this have for capitalist profit? There is a simple accounting relation between price and profit. Designating the price at time *t* as p_t. The profit is the difference between $160p_{t+1}$, which the capitalist receives, and $100p_t$ which she spent. The profit rate *r* is therefore,[5]

$$r = \frac{160p_{t+1} - 100p_t}{100p_t} \tag{6.2}$$

The problem is that this equation tells us nothing about what p_{t+1}, p_t and *r* actually are. The best we can get is an algebraic identity obtained by re-organizing (6.2):

$$100\,p_t(1+r) = 160\,p_{t+1} \tag{6.3}$$

These relations are, however, hopelessly indeterminate.[6] They add nothing to our knowledge of why money sales are bigger than money expenditures. They are mere algebraic relations between two independently determined magnitudes.

Thus, suppose the price of the consumed inputs is £100 and the price of the sold product is £180. 'Production' has added £180. We would get the same result if, for example, we produced nothing, but prices increased by 80 percent through inflation. And, indeed, it is equally possible that the output might sell for £170, or £110, or even £90. There is no way of distinguishing which part of the money profit is really 'produced' and which arises from monetary changes.

At this point equilibrium is introduced, in a form which TSSI authors term 'simultaneism.' If we abstract from all the vicissitudes that might make p_{t+1} different from p_t, that is, if we suppose that the market works so perfectly that there is no need for prices to change, we can write

$$p_{t+1} = p_t \tag{6.4}$$

Physical increase is then the only effect of production. There is no price effect because we have eliminated it. Although we have no more knowledge than before about the actual magnitude of money output, we can calculate the *relative* increase in output – that is, profit:

$$r = \frac{160p_t - 100p_t}{100p_t} = \frac{60}{100} = 60\% \qquad (6.5)$$

Nevertheless, the approach does not actually solve the problem. The profit rate is completely independent of price and we have still not determined what p_t actually is. The money price p_t could be £1 or £100.

The solution offered is characteristic of the equilibrium paradigm. When there is more than one product, it turns out that the same method will tell us in what ratio commodities must exchange with each other to insure that the profit rate is the same in all branches. This is price, but not as we know it. It still does not tell us how much money any given commodity costs. As Townshend (1937) devastatingly points out, general equilibrium theory does not actually determine absolute prices, and the price level makes no difference to profit.

Physicalism: necessary outcome of equilibrium

Implicit, but never stated, is that this exercise does not just determine profit and prices but defines them. The meaning assigned to the concept 'profit' is no longer 'the extra money made by the capitalist' but 'the solution to the simultaneous equations constructed by supposing prices do not change and that all profit rates are equal.' The meaning assigned to 'price' is no longer 'the money paid for something' but 'the relative prices that satisfy the same set of equations.'

Furthermore, 'cause' is reduced to 'calculation,' and is banished from the realm of time to the realm of algebra. If we want to find out whether one thing causes another, all we do is substitute a new value for the allegedly causal variable in the equations and, if another changes, the independent variable is said to have 'caused' it.[7]

Thus 'determination' does not merely calculate price or profit, and does not merely facilitate the identification of causes; it redefines what price, profit and cause actually mean. 'Determination' itself really means 'definition.' This is why the equilibrium method is not neutral; it imposes a set of concepts. When an economist says that she or he has determined profits, she does not mean profits as anyone else understands them; she means 'the profits that would occur, if the market worked.'

This brings us to a full circle. The argument against accounting for production in terms of an independent and quantifiable magnitude is that there is no need because price and physical quantity are visible on the surface, and so we should deal with them directly. But, we cannot measure quantity in aggregate in any case, and price is replaced with something else. Whether or not the v-word is used, this is a value-concept. To determine whether it is an adequate concept, it should be tested both against reality, and against alternative such concepts.

Intrinsic dogmatism

The problem is now the following: the equilibrium paradigm is incapable of recognizing any other value concept. We have seen that equilibrium renders physicalism coherent. It now emerges, however, that it renders nothing else coherent. In the calculations made above there is only one possible profit rate, and it is equal to the physical profit rate. The equilibrium paradigm defines value to mean use-value: it makes physicalism the only possible value concept. Indeed this is why the post-Sraffians claim that the 'physical quantities' method constitutes a sufficient foundation for economics and that 'value' is a redundant category.

Without the calculation, there is no definition, no ontology, just an atheistic void. The fear of this void seems to make it impossible for equilibrium theorists to step into the light and consider even the possibility of a non-equilibrium world. It appears to them a kind of madness. In Foucault's sense, equilibrium theory is literally dazzled by reality.

This leads to what I term the *intrinsic dogmatism* of the equilibrium paradigm; it leaves no discursive space for any other concept. Physicalism emerges not as one concept among many, but as the only possible concept. The equilibrium paradigm not only makes it impossible to conceive of the possibility of temporalism; it makes it impossible to conceive of the possibility of any other meaning to the words it uses. Van Parijs (1980: 1) can thus write:

> It cannot be shown in general that a rise in the organic composition of capital leads to a fall in the rate of profit . . . A falling-rate-of-profit crisis is not a theoretical *necessity*; indeed, it is not even a *possibility* under conditions of competitive capitalism without pausing to consider that this applies *only* to the equilibrium, physical profit rate.

Since the observed profit rate does indeed fall with rises in the organic composition, there is at least some basis to question an approach which says this is logically impossible.

This dogmatism extends to Marx, whose views are tested not against reality but against logic. His equilibrium interpreters seem unable to conceive that the inconsistencies they claim to find in his theory might flow from their own interpretation, and not from the theory itself. They mostly do not even consider it necessary to examine the evidence of Marx's own writings. Marx *must* have shared these conceptions: why? Because no others are possible.

The paradigm inhabits a sealed world of its own conceptions. It does not merely reject the alternative as absurd and impossible; it cannot even understand what it is. In the same way, the anti-Galileans could not comprehend how the earth could be other than the center of the universe, because as Kuhn explains, 'center of the universe' was what they meant by 'earth.'

Winning a one-horse race

To do the paradigm justice, its substantive (and logically legitimate) claim is not that its prices or profit rates are the real ones, but that they are abstractions that in some sense 'govern' the real ones; the physicalist profit rate is a center of gravity for actual profits that fluctuate around it.

The problem is that even a cursory inspection reveals that the physicalist profit rate cannot possibly govern the money rate. Seventy to ninety percentage of fluctuations in reported rates of return on capital arise directly from changes in the organic composition of capital; but as van Parijs notes above, this is logically impossible within the equilibrium paradigm.

The claim therefore relies, to a great extent, on the very fact that nobody does it better: that there is no other candidate for the status of 'center of gravity.' In a one horse race, a three-legged donkey will win. However, there are other horses, except those that have been disqualified. Not only are there many different temporal profit rates, but as we shall see one particular temporal rate – the labor-time rate – does indeed fall as a result of rising organic composition, above all during long periods of technical progress.

Where does the error arise? From the abstraction employed, which does away with changes in price – the actual cause of the variations. Equilibrium abstracts from the most important determinant of all – motion.[8]

Money, motion and markets

Price movements and the rate of profit

The equilibrium paradigm, to be precise, does not suppose prices are constant, but that they do not change during production. Consequently, price changes have no impact on the profits. In point of fact, prices at the start of production never equal prices at the end. This is not just a random difference: technical progress drives down prices. This has been obscured by systematically inflationary policies, but is evident in the relative prices of commodities in which technical progress is most rapid, such as computer chips, which fall fastest.

There is now a marked tendency for a return to a régime of generally falling prices, definitely in world commodity markets and in the case of Japan, in almost all markets in terms of the national currency. This has enabled Brenner (1998), for example, to theorize the fall in the profit rate explicitly in terms of falling prices.

Brenner attributes this to competition, which is a matter for empirical observation. However, it is only *logically possible* under temporalism, a fact he himself has yet to acknowledge. Within the equilibrium paradigm, no change in prices or values can possibly affect profits. In any simultaneist expression for the profit rate, the denominator – capital stock – and the numerator – current profits – are expressed in terms of the same set of prices. Prices always cancel out, top and bottom. No price change for any reason whatsoever can possibly impact the profit rate.

Actually, price changes do clearly affect profits and we can show, and indeed calculate, this effect. Suppose, to fix ideas, inputs were purchased at £1 per unit, so that £100 was laid out altogether. But suppose the sale price is £150, the money profit rate would be £50 and the profit rate is not 60 percent but 50 percent. Why? Because while production was in process, prices rose. This is an effect of motion.

Let us deal with this in a more general way. To simplify matters and focus on the effect of the change, we will write p in place of p_t and $p+\Delta p$ in place of p_{t+1}.

The basic production equation (6.3) becomes

$$100\,p(1+{}^{£}\mathrm{r}) = 160(p+\Delta p) \tag{6.6}$$

where ${}^{£}\mathrm{r}$ is the money profit rate, from which it is not hard to show that

$$^{£}\mathrm{r} = {}^{e}\mathrm{r} + (1+{}^{e}\mathrm{r})\left(\frac{\Delta p}{p}\right) \tag{6.7}$$

where ${}^{e}\mathrm{r}$ is the equilibrium rate. The money profit rate is equal to the equilibrium, physicalist profit rate plus an extra term governed by the rate of change of prices. Where prices are falling, as is generally the case with technical change, it will sink below.

The effect becomes even clearer if, instead of von Bortkiewicz's (1984) very schematic assumption that advanced capital is consumed in a single period, we recognize that fixed capital persists and grows from one period to the next. Profit is calculated over the whole of the advanced capital and not just that which is consumed. The greater this is, the greater is the price effect since the capitalist' profit is reduced by the fall in price of the whole of her or his tied-up capital.

This corresponds exactly to what is observed in reality. If a capitalist lays out £1,000,000 on a brand new factory then this sum of money must be found before any surplus can be realized as profit. If, while the process is going on, the price of a new factory sinks to £500,000 then the capitalist is not entitled to write this £500,000 off on the books without paying it. £1,000,000$\times(\Delta p/p)$ is deducted from the realized profit which is substantially lower than the hypothetical physical equilibrium rate.

The temporal determination of the magnitude of value by the time of labor

Can we, in the light of the above, simply construct the dynamics of capitalism from the dynamics of prices and quantities? This Post-Keynesian idea is essentially the project of Kalecki, and has a lot more in common with Marx's theory than much Marxist theory. The problems remain those identified above: with *what* does the money interact? What is it that gets allocated when money prices change? In the equilibrium paradigm, there is only one choice: use-value. In the temporal paradigm, there is a variety of choices and, in particular, value can be theorized in a non-contradictory way as the 'quantity of production' that gives rise to output.

We begin by noting that a commodity's physical size is by no means its only visible surface property apart from money price. For example, the living labor employed in its production is a perfectly measurable and accessible magnitude.[9]

The principal difficulty arises because first of all, there are other inputs to production and second, labor is generally involved in producing them. The question is then what these inputs contribute to value or, which is the same thing, what does past labor add to value?

Ricardo's solution is really quite simple: past labor adds itself. If a ton of steel is made of a year of labor and a ton of iron, and if we know the iron contains two years of labor, we can deduce that the steel contains three years of labor – one current year and two past years. The problem is, however: how do we know the iron contains two years of labor? The equilibrium approach asks how much labor would be required to reproduce the whole of society unchangingly. The temporal approach takes the labor at some given point as an initial condition; as a datum given externally.

To fix ideas, suppose at the start of our example production process that goods containing 100 days of past labor are consumed in production, and that 20 days of living labor transform them into an output. Just as Laplace did not need to know where God put the planets in order to calculate their subsequent motion, we do not need to enquire why this past labor was 100. The value of the output is

$$100+20=120 \tag{6.8}$$

Provided we can calculate how much of the produced 120 units of value remain unconsumed and pass into the next period of production, we may repeat this calculation by adding in the living labor of this next period, and so on indefinitely.

It may seem that value is indeterminate because there is no basis to ascertain the initial condition. Actually this problem has two quite separate aspects; first, do we know its actual magnitude and second, does it exist?

Whether *we* know this magnitude should not be confused with whether it exists. For the equilibrium paradigm, a magnitude is determinate only if we can calculate it, but the stars pursue their majestic course regardless of whether we count them. Capitalism itself establishes the labor in a commodity, regardless of whether we measure it.

This would be of limited use if capitalism also made this magnitude unknowable. But this is not so. It turns out that if the initial condition is misestimated, the error does not propagate but decays exponentially and effectively vanishes after a few periods. We may thus begin with almost any reasonable initial estimate of the labor content of consumed capital and, within five periods, derive labor values whose magnitude is statistically indistinguishable from the true value.

This is temporal determination. Its conceptual basis is a sound technique known as mathematical induction, which underlies much foundational mathematics. Its method of calculation is behind virtually all modern physics.

The true content of equilibrium, from a temporalist standpoint, is that if all exogenous sources of change are held constant, endogenous change will, under very general conditions, also die out and the system will, mathematically, settle into an equilibrium state. This is why, theoretically, equilibrium is a special case of temporal motion and not vice versa. Ricardo's attention centered on this 'long-run' condition of the economy without, I suspect, ever fully understanding the difference between the temporal and equilibrium determination of this long-run condition.

Marx found value theory in this state when he absorbed it from Ricardo and transformed it in two vital respects: first, he made the motion of the economy its principal determinant and second, he derived from this a diametrically opposite understanding of money.

Value, money and price

For Ricardo, as for the neo-classical economists, the purpose of value was to determine the magnitude of price. For the Ricardians, therefore, the theory had failed if they could not calculate prices. But in reality, for a variety of reasons (of which the equalization of profit rates is only one), price is not quantitatively equal or at least proportional to value, and so the Ricardians concluded that the primary mission had failed.

Marx inverted the problem. From the outset he insisted that price could not be equal to value because the market itself, with its ceaseless failure to equate supply to demand, systematically raised price above and below value both in individual spheres and, during the course of the business cycle, for all goods taken together. Value for Marx was not, therefore, the proximate determinant of price.[10] To the contrary, deviations of price from value are the only way that value can come into being at all:

> If M. Proudhon admits that the value of products is determined by labour time, he should equally admit that it is the fluctuating movement alone that makes labour time the measure of value. There is no ready constituted 'proportionate relation' but only a constituting movement (Marx 1935: 62).

For Marx, value was the *content* of price; it was a quantitative estimate of the amount of labor that a given money quantity represented in exchange. If, therefore, a commodity whose value was 100 hours exchanges on the market for an amount of money which represents 100 hours of past labor, it sells at its value. If, however, it sells for an amount of money representing 200 hours of past labor, then its price is double its value; that is, the commodity exchanges for more labor than that went into its production.

But, for Marx, the total value produced by society cannot so be altered. It is impossible, in circulation alone, to increase the value in existence. Therefore exchange is a zero-sum game. If one capitalist successfully appropriates 100 hours more than that was added in production, other capitalists somewhere else lose, and the total losses equal the total gains.

> The sum of values in circulation clearly cannot be augmented by any change in their distribution... the capitalist class of a given country, taken as a whole, cannot defraud itself. However much we twist and turn, the final conclusion remains the same, if equivalents are exchanged, no surplus-value results, and if non-equivalents are exchanged, we still have no surplus-value. Circulation, or the exchange of commodities, creates no value (Marx 1977: 265–66).

The price system, for Marx, is therefore *the means by which* past social labor is transferred from one capitalist to another. Prices are simply disguised past labor. The requirement of an analytical framework is to penetrate the disguise. The most decisive element of this analytical framework is established at the very beginning of Marx's work, in Chapter 5 of Volume 1 of *Capital*: price movements cannot create or destroy total value. This is why, and how, the price system is the disguised form of social competition. The money measure of the social resources at stake may vary, but the resources themselves are not altered by this. Therefore, whatever one gains, another loses. This is the core which underlies the mechanisms of unequal exchange, periodic crisis, structural crisis, and class struggle.

Three magnitudes, three profit rates

Now consider the physicalist proposition that profit cannot be determined independent of prices. I will bring together the three numerical accounts of our system scattered around the text.

	Used	**Produced**
Use-value	100	160
Value	100	120
Money	100	180

There are three profit rates and they can be calculated without reference to unit values or prices, being simply the surplus divided by what is advanced. These rates are thus *dependent on the unit* – in essence, on the value concept. Thus the value rate is 20/100, the physical rate is 160/100 and the money rate is 180/100. The money profit rate is above the physical rate and the value rate is below it.

Now consider unit values and unit prices. The unit value of the commodity in each period is simply the total labor time embodied in the output divided by the size of the output, and the unit price is simply total price likewise divided by the size of the output.

	Time (t)	**Time (t+1)**
Use-value	100	160
Value	100	120
Money	100	180
Unit price	1.00	1.12
Unit value	1.00	0.75

We thus have falling unit values and rising unit prices.

Money, representative of social labor

A third ratio can be calculated, which unlike unit value and price applies to individual commodities and to the whole of society. This is the quantity which, following Ramos (1995), TSSI authors term the Monetary Equivalent of Labor Time (MELT).

In the example above, the value in society is initially 100 and its price is £100. Consequently the 100 hours are represented, in exchange, by £100. Anyone who owns £1 can purchase a share of society's stored-up labor equal to 100/£100 = 1 hour.[11] One hour is *equivalent* to one pound.

This is a direct relation between money and labor, independent of the physical medium. This magnitude, just like unit value and unit price, is variable. Its variation is the decisive link between the money and value profit rates.

	Initial	**Final**
Value	100	120
Money	100	180
MELT	1.00	1.50

The money profit rate is affected by three independent factors: the value profit rate, the rate of productivity growth, and the rate of money inflation relative to goods. Each factor has a bearing on the actual course of accumulation and each must be independently analyzed.

Notwithstanding, we can decompose the money profit rate in one of two ways. We can think of it as the physical rate, augmented by price inflation relative to goods. Or we can think of it as the value rate augmented by the rate of change of the MELT. Representing the MELT by e_t, total value by V_t, total price by P_t, the value profit rate by ${}^{h}\mathrm{r}$ and the money rate by ${}^{£}\mathrm{r}$, it is not difficult to show that

$$ {}^{£}\mathrm{r} = {}^{h}\mathrm{r} + e'(1 + {}^{h}\mathrm{r}) \tag{6.9} $$

Where, $e' = \delta e/e$ is the rate of change of the MELT. In the example above we thus have

$$ {}^{£}\mathrm{r} = 0.8, \quad {}^{h}\mathrm{r} = 0.2, \quad e' = 0.5 \quad \text{and} \quad {}^{£}\mathrm{r} = {}^{h}\mathrm{r} + 0.5 \times (1 + {}^{h}\mathrm{r}) \tag{6.10} $$

Both the movement of the value rate, and the relation between it and the money rate, can thus be expressed independently of physical quantities.

Anticipating the discussion below, suppose for illustrative purposes that prices are proportional to the values and that the productivity of living labor rises at a steady rate, the general price level would systematically fall, and the factor e' in equation (6.9) would be negative. Thus, the *effect of technical accumulation is to lower the profit rate below the physical rate*. It is not difficult to show that values will fall in such a way that the price effect is greater than the productivity effect. Under a wide variety of circumstances this is the case, and in particular it is invariably true for the case of maximum expanded reproduction in which the whole surplus is reinvested. The first result was established by Kliman and McGlone (1988); the general case was stated by Freeman (1995b). A definitive debate on this question was conducted in the pages of *Research in Political Economy* at the end of which Foley (2000b) concluded that:

> I understand Freeman and Kliman to be arguing that Okishio's theorem as literally stated is wrong because it is possible for the money and labor rates of profit to fall under the circumstances specified in its hypotheses. I accept their examples as establishing this possibility.

The argument has been in existence in one form or another for 15 years, no one has provided a refutation, and all those who have examined it have had to accept that the argument is logically sound. In short the labor rate of profit can, and does, fall as Marx stated, under cost-reducing technical innovation.

The appropriation of value by means of money

The exogenization of money

It is not hard to see why, from an equilibrium standpoint, it makes no sense to construct an independent measure of value in terms of productive resources. For, this magnitude cannot possibly affect the profit rate which is given solely by the physical proportions of inputs and outputs. Value 'is redundant.'

Unfortunately, however, so is price. The equilibrium profit rate is unaffected by prices except for the wage which is in any case represented as a collection of goods, rather than a money price.

This is one aspect of a much deeper problem: within equilibrium, *money* is redundant. It is a veil, a mere numéraire. As Bridel (1997: xiii) notes, citing Hahn (1982: 1):

> The most serious challenge that the existence of money poses to the theorist is this: the best developed model of the economy [the Arrow-Debreu version of a Walrasian equilibrium] cannot find room for it.

Within such theories therefore money cannot, logically, play any determinative or causal role. It is recast as an external, as something that has to be 'properly managed' – that is, exogenously determined – because in the equilibrium determination of prices and profits, it is the great undetermined, an ironic recognition of the market's inability to regulate its own supreme variable. Modern economics sets great store on money but at its heart all is a large black hole: namely, it has no endogenous theory of it.

The reason for this difficulty is that economics has purged its conceptual vocabulary of the thing money really consists of, namely, value. Money represents social effort. It does so not because the market works, but because it does not. If the market did work perfectly, money would not be necessary and every economic transaction could be conducted in terms of barter.[12] Producers seek money itself because it represents a fluctuating, and not a fixed, social power of acquisition. If all rates of exchange were perfectly stable, and all goods could always be sold, there would be no need to single out one particular commodity as a store of value. Any commodity could be money and the only issue would be technical convenience.

But prices are not stable and sale is not guaranteed. Capital retreats into money during a slump because as a universal, unlike any particular, commodity it guarantees the next purchase. But insofar as modern money takes the form of debt, money itself fails as a store of value and is not repaid. When universals fail, no particular is safe. This puts money itself at the center of all the market's storms, since it incarnates in itself all the market's contradictions. An adequate value theory must, therefore, provide an integrated account of the relation between money and value.

Money as the agent of value appropriation

In the literature on Marx's theory, the principal focus of the discussion concerns the so-called transformation problem and far too little attention is given to the substantive issue of endogenous market failure. The concept of money is the link between the two because money is the form in which the capitalist acquires value.

Consequently, there is no transformation problem in the form it is normally discussed. Marx did not 'forget to transform inputs' which, being expressed in money, are already transformed. Inputs transfer a value to the product given by the labor time this money represents in circulation, an aliquot share of the total value in society.

The value-price distinction then has two, completely operational and quantitative, aspects. In the first place, every money price expresses a quantity of labor. If the MELT is, for example, £52,000 per year, and the price of a computer is £2000, then this represents two weeks' labor on the market. But this price will be higher or lower than the labor time required to produce the computer. If, for example, the manufacturer spent £500 on parts and machinery, and if half a week's labor was expended on it, then its value is one week or, in money terms, £1000. It is hence overpriced; its price is above its value. The quantitative distinction between value and price is not abolished, as in the value-form school approach.

What happens when the price of a computer rises above its value? From a monetary standpoint, £2000 now acquires £1000 worth of goods, from a social standpoint, two weeks of social labor acquire one week in return.

The exchange is unequal. This is what really 'lies behind' the price mechanism – the competitive appropriation of social resources through the constant rise and fall of prices.

Profit as the agent of capital movement

Were this the only function of the price mechanism, production would probably not occur. The difference between capitalism and precapitalist trading societies is that production is itself organized by past labor in the form of capital. The 'interest taken by the capitalist' is not a quick bargain but a long-term high profit which arises from placing capital where it can make more money than elsewhere.

The laws of motion of capital arise because this individual placement reacts back on general social conditions. Market breakdown arises when these general social conditions fail to maintain the conditions necessary for individual capitals to function.

All capitalists seek to appropriate labor as much in excess of the labor they part with as possible, in proportion to the labor they advanced. The average profit rate is an ideal never attained in Marx's words:

> Between these spheres that approximate more or less to the social average, there is again a tendency to equalization, which seeks the 'ideal'

> mean position, i.e. a position which does not exist in reality (Marx 1981: 273).

The average rate has occupied the attention of most theory, again driven by the equilibrium obsession with equal profit rates. But capital as such is concerned only with excess, super or *surplus* profit:

> In fact the direct interest taken by the capitalist, or the capital, of any individual sphere of production in the exploitation of the labourers who are directly employed is confined to making an extra gain, a profit above the average (Marx 1971: 197).

This difference is also more important than price-value deviations:

> The tendency of price of production is only to tolerate such surplus profits as arise, under whatever circumstances, not from the difference between the values of commodities and their prices of production, but rather from the general price of production governing the market and the individual production prices differing from this; surplus profits which therefore do not arise between two different spheres of production but rather within each sphere of production (Marx 1981: 895).

The market reconciles these divergent individual actions to produce social results by averaging them, not by forcing them into uniformity. General conditions are established in the market which regulate all producers: a single price for each commodity, an average rate of profit, and so on.

The market exists because these social results are also the social conditions that sustain it. However, it can, and does, produce social results that act in a quite contrary direction, and remove conditions essential for its own existence. The function of value analysis is to uncover how these failures happen.

Value and the course of capitalist accumulation

Bonsai capitalism: the myth of the static economy

The focus of equilibrium theory is to explain how the market stabilizes. The most fundamental mistake of this approach is that a stable market cannot exist. Like any organic entity, the market maintains itself by moving. As Marx (1978: 199) notes:

> This assumption [simple reproduction – AF] is equivalent to assuming the non-existence of capitalist production and therefore the non-existence of the industrial capitalist himself. For capitalism is already essentially

> abolished once we assume that it is enjoyment that is the driving motive and not enrichment itself... It is moreover technically impossible.

The two most general laws of capitalism are therefore technical progress and accumulation. When either slows, an essential function of capitalism is removed.

Technical progress is the quintessentially capitalist source of superprofit. Market value is an average which is normally well below the individual value of the most advanced producer. If, say, a computer chip manufacturer doubles her output then until the industry as a whole catches up, she gets twice as much money. Without technical advances, there is therefore no motor driving force behind capitalist investment.

Without accumulation, the individual capitalist cannot benefit from superprofit. No matter how high the profit rate, the volume of returns depends on how much capital is invested. A profit rate of 500 percent will still yield only £5, if only a pound is invested. Each capitalist therefore strives to increase the total invested and, aside from mutual swindling, the only stable way to achieve this is to invest the surplus.

Accumulation and technical change are not, therefore, just by-products of the market but a condition of its existence. Breakdown occurs when either ceases or is interrupted. The key to understanding breakdown is, therefore, to understand how these processes themselves bring about their own cessation.

Accumulation and the rate of profit

The rate of profit is the most general variable governing the historical evolution of capitalism. However it is easy to misunderstand why. Its level as such is not the source of breakdown, since monetary inflation can raise it arbitrarily. It is, however, the average of a distribution. Individual producers compare their rates with other options. Breakdown arises, therefore, because price movements create alternative sources of superprofit to production.

As Farjoun and Machover (1983) argue and Wells (2001) definitively establishes, actual profits are never equal but are distributed around the average. Consequently, actual prices are always above or below the equal-profit rate and ceaselessly fluctuate around it.

When the average rate sinks the whole swarm of rates around it also shifts. The swarm's behavior is then determined, not by its center but by the outlying capitals. Beyond a certain point their profits in value terms are negative which, as stressed from the outset, signifies that they represent a declining share of total value.

Were production the only possible destination for capital seeking to expand, the absolute profit rate would make little difference, since surplus profit would compete only with private consumption. But in fact, price movement brings into existence non-productive destinations for capital which, when the rate sinks beyond a certain point, become dominant and throw accumulation into reverse.

The absolute level of the profit rate therefore, fixes what proportion of total capital is thrown into production, and what proportion into unproductive speculation.

To see what drives it, I extend the illustration to three periods. To study the effect of accumulation alone, isolated from distribution, I suppose the whole of the product re-enters production but that in each period, 20 days are still employed, which implies some technical progress. I also suppose the entire product is invested, and study the maximum rate of profit, assuming the wage is zero. Technical progress is assumed and the physical product rises relative to both labor and physical inputs. Inflation is assumed and the money rate of profit rises faster than the physical rate. Profit rates, unit prices, and unit values are calculated as before.

Period	1			2			3		
	In	Out	r (in %)	In	Out	r (in %)	In	Out	r (in %)
Use-value	100	160	60	160	300	87.5	300	600	100
Value	100	120	20	120	140	16.7	140	160	14.3
Money	100	180	80	180	360	100	320	800	150

The value profit rate will continue to fall as long as value is invested. This law proceeds independent of technical progress. Because and as long as value is accumulating, the invested value sum will rise until and unless the capitalists stop plowing value into the system and start taking it out – disinvesting in value terms.

Countervailing tendencies and the short cycle

Does this mean that the profit rate necessarily declines for ever? No – it continues as long as, and to the extent that, accumulation proceeds in value terms. This is not identical to physical accumulation and Marxist authors look in vain for a recovery mechanism expressed in terms of the physical liquidation of stock. The profit rate is not about physical stock. A capitalist who loses a factory has lost her money; destroying the factory does not make things better.

Nor is bankruptcy or debt default an adequate mechanism for the reduction of accumulated value although it certainly is one of the means by which accumulation itself is brought to a halt. The non-payment of a debt simply transfers the problem of payment from the debtor to the creditor, whose money worth is reduced by the amount of the loss but who still has to pay her own creditors.

There is only one permanently effective mechanism for stably restoring profitability, which is to run down the value of stocks by using up the accumulated value – by disinvesting. In short, the only definitive way for capitalism to offset accumulation is to stop accumulating.

This can happen while physical accumulation proceeds, albeit at a slower rate. A slump is, in effect, the slowing down of physical accumulation to the point where the decline in the value of existing investment proceeds faster than the physical additions to investment. This is the mechanism that permits a recovery in the profit rate and the reason that the rate varies rhythmically over the period of the business cycle. It is possible only to the extent that a degree of technical innovation persists; if to take the extreme case there is no innovation and therefore no general decline in values, then the slump can succeed in restoring profits only by running down physical accumulation itself, and disinvesting in physical terms.

Why inflation does not work for ever

Why does an inflationary increase in money prices not offset falling profits? A little bit of thought reveals what this idea really entails. An additional profit arises when goods are increasing in price. But this also means that merely holding onto goods becomes a source of profit. In our example, since the product rises from 1 to 1.12 in the first period, a capitalist could make a healthy profit of 12 percent without producing anything. Since in the course of the cycle all prices do not rise together, profit in value terms can always be found where they are rising exceptionally fast. Alongside all the multitude of productive profit rates a new destiny for capital emerges – speculation.

This is reinforced whenever and wherever the capitalist can secure an additional guaranteed income stream by securing a monopoly over a particular necessary function for the rest of capital. *Rent* arises in every case, above all land but also on machinery in the form of lease arrangements, buildings as such, and so on, and becomes part of the expected income from mere ownership.

This is enormously accelerated by the credit system and the emergence of fictitious capital. Credit itself becomes a source of income, and every capital automatically compares the rate of return on investment with the general rate of interest. Financial instruments, representing claims on future income, outstrip the general rise in the price level in the boom phase. Finally money *itself* becomes a source of value profits in the slump phase, since during a period of falling prices, it represents an increasing claim on value. Liquidity preference under conditions of falling prices is a perfectly rational strategy and brings about the growth of money capital at the expense of industrial capital.

The mechanisms of the short cycle remain to be fully explored. As is clear from Evans (2003), the most innovative work on the business cycle comes from writers unhampered by the blindness to financial and monetary phenomena which has blighted Marxist work. The problem is that without an underlying value framework, mechanism and cause are confused. The driving force of the cycle is the repeated oscillation between productive accumulation and speculative accumulation, and this is driven by the dynamics of the productive sector, not the financial sector. It is driven, above all, by the relative levels of superprofit to be obtained from investment in technical innovation and in speculation, which is in turn driven by the overall movement of the profit rate.

The next and final stage of analysis, therefore, concerns the effects of technical change as such.

Divergence and unequal exchange: the limits of technical change

Perhaps the two most striking facts of contemporary capitalism are that, in the age of space travel, the internet, and global communication, the majority of the world's population do not have a telephone; and that while medical science challenges mortality, hundreds of millions are dying of curable diseases. The second great limit that capital sets on itself is that, to the degree that it develops human capacities by the boundless advance of science, it denies access to these advances to an ever growing part of humanity.

The secular divergence of wealth is in a certain sense the most decisive tendency in capitalism because unlike the falling profit rate, it never stops. The difference between the richest and poorest nations at the end of the twentieth century is seven times bigger than it was at the beginning.

The neglected process of unequal exchange has been explored by writers such as Amin (1976a), Palloix (1973), Emmanuel (1972), and Dos Santos (1970), but its workings do not make sense outside of the temporal paradigm. Mandel stands alone in having attempted a serious temporal analysis. This inadequacy is further testimony to the crippling legacy of the equilibrium paradigm.

Secular divergence arises from the coexistence in the market of many producers of the same product employing different technologies. It is the outcome of a self-reinforcing process – in technical terms, a positive feedback loop.

There are two basic mechanisms. First, superprofit arising from technical superiority never vanishes. As fast as it is reduced to zero in one branch, a new source of superprofit emerges in another and the capital always pursues the highest rate around. To this must be added a distinctive mechanism which is very characteristic of modern globalization. Consider what happens if the price of the computer considered above falls from £2000 to, say, £1500 – as happens all the time. The difference is pocketed by the sellers of the computers, who thereby transfer the costs of technological change entirely to the purchasers.

The mechanism is dynamically self-reinforcing. There *is* no long-term steady state; the excess profits of the advanced producers are invested in even more advanced technology, sustaining and extending their lead. The 'development of underdevelopment,' as Andrew Gunder-Frank so accurately designated it, is a product of the market itself and not of any special historical circumstance.

Long waves

What, then, is the actual historical course of events unleashed by these processes? It is empirically clear that once a certain organic composition of capital has been reached, each successive cycle restores profit rates to a lower level than before. The cyclic process is, therefore accompanied by a long-run, secular decline of the profit rate over a 30–50-year period – the Kondratieff or long wave. Unlike the business cycle, there is no endogenous mechanism of recovery from this decline and it therefore brings into play exogenous, social forces on a vast scale that seek to re-organize the entire organization of world production so that one *particular fraction* of capital can rise above all the rest, by extracting an exceptional share of world value production.

The scale is vast. Endogenous recovery from the business cycle ruins individual capitalists and businesses. Exogenous recovery from long declines lays waste peoples and nations. The fractions that gain and lose in the short cycle are banks, corporations, and industrial sectors; in long waves, the winners are the charmed circle of dominant nations and their retinues in the third world, and the losers everyone else. This is why the recovery, if and when it happens, only follows an intrusion of rude politics into the smooth flow of the market; war, revolution, and barbarity. It is why, and how, technology has become the fifth horseman.

The particular form in which divergence now irrupts into politics is war. War is nothing more than the ultimate form of economic competition, which arises when the purely economic mechanisms described above render countries ungovernable or threaten them with economic destruction.

Such exogenous interventions have, in the past, however, achieved the launch of a new phase of expansion and this has been the clear and even stated goal of US economic policy in the last two decades. Essentially, the United States has functioned, through financial deregulation, as a vacuum cleaner for the world's savings. Importing several hundred billion dollars annually, it has sought to re-establish its productive lead of the fifties by a focused drive for world domination in Information and Communications Technology.

This rational is for United States. The endogenous process behind a long wave of expansion, once launched, has been documented by researchers (see for example Perez 2002) and arises because technology revolutionizes a *core branch* of the world economy; an industry which is an input to all others. The year 1848–73 was the age of steam and the railway; 1893–1914, the age of steel and electricity; 1947–65, the age of oil and cars. This becomes the target of a prolonged wave of investment and also revolutionizes all other branches of industry, providing the basis for an investment surge throughout the economy. Any nation producing this core technology rises up the pecking order.

The contradiction is, first, that accumulation itself leads to a declining profit rate for the reasons already discussed, choking off the expansion and, second, the process is phenomenally uneven. It divides the world even more sharply between producers of the new technology, whose domination is at each stage further reinforced, and consumers of it who become dependent. The world market does not spread the technology; it concentrates it. The phenomenon of capital export, observed by Hilferding, Hobson and Lenin, and still a vital part of advanced country operations today, is only one aspect of an overall pattern which *organizes the world labor market* on a world scale under the direction of the new technology. The typical structure of the world corporation, repeated in each phase of expansion, is a core in the center, serviced by outsourced labor-intensive activities in the periphery. This is no different today when the core technology is service-driven and the tributaries are mass industrial production, than a hundred years ago when the core technology was industrial and the tributaries were agricultural.

Inevitably therefore, nations and corporations strive to convert the source of superprofit of the core technology into a monopoly and to extract from it a rent, a stable superprofit. Rail cartels in the 1870s, the steel and electricity cartels of the early part of the last century, the oil cartels in the modern age, and the rise of Microsoft are all classic manifestations of this process.[13] Governments and nations are only too conscious of the benefits to their own capitalists, and the regulatory régimes surrounding core products are the focus of much international politics.

Today the most vivid, and advanced, expression of the process is the legal formalization of intellectual property rights via the Trade-Related Aspects of Intellectual Property Rights (TRIPS) agreement of the WTO. Effectively, this serves to convert technical advantage *as a whole* into a source of rent. The role of technology in dividing the world to haves and have-nots is nowhere clearer than in the conflicts over this new commodity form. Yet the contradictions of the form highlight the reasons that capitalism cannot generalize the gains from technical progress; for the first time, 'free trade' in a commodity depends on the restraint of trade in all other commodities. The pharmaceutical and agricultural companies rushing to patent genes, drugs, seeds and animals are battling not to provide them to the third world, but to prevent the third world making them.

The age of war

We do not yet know if Greenspan will achieve his lifelong objective of launching the fifth Kondratieff. The evidence, overwhelmingly, is that it has not started yet. Not only is world growth at its lowest in 30 years, but US growth is no higher than 20 years ago, and still well below golden-age levels. It has outstripped the rest of the world only by driving all others down. More decisively still, the telltale sign of a productive lack of competitiveness – a huge and growing trade deficit – shows no signs of going away.

In consequence, the United States' relation to the rest of the world bears a far stronger resemblance to the relation, which the United Kingdom held in the 1890s, than that of the United States in the 1950s, or the United Kingdom in the 1850s. Does this rule out a new Kondratieff? No: despite the structural instability imposed by the United Kingdom's weakness, the period 1890–1914 saw the 'Belle Époque,' a prolonged phase of technical revolution and expanded growth.

The problem is that the Belle Époque ushered in World War I. This highlights a crucial difference in modes of super-power domination. In the first type, seen in 1848–73 with Britain, and 1947–65 with the United States, one power establishes exceptional productive dominance providing it with exceptional technical superprofits. It runs a trade surplus and finances the expansion of capital outside its borders, which is why the United States could build a new Germany in 1945 where Europe signally failed in 1918. The second type, however, arises when a power that has lost productive dominance nevertheless organizes the commercial, financial and military system of world capitalism to recapture on this terrain what it can no longer appropriate technically. It monopolizes, in short, the non-productive sources of superprofit to its exclusive advantage, leading to a hypertrophy of finance capital and all the other phenomena associated with classical imperialism.

As the Belle Époque demonstrates, a system of great-power relations based on such economic relations is structurally unstable even if a phase of expansion ensues. The dominant power cannot hegemonize its partners because it cannot offer them anything, and competition between dominant powers becomes the highest form in which economic competition is organized.

A Kondratieff expansion, whether or not it occurs, is not therefore a solution to the current fairly marked tendencies towards market failure. The solution lies in a different quarter, to which Marx would of course have turned: the conscious forces flung into movement by this failure and their capacity to replace the market by something better. Whether or not they succeed will depend on whether or not they understand the tasks facing them; theoretical clarity, in this situation, is not an optional extra but a militant duty.

Notes

1. It may seem that my use of the word 'paradigm,' differs from Kuhn (1962) because I define it to mean the method by which an economic approach determines its variables. I will argue that the equilibrium method imposes a meaning on concepts, and dictates procedures shared by all practitioners; this constitutes it as a paradigm in Kuhn's sense.
2. See Kliman (2001) and Freeman (1997b).
3. See for example Dobb (1973: 184).

4. Sraffa does not differ from the marginalists in this respect. The 'physical size' of a commodity cannot be isolated from its utility and each is just an aspect of the more theoretically adequate concept of *use-value*: thus, I cannot consume the experience of an egg separately from the egg. The claim that Sraffa created an alternative foundation for political economy is questionable; rather, in exhibiting the logical incoherence of marginalism, he demonstrated the logical incoherence of the use-value concept itself.
5. The time subscript will be omitted for simplicity where it is not necessary to the calculation.
6. In the marginalist variant, there would have to be more than one commodity and the equations resulting would be different, being derived from a supposed knowledge of marginal utilities and production functions. However, in both cases, the end result is a set of equations like (6.2) in which the rate of profit is a function of physical quantities, input prices and output prices. We illustrate our point with the physical quantity variant.
7. Compare this with the traditional view of science: 'The sequence in time is thus the sole empirical criterion of an effect in its relation to the causality of the cause which precedes it' (Kant 1933: 288).
8. *In general*, a temporal average must diverge from a moving fixed point solution. Given exogenous parameters a_t and an endogenous state vector $\mathbf{x}_t$, the general temporal trajectory is given by $x_{t+1}; a_{t+1} = f(x_t; a_t)$ for some f or in the continuous case $x'; a' = f(x; a)$. The general equilibrium or comparative static trajectory is $x_t; a_{t+1} = f^*(x_t; a_t)$, or in the continuous case $f^*(x; a_t) = 0$ where f^* is the fixed point of f with respect to x. The exogenous vector a becomes the only source of change. If, however, a is changing secularly (which is the case, given technical change) then f^* cannot possibly equal f.
9. One may conceive of value as the result of any particular input and this is by no means a stupid idea. Thus the physiocrats conceived of output as the contribution of agricultural produce. It is perfectly meaningful to construct an 'energy value,' as the energy expended in producing of a commodity. The issue is not to exclude such ideas by pure logic but to enquire what they can actually explain.
10. The quantitative relation between value and price appears in Marx as a law of *motion*, in the average and over time: as the labor content of any commodity falls, so will its relative price.
11. This is not the same as Adam Smith's 'labor commanded' which refers to the price of living labor. If the wage is £1, and an hour's work produces on average £2 worth of goods, the MELT is £2/hour, not £1.
12. Indeed if the market worked perfectly the *market* would not be necessary. Agents should be able to implement the rationally obvious rates of exchange, production and consumption without the tedious intermediary of actually buying and selling.
13. The relation between monopoly rent and profit has often been mistakenly reversed because from an equilibrium standpoint, any deviation of profits from the average must be caused by something exogenous. Rent is tribute exacted from stream of surplus profit, and monopoly is the fixation of the right to this rent in a particular form of property. No one exacts rent from an unused building. The profit causes the rent, which brings about the monopoly, not the other way around. Baran and Sweezy's account of 'State Monopoly Capitalism' inverts this essential causative relation.

7

Value Production and Economic Crisis: A Temporal Analysis

Andrew J. Kliman

During the past few years, an economic crisis threatened to destabilize the global economy as it spread from East Asia to Russia, Brazil, and elsewhere. Argentina went into a deep, accelerating collapse, and has not recovered. Meanwhile, the 12-year-long deterioration of Japan's economy has intensified, bringing on serious deflation. And shortly on the heels of one worldwide recession, another slump, potentially more severe, may be looming on the horizon, along with worldwide deflation. Globally, share prices have fallen by almost one-half since early 2000, and the current growth path of the United States appears unsustainable, given its whopping current account deficit, negative private saving rate, and real estate market bubble.

Owing to policy makers' adroitness – or perhaps luck – their interventions have thus far succeeded in holding the global economy together. Yet the crises keep erupting. It should thus be clear that the interventions have been *ad hoc* 'quick fixes,' not solutions to capitalism's crisis tendencies.

The fundamental reason why capitalism cannot resolve its crisis tendencies, I suggest below, is that the capitalist mode of production is founded on an unsolvable contradiction between the production of use-values (physical goods and services) and the production of value. *As physical productivity rises, commodities' values fall.* In other words, costs of production fall, and prices tend to fall as a result. This failure of value to 'self-expand' sufficiently leads to slumps in physical production because physical production under capitalism is always tied to value production and engaged in only insofar as it expands value.

Demand-side theories, in contrast, attribute economic crises to inadequate demand (or 'overproduction') and debt crises to excessive debt expansion. *Yet why is demand inadequate? What has made the volume of debt excessive?* The section 'Demand-side theories' argues that demand-side theories cannot answer these questions;[1] in the section 'Value production and crisis tendencies,' I suggest that the answer is, in large part, that value has failed to 'self-expand' sufficiently. Yet this raises a further question: what determines the growth rate of value? According to Marx's theory, its most fundamental determinant is employment growth (or, more precisely, growth of living labor extracted in production). I argue that this theory alone provides a foundation for explaining the coexistence of some key macroeconomic phenomena – rapid technological advance, sluggish or negative employment growth, the tendency of prices to fall, rising debt burdens, and economic crises – as a *coherent unified whole*.

A very different theory – the 'physical quantities approach' (Steedman 1977: 72, 216–17) – dominates today's 'Marxian economics.' Duménil and Lévy (2000: 142), like other proponents of physicalism, hold that '[t]he labor theory of value is not . . . [the foundation of] the theory of crisis or of historical tendencies. . . . [It] does not provide the framework to account for disequilibrium and dynamics in capitalism.' Physicalist authors do recognize that technological progress tends to reduce commodities' values and prices. Curiously, however, they deny that these reductions impair profitability, holding instead that profit rates are determined solely by 'physical quantities.' As a founder of this approach Bortkiewicz (1952: 40) wrote, 'it is wrong to connect a change in the rate of profit with a change in prices, since, as can be seen from our formulae, . . . price movements affect the capitalist's product [i.e. sales revenue] to the same degree as they do his outlay'; the profit rate thus remains unchanged.

What is actually wrong, I argue in section 'physicalism vs Marx's theory,' are the physicalist formulae. They misconstrue what profitability is (in the world outside physicalist models) and mismeasure it. The physicalist profit rate would measure profitability correctly only in a world in which technological advances did not tend to reduce prices.

Demand-side theories

Tautologies vs explanations

One widely held view on the Left attributes economic crises to the anarchic and competitive nature of private capitalism, which causes firms systematically to expand faster than demand will permit in the long run. Periodically, this results in excess capacity and overproduction, that is, production in excess of demand.[2]

This account is actually a tautology, not an explanation. As Marx (1978: 486) noted, '[i]t is a pure tautology to say that crises are provoked by a lack of effective demand or effective consumption. . . . The fact that commodities are unsaleable means no more than that no effective buyers have been found for them.' To attribute crisis to an excess of production over demand, in other words, is merely to restate that there is a crisis. It does not explain what has caused it. To do so, one needs to explain *why* the volume of output has proven to be excessive – why, that is, demand has been too sluggish to enable everything to be sold at existing prices.

Attempts to attribute the Asian economic crisis to an overexpansion of credit also substitute tautology for explanation. That the region experienced a sudden outflow of capital *means* precisely that the prior inflow of capital was, in retrospect, excessive. The phenomenon has been restated but not explained.

A similar observation can be made with respect to Minsky's (1982) 'financial instability hypothesis.' Emphasizing the excessive increase in indebtedness – speculative and 'Ponzi' financing – that takes place in tranquil times, Minsky offers valuable insights into the conditions that permit 'shocks' to the economy to develop into crises. Yet the excessiveness of the debt burden is itself left unexplained. With reference to what has it become excessive? Why is the economy unable to absorb credit at the same pace as it is created? Only by answering such questions does one move from tautology to explanation.

Underconsumptionism

Underconsumption theories have indeed tried to explain what determines the growth of demand. They hold that total demand is ultimately determined by the demand for consumer goods, which is strictly limited by biological needs and/or the restricted development of new needs under capitalism.

Underconsumptionists recognize that investment spending, an additional source of demand, is not determined directly by consumer demand, but by the extent to which firms desire to increase production. Yet, they maintain, consumer demand limits the increase in production, and thus investment demand, because, directly or indirectly, 'the process of production is and must remain, regardless of its historical form, a process of producing goods for human consumption' (Sweezy 1970: 172).

Given the restricted growth of consumer demand, and the quicker growth of *potential* output that results from technological progress, it follows that a chronic tendency exists for aggregate supply to exceed aggregate demand. This is unsustainable in the long term, so it leads to crises of overproduction. Either production and employment must decline, or prices must fall, or some combination of the two.

Underconsumptionists deserve considerable credit for attempting to explain forthrightly why demand does not keep pace with production. Yet their crucial claim that the expansion of capitalist production is limited by consumer demand happens to be false. This was first demonstrated in the schemes of reproduction in Volume 2 of *Capital*. Marx did not dispute the tendency toward underconsumption, but showed that it constitutes no insurmountable obstacle to the expansion of production (Dunayevskaya 1989: 126).

One part of output consists of consumer goods. Another consists of means of production that are used, directly or indirectly, to produce new consumer goods. Consumer demand sets a limit to the expansion of these parts of output. Yet Marx's schemes demonstrated that there exists a final part of output that does not enter into consumption either directly or indirectly. Iron is used to produce steel, which is used to produce mining equipment, which is used to produce iron, and so on. The growth of *this* part of output is not constrained by 'human consumption,' since its demanders are not humans, but capitals.

The schemes also demonstrated that growth under capitalism generally requires that this final part of output grow faster than the others.[3] Thus, rather than being a system that produces for consumption's sake, capitalism increasingly becomes a system of production for production's sake.

Instead of attempting to disprove these demonstrations, underconsumptionists merely dismiss them in favor of what they believe to be reality, namely the dogma that even capitalist production is production for consumption's sake.[4] Explanations must of course correspond to reality; the problem is that the reproduction schemes *demonstrate* that this dogma does not.

Because the part of output that is not constrained by consumer demand grows faster than the other parts, production can indeed grow faster than consumption, even in the long term. Yet if the expansion of production is not limited by consumer demand and, again, investment demand is governed by capitalists' desire to expand production, it follows that consumer demand can set no insuperable limit to investment demand. Appeals to underconsumption are thus unable to explain what determines *total* demand.

This also implies that underconsumptionism cannot adequately account for crises. If investment demand is sufficiently strong, no crisis will occur, despite constraints on consumer demand. If, on the other hand, investment demand is weak and a crisis does occur, the crisis cannot be due to underconsumption, since what has constrained investment is something other than underconsumption.

It is widely recognized, even by demand-side theorists, that falling rates of profit (actual and expected) are what lie behind weak investment. They contend, however, that what lies behind falling profitability is weak demand in the market. Yet we have seen that, in order to explain the weakness in demand, weak investment spending must *first be presupposed*. Thus the demand-side explanation reduces to the circular claim that weak investment causes weak investment!

Breaking free from the circularity requires a reversal of the causal relation. It is the profit rate that regulates investment demand, and thus total demand, not the opposite. Thus the falling tendency of the profit rate does not result from 'realization' problems in the market, since these problems are not its cause, but its consequence. As Dunayevskaya (1991: 43) noted, 'it is the crisis that causes a shortage of "effective demand." The ... "inability to sell" manifests itself as such *because of the fundamental antecedent decline in the rate of profit, which has nothing whatever to do with the inability to sell.*'

Value production and crisis tendencies

A brief sketch

A brief sketch of the view that I will develop further below runs as follows. When technological advances displace workers with machines, commodities' values (costs of production) fall. Their prices therefore tend to fall, too. This causes the devaluation of existing capital investments, as do technological advances directly, by making older equipment obsolescent. Devaluation leads to crises because the losses of value must eventually be written off and charged against profits, causing current profit rates to plummet. (But the same process restores future profitability since, after the write-offs, profit is larger in relation to the now-devalued capital.)

Declining prices – deflation – and even declines in their growth rate – disinflation – also depress profitability by reducing sales revenues. The decline in profitability can trigger a drop in investment, leading to a crisis of 'overproduction.' Deflation and disinflation also raise the real burden of debt, which tends to cause bankruptcies and financial instability. By heightening the risk of default, rising debt burdens can also bring about credit crunches, another cause of falling investment spending.

The falling tendency of prices can often be neutralized, as it has been throughout most of the past 70 years, by means of excessive credit expansion. I maintain, however, that this does not *negate* the system's crisis tendencies, but merely *displaces* them. The crises now appear more often in the form of debt crises, including State fiscal crises.[5]

It should be clear that I am not putting forward a 'millennial' model in which the profit rate falls 'mechanically' and 'inevitably' throughout all time (Laibman 1999: 224, 2001a: 81, 92). Some physicalist authors have characterized an earlier paper of mine in these terms, but in fact the paper contained *no model whatsoever*. I explicitly noted that I was not trying 'to model the movement in the observed profit rate' and that I was abstracting from the restoration of profitability by means of crises (Kliman 1996: 213). What has been mistaken for a model was simply a *counterexample* that I constructed in order to disprove the physicalist Okishio Theorem (Okishio 1961), which had long been thought to have refuted Marx's law of the tendential fall in the profit rate.

Productivity growth, values and prices

Marx (1977: 137) held that '[t]he same labour, ... performed for the same length of time, always yields the same amount of value, independently of any variations in productivity.' But when productivity rises, a given amount of labor yields more physical output, so values – that is, costs of production – per unit of output decline. Because innovating firms face lower costs than their rivals, they can boost their market shares by lowering their prices and still maintain or even increase their own profit rates. The rivals must either match the price reductions in order to remain competitive, or go out of business. In either case, the end result is that the firms which remain now sell at lower prices, *ceteris paribus*.

Even opponents of this supposedly 'metaphysical' value theory recognize that it correctly explains the effect of technological progress on prices. For example, Greenspan (2000) has stated that:

> Faster productivity growth keeps a lid on unit costs and prices. Firms hesitate to raise prices for fear that their competitors will be able, with lower costs from new investments, to wrest market share from them.... Indeed, the increased availability of labor-displacing equipment and software... is arguably at the root of the loss of business pricing power in recent years.

Let Q stand for aggregate output and L for the total (dead + living) labor needed to produce the aggregate output. Productivity can be expressed as $\Pi \equiv Q/L$. The aggregate value of output is $V \equiv vQ = aL$, where v is an index of per-unit values, and a is a constant. Its constancy reflects Marx's theory that a given amount of labor always produces a given amount of value. Yet the monetary expression of this value varies over time (see, e.g. Marx 1981: 266). The aggregate money price of commodities can thus be represented as $P \equiv pQ = mL$, where p is an index of per-unit prices, and m is the (variable) monetary expression of labor-time (see Ramos 2003). The associated percentage growth rates (denoted by dot superscripts)[6] are thus

$$\begin{aligned}
\dot{\Pi} &= \dot{Q} - \dot{L} \\
\dot{V} &= \dot{L} \\
\dot{P} &= \dot{m} + \dot{L} \\
\dot{v} &= -\dot{\Pi} \\
\dot{p} &= -\dot{\Pi} + \dot{m}
\end{aligned}$$

If $\dot{m} > \dot{\Pi}$, then $\dot{p} > 0$ – productivity growth will be accompanied by higher, not lower, prices. This does not contradict the point that Marx's theory predicts that technological advances *tend* to reduce prices. *Ceteris paribus*, an increase in productivity growth will reduce $\dot{p}$, and to the exact same degree that it reduces $\dot{v}$ – by one percentage point for every percentage-point rise in $\dot{\Pi}$. My preliminary estimate for the US economy between 1949 and 2000 indicates that a one-point rise in $\dot{\Pi}$ did indeed reduce $\dot{p}$ by roughly an amount, 0.987 point (Table 7.1).

Table 7.1 Effect of productivity growth on prices in the United States, 1949–2000

OLS Regression Estimate[a]	$\dot{p} = 2.50 - 0.987\ \dot{\Pi} + 0.456\ \dot{Y} + 4.39\ \boldsymbol{D}$
	(4.89) (–4.33) (2.67) (7.45)
	$R^2 = 0.68$; $F = 33.7$; $DW = 1.52$; $N = 52$. *t*-statistics are in parentheses.

[a] $\dot{p}$, $\dot{\Pi}$, and $\dot{Y}$ are the annual growth rates of the CPI-U price index (year-on-year rate), the Bureau of Labor Statistics' multifactor productivity index for the business sector, and real gross domestic product. D is a dummy variable, equal to 1 for the years 1969–82, and 0 otherwise, that I introduced in order to account for an increase in $\dot{m}$ during that period. I introduced $\dot{Y}$ to control for cyclical effects. Multifactor productivity growth rate data are currently available for the years 1949–2000 only.

Profit rate dynamics

The general rate of profit is $r \equiv S/C$, where S is aggregate profit (which equals aggregate surplus-value under Marx's theory) and C is aggregate capital advanced. This implies that $\dot{r} = \dot{S} - \dot{C}$.[7] One important determinant of the rate of capital accumulation $\dot{C}$ is the '*destruction of capital* through crises' – both the destruction of 'real' or physical capital, and the destruction of 'nominal' capital, the 'depreciation of *values*' (Marx 1968: 495, 496). But assuming – for the moment – that no such destruction occurs, $\dot{C}$ is simply the ratio of new investment to capital advanced, I/C. I can be expressed as αS, where $\alpha \equiv I/S$ is the share of profit that is re-invested. Thus $\dot{C} = \alpha S/C = \alpha r$, so that

$$\dot{r} = \dot{S} - \alpha r$$

Assume that $\dot{S} \geq 0$ and $\alpha > 0$. Then the profit rate falls ($\dot{r} < 0$) if $r > \dot{S}/\alpha$, and rises if $r < \dot{S}/\alpha$. Thus r converges over time to $\dot{S}/\alpha$, which we can call r_{LR}, the long-run profit rate.

It seems reasonable that movements in α are principally short-term ones, associated with the business cycle, and thus that α is essentially trendless in the long run. Nor is there good reason to predict any specific trend in $\dot{S}$. Strong theoretical and empirical arguments suggest that profit will be a more or less constant share of the aggregate price of output over the long haul, since wage-increases that threaten profitability will be temporary and self-negating.[8] Thus S will grow at a rate close to the same rate as P, and there is little, if any, reason to presume any particular trend in the latter's growth rate.

There is consequently little, if any, reason to suppose that the long-run profit rate will fall over time! How, then, can the profit rate have a falling tendency?

The answer is that the falling tendency is not a matter of a different steady state (a decline in r_{LR}), but of 'transition dynamics,' that is, adjustment toward the steady state. As we saw above, if the profit rate is initially greater than r_{LR}, it will tend to fall over time. *The tendency of the profit rate to fall is precisely this tendency of the profit rate to adjust downward toward* r_{LR}.

Put differently, the profit rate will decline if r_{LR} is too low to allow the current rate to be sustained. But what makes r_{LR} too low? It is limited by the growth rate of profit, which in turn is held in check by sluggish employment growth and reduced by productivity growth. To see this, assume as before that profit is a roughly constant fraction of the aggregate price of output over the long haul. Profit then grows at essentially the same rate as does aggregate price, $\dot{L} + \dot{m}$. Thus the profit rate is limited in the long run by the growth rate of value, which in turn depends upon the growth rate of employment. And since $\dot{L} + \dot{m} = \dot{p} + \dot{Q}$, and technological advances tend to reduce $\dot{p}$, they likewise tend to lower the profit rate.

Note that any reduction in $\dot{p}$ – any disinflation – will tend to reduce profitability. Outright deflation – $\dot{p} < 0$ – is not necessary. Nor is the supposed distinction between 'bad' deflation, 'caused' by inadequate demand, and 'good' deflation, caused by technological progress, relevant here. 'Good' deflation depresses profitability no less than does 'bad' deflation, because it, too, reduces revenues today in relation to costs incurred in the past.[9]

Yet technological advances not only reduce profitability, they also restore it. By lowering prices and causing early obsolescence of old equipment, they bring about economic crises in which capital-value is destroyed. From that point forward, the profit rate increases because the destruction of capital reduces its denominator. Thus the profit rate is once again greater than r_{LR}, and the process is set to begin all over again.

The tendential fall in the profit rate therefore expresses itself not through a secular decline in profitability, but through recurrent crises. This was Marx's (1981: 367, emphasis added) view as well: 'the falling rate of profit . . . has *constantly to be overcome* by way of crises.' The destruction of value 'overcomes' the falling tendency and sets the stage for renewed expansion. And since profitability can always be restored if enough capital-value is destroyed (which requires only a sufficiently long and severe crisis), no crisis is permanent.[10]

Value and the debt burden

The framework developed above can help clarify that what makes debt burdens excessive is debt expansion that is too great *in relation to* the surplus-value that has been produced. The same imbalance is what makes Ponzi finance a destabilizing factor, rather than something sustainable in the long term.

A common measure of the business sector's debt burden is the ratio of debt to profit. This ratio will rise if profit grows more slowly than debt. The proportional growth rate of debt is the interest rate, *i*, plus the ratio of net borrowing (new borrowing minus retired debt) to existing debt, *b*. Thus the debt/profit ratio will rise as long as

$$\dot{S} < i + b$$

If $\dot{S} < i$, the debt burden is clearly unsustainable. The debt/profit ratio will rise indefinitely and without limit, even if $b=0$. Short of massive default, the only solution for businesses is to pay back more of their existing debt than they borrow. But even when $\dot{S} > i$, businesses still have to reduce their rate of net borrowing. In either case, the drop in b causes a drop in investment spending, which in turn causes $\dot{S}$ to fall, making yet another decline in b necessary, and so on (If the fall in b causes $\dot{S}$ to fall by a larger percentage, it is impossible to halt the growth of the debt burden.)

'Ponzi finance' refers to an increase in indebtedness not for the purpose of acquiring new productive assets, but simply to pay interest on outstanding debt (Minsky 1982: 28). If the ratio of debt to the value of capital assets is rising, Ponzi finance is taking place. But the debt/capital ratio rises insofar as the growth rate of capital, $\dot{C}$, is less than the growth rate of debt,

$$\dot{C} < i + b$$

As noted above, the profit rate will almost certainly be convergent. This implies that capital-value and surplus-value grow at the same rate in the long run, that is, that $\dot{C}$ converges to $\dot{S}$. Thus if surplus-value fails to grow or grows very slowly (at a rate less than $i+b$), Ponzi finance is almost inevitable. The financial structure becomes unstable, increasingly prone to crisis when confronted with a 'shock.' A decline in the interest rate, perhaps engineered by central banks, could conceivably offset this tendency. On the other hand, as debt rises in relation to the asset base, lenders will demand higher risk premiums, and the interest rate will instead tend to rise.

By using the terms surplus-value and profit interchangeably here, I have implicitly assumed that the monetary expression of labor-time, m, remains constant. During the expansionary phase of the business cycle, however, m increases – the nominal price of aggregate output grows faster than its real value. This temporarily raises the nominal profit rate and temporarily ameliorates the tendency toward excessive indebtedness.

A considerably longer-term discrepancy between the nominal price and the real value of aggregate output arises when government debt is used as a policy tool, and when easy money policies encourage private sector borrowing. Aggregate demand increases more quickly than does the production of value, so commodities' money prices rise above their values. This process, too, tends to counteract the tendency of the (nominal) profit rate to fall.[11]

In contrast to the expansion-induced discrepancy between nominal prices and real values, however, this one *exacerbates* the debt problem, precisely because excessive debt buildup – a buildup of debt in excess of the underlying values – is the very mechanism that is propping up prices. On the one hand,

Table 7.2 Public debt burden in OECD countries, 1979–2001

Country	Public Debt/GDP[a]		Percentage Change[b]
	Low (in %)	High (in %)	
United States	36.2 (1981)	75.8 (1993)	109
Japan	45.6 (1979)	132.8 (2001)	191
Germany	30.8 (1979)	63.2 (1998)	105
France	30.1 (1981)	65.0 (1998)	116
United Kingdom	44.3 (1991)	61.4 (1998)	39
Italy	57.7 (1980)	124.0 (1994)	115
Canada	43.7 (1979)	120.4 (1995)	176
Spain	16.5 (1979)	81.3 (1998)	393
Netherlands	44.1 (1979)	78.8 (1993)	79
Belgium	70.6 (1979)	138.1 (1993)	96
Austria	36.0 (1979)	69.2 (1995)	92
Sweden	39.6 (1979)	77.9 (1994)	97
TOTAL, OECD[c]	39.7 (1979)	75.6 (1996)	90

[a] General government gross financial liabilities, as a percentage of nominal gross domestic product.
[b] From lowest to highest year.
[c] Includes other OECD countries not listed above.

Sources: *OECD Economic Outlook* (Paris: Organization for Economico-operation and Development), No. 59, June 1996, Annex Table 34; No. 71, June 2002, Annex Table 33.

then, the tendency of the profit rate to fall is less likely to find *immediate* expression; the profit rate, in other words, is less likely to fall. On the other hand, these Keynesian policies do not negate, but only *displace*, the system's crisis tendencies. Instead of the crises appearing in the goods market, they crop up mostly in the forms of debt crises and of fiscal crises of the state.

Table 7.2 helps to indicate the magnitude as well as the ubiquitous nature of the fiscal difficulties faced by Organization for Economic Co-operation and Development (OECD) countries in the last two decades. The twelve countries, listed in order of GDP, together produce more than 70 percent of the value of world output. Except for the United Kingdom, all of them have experienced massive increases in the burden of public debt. The overall debt/GDP ratio fell somewhat during the boom years of the late 1990s, but the OECD expects it to rise again.

Physicalism vs Marx's theory

The physicalist profit rate

The 'physical quantities approach' is rooted in static general equilibrium models formulated by Dmitriev (1974), Bortkiewicz (1952), and later writers. Such models suppress intertemporal changes in prices and values, and thus the profit rate becomes a function solely of 'physical quantities' – technology and real (i.e. physical) wages. In diametrical opposition to Marx's (1968: 439; cf. Marx 1981: 347) theory, in which '[t]he rate of profit... falls, not because labour becomes less productive, but because it becomes more productive,' these models imply that productivity increases *raise* the profit rate. For the profit rate to fall, some kind of *falling* productivity is therefore necessary. If the real wage rate is constant, the physicalist profit rate falls only if total factor productivity falls. If instead, the value of the wage is constant, this profit rate becomes a function solely of capital productivity (output per unit of physical capital) and falls only if capital productivity falls (see Brenner 1988: 11). Thus Laibman (1997: 56) posits 'severe diminishing returns to mechanization' in order to derive a falling profit rate. Clearly, the implications of physicalism are, in Brenner's (1998: 11) apt phrase, 'impeccably Malthusian.'

Although proponents of physicalism recognize that technological advances create a tendency for prices to fall, they deny that this impairs profitability. They do so in one of four ways.

Static equilibrium

Prices in their models are stationary; each good's input and output prices are equal. How, then, do technological advances tend to reduce prices? The answer is that there has been history, but there is no longer any. Productivity increases *did* reduce prices, but they have since stabilized. Since they are no longer falling, the profit rate now depends solely upon physical quantities. This answer might seem reasonable, since surely no single technological innovation will reduce prices forever. Yet technological advance is an ongoing process. Continuous technological change tends continually to lower output prices in relation to input prices. So today's revenues decline continually in relation to costs incurred in the past, which does depress profitability.

The 'tracking' argument

In light of this problem, some theorists have conceded that physicalism's stationary-price profit rate does not accurately reflect the actual rate. Nonetheless, they have countered, the value rate of profit must 'track' the physicalist rate. This claim was debated in two symposia in *Research in Political Economy* (Volumes 17 and 18). In the end, Foley (2000b: 281) agreed with Alan Freeman and me that 'it is possible for the *money* and *labor* rates of profit to fall [under conditions in which the physicalist rate must rise], if the money price level or labor productivity... change in certain ways.' David Laibman held fast to the tracking argument, but only by redefining 'tracking.' According to his revised definition, the value rate of profit tracks the physicalist rate even if the former falls *forever* while the latter rises forever (Kliman and Freeman 2000: 292; Laibman 2000b: 274).

Irrelevance of absolute prices

Some proponents of physicalism appeal to corn models and standard commodities in order to argue that values and prices are mere veils. In an economy in which corn was the only output and non-labor input, they maintain, the profit rate would be determined 'directly between quantities of corn without any question of valuation' (Sraffa 1982: xxxi). And the real-world profit rate is *fundamentally* determined in the same way.

Yet even in the corn-model case, profitability does indeed depend upon the self-expansion of value. Imagine a firm that invested $100 a year ago for 4 bu of seed corn, which it used to produce 5 bu of corn, harvested today. Also imagine that, owing to rising productivity, the latter are worth only $100. Sraffians insist that the firm's profit rate is not zero percent, but 25 percent – the rate of increase in corn. To see what's wrong here, imagine that the firm *borrowed* the original $100 for one year. Will its creditor be content with a repayment of $80, on the ground that the $100 loan was equivalent to 4 bu, which are worth a total of $80 today? It will more likely demand the whole $100 – plus interest, which the firm cannot pay.

The Sraffians' error stems from their misunderstanding of the doctrine that only relative prices, not absolute money prices, affect profitability. Since corn is the only 'commodity,' they reason, it has no relative price, and thus profitability depends upon the physical data alone. But the corn *does* have a relative price, one that falls and thereby lowers the profit rate: each bushel is worth 1/4 of the $100 loan asset before the harvest, but only 1/5 thereafter. This phenomenon is known as debt deflation. As the Bank of England's Mervyn King (1993) has emphasized, 'debt deflation is a real[,] not a monetary[,] phenomenon, and is concerned with a change in relative prices.'

Hence, the fact that value and price are relative concepts does not mean that '[v]alue is a relation between *contemporary* commodities... only' (Bailey 1825, quoted in Marx 1971: 154), which is the real significance of the Sraffians' 'relative price' doctrine – and which, ironically, was the crux of Bailey's attack on Ricardian value theory! Financial relations are temporal relations, relations that link the past and the present, the present and the future, relations in which value *persists* over time.

Replacement-cost valuation

Finally, some physicalist theorists are able to deny that falling prices reduce profitability because they use post-production replacement costs, not costs actually incurred in the past, to compute profits and profit rates. Because this procedure makes price changes irrelevant, it yields a 'profit rate' that depends upon physical quantities alone. Yet this 'profit rate' is not a profit rate in the normal sense. It is not the rate that guides capitalists' decisions (the rate they seek to maximize), nor the rate of 'self-expansion' of value, nor the rate that regulates capital accumulation.

Investors, managers, and state planners care about the rate of return on their actual, original investment. Their concept of profit is temporal. Measures of profitability used in investment decisions, such as the internal rate of return (IRR) and net present value, compare sums of value spent and received at *different moments in time*. Marx measured profitability in essentially the same way. For instance, he wrote that '[t]he relation between the value antecedent to production and the value which results from it – capital as antecedent value is capital in contrast to profit – constitutes the all-embracing and decisive factor in the whole process of capitalist production' (Marx 1971: 131). The foremost purpose of his theory of surplus-value is to explain what determines the difference 'between the value antecedent to production and the value which results from it.' Replacement-cost valuation cannot explain this, since it does not use the value antecedent to production to measure cost. Physicalist 'profit' is simply not surplus-value; it is the difference between the value of output and the inputs' replacement costs at a *single moment in time.*[12]

The actual profit rate is also important because it governs the rate of capital accumulation $\dot{C}$. Indeed, $\dot{C} \equiv I/C$ is simply the profit rate (S/C) times the ratio of new investment to profit (I/S). If all profit is re-invested, then the rate of accumulation must equal the profit rate. Yet because the replacement-cost profit rate is not computed on the actual sum of capital advanced C, it fails to govern the rate of accumulation in this way.

An example

The following simple example (Table 7.3); does not attempt to model the real-world movement of profitability. Its purpose is to substantiate the claims made in the last subsection. The economy produces corn by means of seed corn and labor. The wage rate is zero, so profit equals the new value generated in production, and the value advanced for seed corn is the entire capital advanced. The total value of output is the cost of the seed corn plus the new value generated. Capitalists re-invest all output and, accordingly, the total value produced in one year becomes the capital advanced in the next. Employment is constant over time, and since according to Marx's theory the same amount of labor always creates the same amount of value, new value is also constant. Physical quantities, and the first year's capital advanced and new value figures, are data; all other figures are derived. (Using end-of-year (output) prices to revalue the seed corn, we obtain capital 'advanced' in replacement-cost terms; subtraction of the latter from the value of output yields the revised new value = profit.)

Because productivity increases continually, so does the physical profit rate. But the IRR – the (temporal) value rate of profit – falls continually, since capital advanced is increasing by $125/year, while profit is stagnant. The replacement-cost profit rate, equal to the physical rate, rises continually.

Table 7.3 Value, physical, and replacement–cost profit rates

							Replacement-cost calculations			
Year	Capital advanced	New value = Profit	Value of output	Profit rate (in %)	$\dot{C}$ (in %)	Unit price of output (in \$)	Capital 'advanced' (in \$)	New value = Profit (in \$)	Profit rate (in %)	$\dot{C}$ (in %)
1	\$1250 (1250 bu)	\$125 (125 bu)	\$1375 (1375 bu)	10.0 (10.0)	10.0	1.00/bu	1250.00	125.00	10.0	8.2
2	\$1375 (1375 bu)	\$125 (150 bu)	\$1500 (1525 bu)	9.1 (10.9)	9.1	0.98/bu	1352.46	147.54	10.9	7.5
3	\$1500 (1525 bu)	\$125 (180 bu)	\$1625 (1705 bu)	8.3 (11.8)	8.3	0.95/bu	1453.45	171.55	11.8	6.9
4	\$1625 (1705 bu)	\$125 (216 bu)	\$1750 (1921 bu)	7.7 (12.7)	–	0.91/bu	1553.23	196.77	12.7	–

But this means that it diverges increasingly from the IRR and from the rate of self-expansion of value, which is precisely what the IRR measures.

As noted above, the rate of capital accumulation *C* must equal the profit rate when, as in this example, all profit is re-invested. The value rate of profit satisfies this definitional requirement, but the replacement-cost rate does not. It exceeds both the actual rate of capital accumulation and the replacement-cost-based rate by an ever-increasing amount. Thus as time proceeds, *the replacement-cost profit rate becomes a decreasingly adequate measure of the actual expansion of value in relation to the original capital advanced, and of the rate of capital accumulation.*

This example disproves the Okishio theorem, which supposedly refuted Marx's law of the tendential fall in the profit rate. The real wage (=0) is constant, and the technical changes are continually cost reducing, since they reduce the ratio of seed corn to output. According to the theorem, the profit rate cannot fall under such conditions, yet the IRR falls continually.

What creates value?

Is there *any* way, then, that the profit rate might mirror changes in productivity, in the manner of the physicalist rate, but without cooking the books? Is it possible, in other words, to conceive of a physically determined profit rate that nonetheless accurately measures the self-expansion of value and governs investment decisions and the rate of accumulation? Certainly. One needs only to repudiate Marx's theory that living labor creates all new value – but one does need to repudiate it.

One may, for instance, contend that value is determined in the market, not in production. In other words, one may contend that the total value of commodities is just the price paid for them, which is determined by the relation between aggregate supply and aggregate demand. Yet as we have seen above, demand depends on profitability, which in turn depends upon the growth of value. Theories of this sort therefore fall prey to a circularity – the generation of value determines the aggregate demand that determines the generation of value – that makes them truly unable to account for the determination of value.

Another – physicalist – way to repudiate Marx's theory is to claim that new value is determined not by the amount of living labor extracted, but by the amount of net product. Imagine, for instance, that each bushel of net product in Table 7.3 (the physical figure corresponding to new value) generates a constant $1 of new value. If we otherwise retain the same assumptions that were used to generate Table 7.3, we obtain Table 7.4.; The rates of profit and capital accumulation are now identical to the physical rates. In accordance with physicalism, and without using replacement-cost valuation to cook the books, rising productivity causes the profit rate and maximum rate of capital accumulation to rise.

Table 7.4 Corn as value substance

Year	Capital advanced (in $)	New value (in $)	Value of output (in $)	Profit rate (in %)	$\dot{C}$ (in %)	Unit price of output (in $)
1	1250	125	1375	10.0	10.0	1.00/bu
2	1375	150	1525	10.9	10.9	1.00/bu
3	1525	180	1705	11.8	11.8	1.00/bu
4	1705	216	1921	12.7	–	1.00/bu

I noted earlier that proponents of physicalism accept that technological change tends to reduce prices. Yet physicalism *itself* is not compatible with this tendency. As Table 7.4 shows, *once the net product is made the determinant of new value, technological advances cannot cause the price of corn to fall* (unless the books are cooked).[13] Indeed, the reason the rates of profit and accumulation are rising is precisely that, despite continually increasing productivity, the price of corn is not falling.

From Ernst (1982) to the example of the last subsection, twenty years' worth of examples have demonstrated conclusively that Marx's law of the tendential fall in the profit rate does not suffer from the *internal inconsistency* that has been attributed to it. Nonetheless, it might be *false*. That sources of value other than living labor may exist cannot be ruled out *a priori*. Empirical criteria must be used to decide the matter.

I suggest that the well-known tendency for rising productivity to lead to falling prices counts as very strong empirical evidence in favor of Marx's theory. The other theories discussed here cannot predict this tendency. Because demand-side theories cannot account for total demand, they cannot explain movements in aggregate prices. Physicalism fares even more poorly. If changes in the profit rate are to mirror changes in productivity, rising productivity cannot lead to falling prices.

Conclusion

This chapter has critiqued prominent theories of profitability and crisis, especially underconsumptionism and the 'physical quantities approach' that dominates Marxian economics. It has argued instead that economic crises are rooted in capitalism's production of value as an end in itself. The imperatives imposed by the production and accumulation of value lead to recurrent disruptions of physical production. A key policy conclusion flowing from this analysis is that an end to recurrent crises will require a different way of producing and coordinating society, based on a different goal: 'the development of human powers as an end in itself' (Marx 1981: 959).

Notes

An earlier version of this chapter appeared in *Revista da Sociedade Brasileira de Economia Política* 6 (June 2000), under the title 'Endividamento, Crise Econômica e a Tendência de Queda na Taxa de Lucro – uma Perspectiva Temporal.' I wish to thank the many colleagues, too numerous to mention individually, who have commented on earlier versions. The usual caveat applies.

1. I disregard (post-)Keynesian crisis theory, which seems to me ultimately to offer no explanation at all, since the key determinants in this theory, changes in investors' expectations and in central bank policies, are themselves left unexplained.
2. The theory advanced by Brenner (1998) can be read in this manner, though I am not sure it was what he intended.
3. A decline in input–output coefficients could counteract this tendency.
4. 'Any attempt to get away from this fundamental fact represents a flight from reality . . . [The existence of] reproduction schemes which apparently demonstrate the opposite does not change matters one whit: production is production for consumption' (Sweezy 1970: 172).
5. I am not suggesting that this account constitutes a complete explanation of economic crisis, only that the linkages sketched out above are important ones that should not be overlooked.
6. If $Z=XY$, then $\dot{Z} = \dot{X} + \dot{Y}$ and if $Z=X/Y$, then $\dot{Z} = \dot{X} - \dot{Y}$. The growth rate of constants is 0.
7. Only under the 'temporal single-system' – or 'sequential' and 'non-dualist' – interpretation (see e.g. Freeman and Carchedi 1996) of Marx's value theory do these relations hold true. Under this interpretation, C is determined temporally – it is the sum of value *actually advanced prior to production* – and there is a single system of price and value determination in which commodities' values and prices both depend in part upon the *price* of inputs. Physicalist interpreters hold to the contrary that C is determined atemporally; it depends upon inputs' *post-production* (or replacement) cost. As will be shown below, this implies that the tendency of r does not depend upon the rate of accumulation of capital-value ($\dot{C}$). Most physicalist interpreters also subscribe to a dual-system interpretation, according to which commodities' values depend upon the *value* of inputs. Under this interpretation, aggregate profit can deviate from aggregate surplus-value.
8. See Marx (1977: 769–72); Brenner (1998: 16–21). Faced with rising wages which threaten profitability, firms substitute machines for workers, or reduce investment spending and thus cut back on production and employment. In both cases, the drop in employment depresses wages.
9. I suspect that one reason why the negative effect of technological advances on profitability is not recognized more widely is that innovating firms tend to increase their own profit rates since they produce more cheaply than before. But to assume that what is true for the individual firm is true for the whole economy is to commit a logical error, the fallacy of composition.
10. 'When Adam Smith explains the fall in the rate of profit [as stemming] from an over-abundance of capital, . . . he is speaking of a *permanent* effect and this is wrong. . . . Permanent crises do not exist' (Marx 1968: 497n).
11. '[T]he rise in the rate of profit [in England between 1797 and 1813] was due [partly] to rising *nominal* prices of commodities, because loans and government expenditure increased the demand for capital even more rapidly than its supply' (Marx 1968: 460).

12. Moseley (2000b) and others have argued that Marx valued inputs and outputs simultaneously and thus that he measured profitability in replacement-cost terms. This interpretation fails standard tests of interpretative adequacy, since it renders his law of the tendential fall in the profit rate and other important theoretical conclusions internally inconsistent or false. According to a generally accepted hermeneutic tenet, interpretations must understand texts as coherent wholes, and according to leading historians of economic thought, they must be compatible with the author's main analytical conclusions (see Kliman 2002a).
13. This perverse phenomenon was recognized concurrently by Freeman (1997a), and Kliman (1997).

8

Production and Management: Marx's Dual Theory of Labor

Gérard Duménil and Dominique Lévy

Introduction

Yes, the labor theory of value is relevant to the analysis of contemporary capitalism. Apart from the so-called *transformation problem*, there are grounds for a discussion concerning the nature of various categories of labor such as productive and unproductive labor.

The thesis of this chapter is that Marx actually put forward a dual theory of labor, of which the labor theory of value is only one aspect. Marx's identification of a second category of labor is consistent with the separation between productive and unproductive labor, though not equivalent to it. The potential modernity of this framework is underestimated. Although the correspondence is not complete and must be discussed in detail, this dual theory of labor refers to what is now labeled *production* and *management*. Clerical and managerial tasks are useful, in spite of their basic unproductive character. Within capitalism, their purpose is to maximize the profit rate, which relates to what can be called management in a broad sense. Their rising numbers point to new class patterns and technological trends. In our opinion, Marxist economists need to confront these issues rather than calculate hours of labor in the maze of industrial divisions.

The overall question raised in this chapter can be summarized as follows: *Is Marx's dual theory of labor useful?* Or more precisely, *What can we learn about capitalism by referring to the labor theory of value and to the theory of profit-rate-maximizing (PRM) labor?*

This chapter is divided into three sections. The section 'Profit-rate-maximizing (PRM) labor' introduces the concept of PRM labor as the tasks of the capitalist in the reproduction of capital. The transformation of PRM labor from the framework of the formal subsumption of labor under capital to that of real subsumption is discussed. The section 'The delegation of the tasks of the active capitalist' is devoted to the delegation of these tasks to managerial and clerical personnel. This is where the relationship is established between Marx's categories and the contemporary notion of management. The section

'The usefulness of the theories of value and of PRM labor' discusses the usefulness of the theory of labor value and of the theory of PRM labor, as two distinct and complementary theories.

It is noteworthy that the object of this chapter is not the relationship between the labor theory of value and the theory of exchange, or the transformation problem, which has been at the origin of much confusion (Box 8.1).

Box 8.1 Value, exchange, and price

The relationships between the concepts of value, exchange and price are difficult and controversial. Below, we simultaneously emphasize their congenial character and discuss the differences in content. Ultimately, we return briefly to the *transformation* controversy.

Exchange in the definition of labor values The value of a commodity is defined by Marx as the socially necessary labor time required for its production. This definition refers to production but market mechanisms are also implied in the determination of *socially* necessary labor time. The overall idea is that, in a noncapitalist commodity-producing economy, the market would not recognize the specific features of the labor process as executed by one producer. In particular, such a producer cannot claim a price to reward his/her effort if it is inefficient.

The famous 'abstraction' of labor, in particular the reduction of complex to simple labor, can only be realized by the process of exchange in the market and the mobility of producers between various activities. If market and social practices (since such mechanisms are highly dependent on power relations or uses) do not acknowledge the intensity and skillfulness of particular types of labor, producers would be discouraged to undertake these tasks; the deficient or excessive supply of particular goods would then modify behaviors. In other words, the process of abstraction of labor is the product of the behavior of economic agents in an economy. If this were not so, the concept of abstract labor would be an empty shell with no explanatory power.

Since the conditions of production (technology, wages, scarce resources, outputs...) are influenced by the capitalist features of the economy, the determination of values along the above lines rests on the idea of an impossible social experiment in which a number of social relations and mechanisms are set aside: *a fictitious reference state*, used as a tool of analysis. In other words, we compute values rather than observe them.

Box 8.1 Continued

Laws of exchange The labor theory of value – or the *law of value*, an expression that Marx scarcely uses – does not imply that commodities exchange at prices proportional to their values. Marx states two basic *laws of exchange*, which obviously do not sum up the entire complexity of exchange relations:

1. *The commodity law of exchange* The exchange of commodities at prices proportional to their values. This relates to a noncapitalist commodity-producing economy. (Such a commodity noncapitalist economy is more a theoretical reference than the description of a geographically and historically identifiable situation.) This law of exchange is used by Marx as a simplifying assumption whenever a more complex framework is unnecessary (sometimes even when it is required).
2. *The capitalist law of exchange* The exchange of commodities at prices proportional to hours of social labor reallocated to take account of the comparative sizes of the amounts of capital used in their production. These prices are called *prices of production*. This framework can be broadened to include the existence of rent for natural resources. This second law of exchange is more realistic than the previous one, whose purpose is fundamentally theoretical. (Only capitalist economies transform most products into commodities.)

Assuming that prices of production regulate exchange, the market will simultaneously acknowledge the quantities and qualities of labor, on the one hand, and capital invested, on the other.

Values and prices – The price form of value It is obvious from this analysis that the relevance of the labor theory of value does not rest on the actual exchange of commodities according to the first law of exchange. Any more complex law of exchange or disequilibrium may prevail. Surplus-value can be realized according to more complex reallocation procedures (such as the payment of rent), without affecting the relevance of the labor theory of value, or law of value, as evident from the last sentence below:

> Apart from the confusion produced by the transformation of values into prices of production, a further confusion derives from the transformation of surplus-value into various separate, mutually

Box 8.1 Continued

> independent forms related to the various elements of production, into profits and rents. It is forgotten that the values of commodities are the basis and that the breakdown of this commodity value into particular components [...], in no way alter the value determination and its law. Just as little is the law of value affected by the fact that the equalization of profit [...], gives rise to governing average prices for commodities that diverge from their individual values (Marx 1981: 984–5).

This last sentence shows that by 'law of value' Marx does not mean the exchange of commodities at prices proportional to their individual values. The individual values of commodities play no role in the determination of relative prices in capitalist economies, where prices tend to gravitate around prices of production. However, the prices of commodities (contrary to the prices of land) are forms of value[a]: either value (hours of socially necessary labor time) in the enterprises and industries where it has been created (as in the commodity law of exchange) or value as it has been reallocated (as in the capitalist law of exchange). The terminology 'prices of production' is somewhat ambiguous, since the same relation holds between reallocated hours of socially necessary labor time and its price (its expression in money) in a capitalist economy, as between socially necessary labor time and its price expression in a pure commodity economy. What should we call prices of production: reallocated hours or their monetary form ?

The transformation controversy The controversy around the so-called 'transformation of values into prices of production' specifically addresses the issue of the redistribution of labor time in a capitalist economy recalled above. The problem hinges upon the exact content given to this notion of 'redistribution,' in relation to the equality between total values and total prices of production, and total surplus-value and total profits. Years ago, a 'new' interpretation (new when it was formulated) was proposed[1]. It suggests that only the hours of labor time expanded during the period are at stake, while the value of the commodities transferred from previous periods must be reassessed according to the present conditions of production[2]. Correspondingly, the rate of surplus-value must be measured according to the purchasing power of workers in terms of such redistributed hours (thus, independently of what they actually consume).

Box 8.1 Continued

In a discussion of the relevance of the labor theory of value in the analysis of contemporary capitalism, we judge such controversies as secondary technical issues, with little practical consequences if any. Far more relevant is the idea of the dual conceptualization of labor in Marx's analysis to which this chapter is devoted.

[a] Values refer to social relationships. The value of a commodity can only be expressed as a quantity of another commodity, as in the *exchange-value*, or in a quantity of money, as in the *price form*.

Profit-rate-maximizing (PRM) labor

Central to our analysis is the fact that a capitalist performs specific *tasks*. These tasks are not useless, but are a necessary component of the reproduction of capital. Their purpose is the maximizing of the profit rate. Some difficulty is created in this analysis since the content and nature of some of the tasks of the capitalist change with the development of capitalist relations of production. The crucial distinction in this respect is between formal and real subsumption of labor under capital.

We first consider all capitalist tasks related to circulation, for which this distinction is not relevant.

The tasks of the capitalist regarding circulation

Marx analyzes the *reproduction of capital* as the unity of the production and *circulation processes* of capital. Production is simultaneously related to the labor process and the valorization process of capital. The second concept, circulation, refers to the metamorphoses of capital through its various social forms and the simultaneous existence of the fractions of capital under the three forms.

Capital is value taken in a movement through three 'forms': money capital, M, commodity capital, C, and productive capital (in the labor process), P. Each element of capital moves, at its own speed, through a process of metamorphoses through these three forms. To describe it, it does not matter if we begin in M, C, or P. For example, Marx writes: $M-C\ldots P\ldots C-M$.

Each step of this circulation process of capital requires labor: (1) conserving money M (managing liquidities), (2) buying $M-C$ and selling $C-M$ (commercial activity and hiring of the labor force), stockpiling C (managing inventories), and (3) producing P (ensuring the provision of material and labor inputs, managing goods in process...); it is also necessary to (4) collect the necessary financing and (5) to control the entire circulation of capital, as in internal accounting.[3]

In Marx's analysis, all circulation activities are originally part of the tasks or, equivalently, the functions of the capitalist. In particular, buying and selling are components of these tasks:

> Just as the circulation time of capital forms a necessary part of its reproduction time, so the time during which the capitalist buys and sells, prowls around the market, forms a necessary part of the time in which he functions as a capitalist, i.e. as personified capital. It forms part of its business hours.[4]

Three ideas are combined in this passage: (1) Buying and selling require time-consuming activities; (2) These activities are a component of a broader set of activities; (3) They are the responsibilities of the capitalist.

The distinction between production and circulation is related to the definition of productive and unproductive labor (Box 8.2). Very clearly, in Marx's framework, all circulation tasks are unproductive, and the agents who perform these acts are unproductive workers. All categories of labor performed within the production process, under the form *P*, are not productive. The labor that must be expended to impose discipline on the workers does not produce value (discussed below). Thus, the two distinctions are not coextensive.

Box 8.2 Productive and unproductive labor

All labor is not included in the definition of value, only productive labor is included. First, the product must be sold in the market. Labor spent to prepare foods or to produce cloth for the family is not productive labor in this sense; in a similar fashion, the work of a civil servant in a public administration is unproductive labor. Second, in a capitalist economy, where a more sophisticated division of labor prevails within each enterprise and among enterprises, a further broad category of labor is classified by Marx as unproductive. This is, for example, the case of all commercial activities: Buying and selling, although they demand actual work, are not component parts of productive labor and do not create value.

Within the theory of commodity, productive labor creates values; within the theory of capital, productive labor creates surplus-value for the capitalist class. Marx treats this distinction as a straightforward outcome of the extension of the field of analysis:

Box 8.2 Continued

> Only the labour which posits the variable capital and hence the total capital as $C + \Delta C = C + \Delta v$ is productive. It is therefore labour which directly serves capital as the agency of its *self-valorization*, as means for the production of surplus-value.
>
> The capitalist labour process does not cancel the general definitions of the labour process. It produces both product and commodity. Labour remains productive as long as it objectifies itself in *commodities*, as the unity of exchange-value and use-value. But the labour process is merely a means for the self-valorization of capital. Labour is productive, therefore, if it is converted into *commodities*, but when we consider individual commodity we find that a certain proportion of it represents *unpaid* labour, and when we take the *mass of commodities as a whole*, we find similarly that a certain proportion of that also represents unpaid labour (Marx 1867: 1039).

Far from being useless, unproductive labor has a well-defined purpose: the circulation of capital. In particular, the aim of commercial activities is to insure the passage from commodity capital to money capital, $C - M$, in order to guarantee the fastest *rotation* possible.

The formal and real subsumption of labor under capital

Marx distinguishes two historical stages in the evolution of the control that capitalists exercise in the labor process. In both the cases, formal and real subsumption, the activity of the capitalist is required but its content is altered. The formal subsumption of labor refers to the transfer under the sway of the capitalist owner of a basically unchanged labor process. In the second stage, the real subsumption, the labor process is thoroughly transformed in terms of (1) scale (largely increased), (2) technology (much more sophisticated), and (3) complexity, due to the increased division of tasks and through the application of science:

> [...] capital subsumes the labour process as it finds it, that is to say, it takes over an existing labour process, developed by different and more archaic modes of production. For example, handicraft, a mode of agriculture corresponding to a small, independent peasant economy. [...] This stands in striking contrast to the development of a specifically capitalist mode of production (large scale industry, etc.) [real subsumption]; the

> latter [...] revolutionizes their [of the agents of production] actual mode of labour and the real nature of the labour process as a whole. It is in contradistinction to this last that we come to designate as the formal subsumption of labour under capital [...] the takeover by capital of a mode of labor developed before the emergence of capitalist relations.[5]

Marx links the distinction between formal and real subsumption of labor to the two patterns of growth of surplus-value: absolute and relative surplus-value. The relationship is straightforward, since the progress of labor productivity is a central feature of real subsumption and of the mechanism of the relative surplus-value:

> If the production of absolute surplus-value was the material expression of the formal subsumption of labour under capital, then the production of relative surplus-value may be viewed as its real subsumption.[6]

The tasks of the capitalist in production

Formal subsumption

The tasks of the capitalist concerning circulation are not interrupted by the labor process, since capital still circulates under its form *P*: Raw materials cannot be wasted and labor must be expended with the required intensity and care. Thus, there appears a disciplinary component, which is already typical of formal subsumption, but obviously persists under real subsumption:

> As far as the old value is concerned, namely the value of the constant portion, this depends for its maintenance on the value of the means of production entering the [production] process not being greater than necessary. The commodities of which they are made up should contain in objectified form, i.e. as buildings, machinery, etc., no more than the socially necessary labour time essential for their production. And it is the task of the capitalist to see to it when purchasing these means of production that their use-values have no more than the quality needed to manufacture the product. [...] He must also see to it that the work is performed in an orderly and methodological fashion and that the use-value he has in mind actually emerges successfully at the end of the process. At this point too, the capitalist's ability to supervise and enforce discipline is vital.[7]

This passage by Marx states clearly that the purpose of the activity of the capitalist is to diminish the costs and reduce the necessary amount capital to a minimum for a given output.

As a result of the control exercised by the capitalist, it is not possible to state that formal subsumption does not modify the labor process in any respect. Marx insists, however, that the basic organizational and technical process remains fundamentally unchanged despite the control of the capitalist:

> If changes occur in these traditional established labour processes [under formal subsumption] after their takeover by capital, these are nothing but the gradual consequences of that subsumption. The work may become more intensive, its duration may be extended, it may become more continuous or orderly under the eye of the interested capitalist, but in themselves these changes do not affect the character of the actual labour process, the actual mode of working.[8]

In contrast, the transformation of the labor process under real subsumption is of a different nature and has a considerably larger impact.

Real subsumption

In the real subsumption of labor under capital, the production process is revolutionized as capitalist relations of production acquire a social character:

> With the real subsumption of labour under capital, all the changes in the process already discussed now become reality. The social forces of production of labour are now developed, and with large-scale production comes the direct application of science and technology. On the one hand, capitalist production now establishes itself as a mode of production sui generis and brings into being a new mode of material production. On the other hand, the latter itself forms the basis for the development of capitalist relations whose adequate form, therefore, presuppose a definite stage in the evolution of the productive forces of labour.[9]

A crucial element in the transformation of the labor process is the emergence of the *collective worker*. Marx explains how the labor process is organized, under real subsumption, in a manner reflecting the existence of various categories of tasks, such as manual and intellectual labor. Actually, the transformations of the labor process tend to *create* a 'physical' separation between such components:

> The knowledge, the judgement and will which, even though to a small extent, are exercised by the independent peasant or handicraftsman, [...] are faculties now required only for the workshop as a whole. The possibility of an intelligent direction of production expands in one direction, because it vanishes in many others. What is lost by the specialized workers is concentrated in the capital which confronts them. It is a result of the division of labour in manufacture that the worker is brought face to face with the intellectual potentialities of the material process of production as the property of another and as a power which

> rules over him. This process of separation starts in simple co-operation, where the capitalist represents to the individual worker the unity and the will of the whole body of social labour. It is developed in manufacture, which mutilates the worker, turning him into a fragment of himself. It is completed in large-scale industry, which makes science a potentiality for production which is distinct from labour and presses it into the service of capital.[10]

Capitalist relations of production transform the pattern in which intellectual and manual labor are combined. Along the succession of the various configurations (co-operation, manufacture, and industry), the organization of labor gradually displaces the intellectual component from the person of the worker toward an autonomous force (such as the will of the actual capitalist), independent from the individual worker – that actually dominates the worker and belongs to capital. This process coincides with the progress of organization, technology, and discipline within capitalism. Thus, the separation between the intellectual and manual components of the labor process gradually gains empirical relevance, while difficult in the early stages, it becomes an external feature of the labor process. The evolution of relations of production creates a separation that was not inherent in labor *per se*, as labor itself is transformed.

Within the *collective worker* discipline, the actual organization and coordination of production are difficult to disentangle:

> On the one hand, in all labour where many individuals cooperate, the interconnection and unity of the process is necessarily represented in a governing will, and in functions that concerned not the detailed work but rather the workplace and its activity as a whole, as with the conductor of an orchestra.[11]

Marx does not hesitate to describe these tasks of coordination, which belong to the capitalist as such, as productive. The next sentence is:

> This is productive labour that has to be performed in any combined mode of production.[12]

Thus, the production process under real subsumption introduces a new element: a productive contribution of the capitalist to the production process as coordinator (a task of conception, organization, and coordination). The control of production requires an increased involvement of the capitalist in the labor process. In addition to the control of circulation within production and to the discipline imposed on the worker, the capitalist now actually participates in production. Thus, part of his/her activity is now productive labor.

PRM labor in general

Thus, a broad category of tasks, concerning both circulation and production, is implied in Marx's analysis, whose purpose is the *maximizing of the profit rate*. Recall that a profit rate is defined as the ratio of a measure of profits to a measure of capital. Many definitions can be used, however, depending on the purpose of the analysis.[13] The maximizing of the profit rate requires contributions by numerous agents performing different activities, as well as a whole set of expenses and investments:

1. Considered independently of their functions, these expenses and investments always diminish the profit rate (since they diminish the numerator and increase the denominator). What Marx denotes *circulation costs* affect profits negatively. For example, costs must be incurred to accelerate the sale of commodities; the store where commodities are sold is a fixed capital that gradually depreciates like any component of fixed capital used in production.
2. These expenses and investments are, however, required to diminishing other expenses and investments that would be higher, that is, to the maximizing of the profit rate. Discipline, for example, insures that labor is performed with maximum intensity and efficiency. The enforcement of discipline has a cost, but the costs of the wages of productive workers are minimized and the outcome of labor is maximized. Other costs and investments (for example, required by the collection of information concerning markets) insure that the productive capacity of the firm is used at appropriate levels, so that as much possible output is obtained at adequate costs. These expenses and investments are substituted for others, assuming that the profit rate will be larger.

The delegation of the tasks of the active capitalist

With the development of capitalism, the tasks of the capitalist increase in size. New institutional frameworks, such as corporations, also appear. This section is devoted to the delegation of the tasks of the active capitalist to salaried workers in the new framework of capitalist relations. The link is established with the notion of management.

The social framework of real subsumption and the active capitalist

Besides the transformation of organization and technology, Marx is aware that the real subsumption requires a dramatic rise of the scale of production:

> [...] a definite and constantly growing minimum of capital is both the necessary precondition and the constant result of the specifically capitalist mode of production. The capitalist must be the owner or proprietor of

> the means of production on a social scale and in quantities that beggar comparison with the possible production of the individual and his family. The minimum amount of capital in an industry increases in proportion to its penetration by capitalist methods and the growth in the social productivity of labour within it. Capital must increase the value of its operations to the point where it assumes social dimensions, and so sheds its individual character entirely.[14]

Marx states very clearly in this quotation that the transformation of production under real subsumption cannot be separated from the establishment of a new framework of capitalists institutions. First, the increased size of production oversteps the limits of individual or family financing. Thus, the progress of real subsumption requires a credit and, potentially, a corporate economy in which large amount of capital can be more easily collected. In turn, the diffusion of these institutions is linked to the emergence of modern finance and the separation between ownership and management:

> Joint-stock companies in general (developed with the credit system) have the tendency to separate this function of managerial work more and more from the possession of capital, whether one's own or borrowed; [...] the functioning capitalist confronts the mere owner of capital, the money capitalist, and with the development of credit this money capital itself assumes a social character, being concentrated in banks and loaned out by these, no longer by its direct proprietors [...].[15]

Marx witnessed the first stages of these developments and understood their importance and significance.

It is noteworthy that, under the category of the lender, Marx also includes the shareholder who is not directly involved in the control of the functioning of the firm. (In the extract above, Marx uses the term *money capitalist*, but this terminology is misleading because of the possible confusion with the category of money capital, one of the forms of capital in its circulation: Obviously, the money capitalist is not the owner of this fraction of capital!)

Salaried workers performing capitalist tasks

As apparent in the above extract, the delegation of the tasks of the active capitalist to salaried workers is an important component of Marx's analysis. Whenever he discusses the functions of the active capitalist, he is always mindful of their delegation to salaried workers. Marx refers to the substitution of a salaried manager for the active capitalist himself, to such a point that the capitalist disappears from the labor process:

> [...] the mere manager, who does not possess capital under any title, neither by loan nor in any other way, takes care of all real functions that fall to the functioning capitalist as such, there remains only the functionary [the one that assumes functions], and the capitalist vanishes from the labor process as someone superfluous.[16]

But the manager is surrounded by a broad team of salaried aids. This is, for example, true of commercial tasks which are done by salaried employees. In his analysis of the collective worker, Marx also refers to a team of such salaried employees that carry out the tasks of organization and discipline. For example, concerning discipline:

> Just as at first the capitalist is relieved from actual labour as soon as its capital has reached that minimum amount with which capitalist production, properly speaking, first begins, so now he hands over the work of direct and constant supervision of the individual workers and groups of workers to a special kind of wage-labourer. An industrial army of workers under the command of a capitalist requires, like a real army, officers (managers) and N.C.Os (foremen, overseers), who command during the labour process in the name of capital. The work of supervision becomes their established and unique function.[17]

As a result of this delegation, the wages of these salaried workers forms an important component of the cost of maximizing the profit rate. In particular, Marx sometimes mentions the wages of the employees involved in circulation activities such as trade.

This delegation, which existed from the origin of capitalism but grew to dramatic proportions in contemporary capitalism, has important consequences concerning basic theoretical distinctions. Marx is primarily concerned with the fact that the delegation of capitalist tasks, or their realization within a specific industry (for example, commerce), does not transform an originally unproductive labor into productive labor:

> [...] if we have a function which, although in and for itself unproductive, is nevertheless a necessary moment of reproduction, then when this is transformed, through the division of labour, from the secondary activity of many into the exclusive activity of a few, into their special business, this does not change the character of the function itself.[18]

Delegation and polarization

Marx is aware of the broad spectrum of situations from which the delegation of the tasks of the active capitalist may result: from the rank-and-file employee to a salaried manager. He does not, however, elaborate much on this issue. In our opinion, this polarization is very similar to that described earlier concerning the separation of intellectual and manual activities in the labor process, since class patterns and relations of production are gradually manifested in the organizational and technical features of PRM labor.

Each component of the activities of the active capitalist requires initiative, authority, as well as routine and repetition. From the origin, these tasks were separated into various components and delegated to distinct categories of salaried workers. *The contents of the tasks were adjusted in order to match such a hierarchical separation.* The manager thinks, discusses, decides, and so on, his/her secretary writes, classifies, initiates, contacts, and so on. Accounting procedures are defined by managers, who also analyze the results; the accounts are established by accountants, and so on. The sophistication of managerial labor followed specific lines tending to create or strengthen the polarization of the tasks.

Class patterns and relations of production are at issue both in the workshop and in the accomplishment of the tasks of the capitalist. This polar division of tasks, de facto, isolates the upper component of managerial tasks from the rest of the body of activities devoted to the maximizing of the profit rate. They create an increasingly visible division, as in the case of the labor process.

Production and management

The distinction between basic productive labor and PRM labor can be interpreted by reference to the contemporary notions of production and management. We first discuss this interpretation assuming that all activities other than the labor of the productive worker are performed by the active capitalist, and then in the context of their delegation to salaried workers. The content given to the usual notion of management is altered. (Note that the use that we make of the notion in reference to Marx's analysis is always broad, but to different degrees.)

Management in the broader sense

We assume that the bulk of the intellectual components (conception, organization) of production has been transferred, thanks to the practical way in which production is organized, to the person of the capitalist, who also enforces discipline. Relations of production blur some of these theoretical distinctions. Strictly speaking, some aspects of this activity may be part of productive labor but typically only secondarily. Most of such tasks is unproductive. Nonetheless, all capitalist activity is targeted to the maximizing of the profit rate.

Inasmuch as the maximizing of the profit rate is performed by the active capitalist, there is no difficulty in identifying it with what is now known as 'management.' In this simple framework of analysis, the worker produces and the capitalist maximizes the profit rate, that is, manages the firm. It is possible to draw the following (simplified) correspondence:

Production		**Management**
Productive labor	→	Unproductive labor
Creation of value		Maximizing of the profit rate

Management in a narrower sense

The delegation of the tasks of the active capitalist to salaried workers does not alter their nature. The fact that some productive components may be realized by certain individuals does not modify either their position within relations of production.

Given this delegation, and due to the polarization of tasks, it becomes less obvious, however, to include all of these tasks under the general category of management, or the notion must be given the above very broad content (as we often do for simplicity). In the contemporary terminology, a cashier or employee of a supermarket is not performing management functions, although he/she is involved in a task of circulation. The notion of management, as it is now used, seems more appropriate to designate the tasks of the upper fraction of the salaried workers to which the tasks of the capitalist are delegated (including engineers, lawyers . . .). This is true at the upper levels of conception, coordination, as well as discipline, which relates to both production and circulation activities. A store must be organized as well as a workshop; discipline must be imposed in both contexts, and so on.

The usefulness of the theories of value and of PRM labor

The dual feature of Marx's analysis of labor does not make the labor theory of value irrelevant. The two components must be combined in the analysis of contemporary capitalism.

The usefulness of the labor theory of value

It is important to assess the explanatory power of the labor theory of value and simultaneously recognize its limits: The labor theory of value explains a lot but not everything.

The structural and collective character of exploitation

The usefulness of the labor theory of value is the clarification of the nature of exploitation within capitalism. Marx's central contention in this respect can be summarized in three points: (1) capitalism is a class society where a fraction of the result of the labor of basic producers is appropriated by the owners of the means of production, in a relationship of exploitation; (2) this exploitation can be portrayed as *structural* (an expression that Marx does not utilize) in the sense that it does not violate the laws of exchange (exploitation is part of the normal functioning of capitalism); and (3) it is also *collective* in the sense that the total surplus-labor appropriated by capitalists is realized according to rules (according to the capitalist law of exchange, including rent, interest, or not...), that differ from the individual extraction of surplus-labor by individual capitalists (a capitalist does not realize the surplus-value extracted in his/her own enterprise).

Marx calls *exploitation* the process by which one group of people benefit from the outcome of the labor of others; these groups of people are called *classes*.[19] Note that this exploitation is one among many related either to other categories of labor, age, sex, ethnicity, and so on.

The usefulness of the labor theory of value can be summarized in two points:

1. In the exposition of the structural character of exploitation in capitalism, Marx makes the simplifying assumption that commodities exchange at prices proportional to their values. He treats the labor force of the workers as a commodity, with a use-value and an exchange-value. The labor force is purchased at its normal price, and workers buy commodities at such prices. Exploitation arises from the existence of surplus-labor. This is the well-known theory of surplus-value.
2. The collective character of exploitation is addressed within the theory of the capitalist law of exchanges, that of prices of production. This is where a concept of value is crucial. Under normal conditions, surplus-labor is appropriated by one firm (or industry) proportionally to the amount of productive labor expended. Exploitation cannot be measured in physical (quantity of product) or price terms. If it were, the rate of exploitation would structurally differ in each industry due to its technical features (the various compositions of capital). Quite the opposite, Marx points to a uniform rate of exploitation.[20] The social substance, socially necessary labor time, is realized by capitalists, still under normal conditions, proportionally to the socially required amount of capital. The appropriation of labor is made as within a single large enterprise covering all activities, and then shared (rather 'antagonistically reallocated') by capitalists in the framework of competitive mechanisms.

This remarkable analysis has been made once for all by Marx, and we do not think that much must be added to it or subtracted. It does not have to be repeated.

What the labor theory of value does not explain

The interpretation of profits in terms of surplus-labor implies that surplus-value is created in each industry proportionally to the amount of productive labor (consequently no surplus-value is created within industries where no productive labor is used). However, this theory has no consequences concerning the realization of surplus-value in various industries. Thus, the theory of labor value does not inform us concerning relative prices in a capitalist economy (Box 8.1). Prices of production cannot be derived from values. Prices reflect costs and the amount of capital required for production in the long run, and disequilibria between supply and demand in the short run. A profit rate expressed in terms of value has no relevance concerning the functioning of capitalism.

None of the basic stylized facts of capitalism, like the tendency for the profit rate to fall, can be derived from the labor theory of value. This tendency is the expression of the entire dynamics of technological change and determination of wages.

The usefulness of the theory of PRM labor

Managerial and clerical personnel

In a framework of analysis where all salaried labor is interpreted in terms of productive labor confronting capital – the traditional dual conception of the *Manifesto* – there is no way of conceptualizing the specific features of these intermediary classes of white collars.

Marx's actual framework of analysis is, however, more complex. PRM labor defines a specific social group, distinct from productive workers. The new intermediary classes of managerial and clerical personnel perform PRM labor, that is, delegated capitalist tasks; in addition, their wages appear as a deduction from profits. To that extent, they can be described as a new petty bourgeoisie.[21]

The acknowledgement of this specificity is, however, not sufficient. A new relation of production emerged from the polarization of PRM labor (as a historical process). The separation opposes managerial labor, on the one hand, and clerical labor, on the other, in a new class relation.[22]

From the coexistence of the two class contradictions (Figure 8.1): (1) capitalist/productive workers, and (2) managerial personnel/clerical personnel, derives a new pattern of class relations in which productive workers and clerical personnel tend to form a new dominated social entity. Besides capitalist owners, managers form a new component of ruling classes. Their relation to capitalists is simultaneously one of co-operation and rivalry.

The dynamics of managerial capitalism

As well understood by Marx, the profit rate is a crucial variable in the analysis of capitalism. From this property derives the importance of the concept of PRM labor. The relative importance of PRM labor has been continuously growing over the history of capitalism. Marx's analysis of what we called

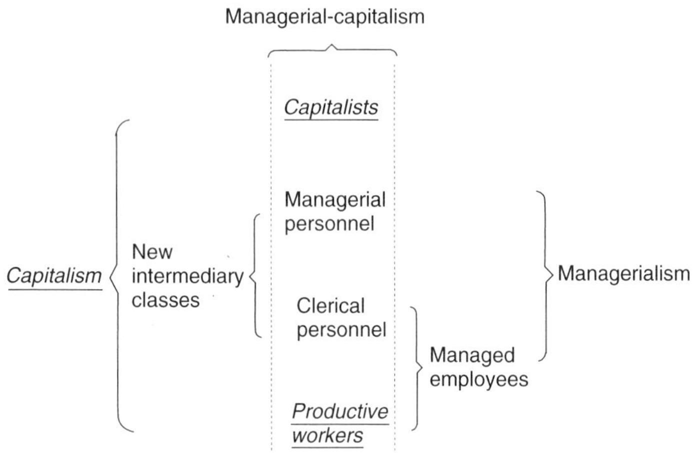

Figure 8.1

earlier the social framework of the real subsumption anticipated on the revolution of capitalism in the United States at the transition between the nineteenth and twentieth century, with its three aspects, the corporate, financial, and managerial revolutions, that we often described.[23]

The notion of *managerial revolution* (from the beginning of the twentieth century) refers to a dramatic movement forward in this respect.[24] The more recent transformations of capitalism during the last decades echo these earlier evolutions, with the new progress of management, in particular with respect to financial activities.

The theoretical and empirical analysis of capitalism, as it can be conducted for the United States[25] points to the progress of management as the main countertendency to the falling profit rate. In this sense, this progress was crucial to the evolution of capitalism.

During the last decades of the nineteenth century, the profit rate displayed a strong downward trend, from which resulted the structural crisis that culminated in the 1890s. In the context of the growing size of enterprises, this crisis was manifested in a crisis of competition, with the development of cartels and trusts. Besides the Sherman Act, the transformation of the laws governing incorporation opened the way to the large wave of incorporation and merger at the turn of the century. Simultaneously the new framework of modern finance emerged, and monetary and financial mechanisms underwent a considerable growth. A component of this assertion of the institutions of modern capitalism was the separation between ownership and management, and the corresponding managerial revolution, which can be interpreted as a dramatic rise of PRM expenses in general, and PRM labor in particular.

The outcome of this revolution was spectacular with respect to the features of technological change, introducing new trajectories in which the traditional unfavorable characteristics of technical change *à la Marx* (which we call the *difficulty to innovate*) were superseded. As in the assembly line, mechanization reached new heights, but labor was used so intensely and continuously by the machine that the composition of capital (the capital–labor ratio) grew at lower rates in comparison to previous decades. The profit rate entered a phase of growth, despite the larger growth rates of wages. This movement was apparently interrupted by the Great Depression, since the sharp contraction of activity diminished suddenly the profit rate, but it actually contributed to the generalization over the economy of the new technology and organization. In a sense, the boom of PRM labor insured the survival of capitalism, although at the cost of a profound transformation, in particular the rise of the new intermediary classes of managerial and clerical workers.

The new configuration of capitalism progressively spread to the entire economy, between the late 1950s and late 1960s. Then, the traditional features *à la Marx* of technological change were re-established, and the profit rate entered the new phase of decline leading to the structural crisis of the 1970s.

It is not the rise of PRM labor during these decades of hardship that caused the decline of the profit rate[26] but rather what can be described as their declining efficiency. More was put in PRM labor, but with diminishing results. The growth of PRM labor (the progress of management) had been very efficient during the first half of the twentieth century, but they gradually lost efficiency.

It is difficult to identify PRM expenses within the available set of data. Even abstracting from expenses other than labor, the measurement of PRM labor costs is practically impossible because of a lack of appropriate data series. There is, in the United States, a category of production labor, which actually corresponds to about 80 percent of total labor, but this variable cannot be considered as a proxy for productive labor in Marx's sense. This difficulty does not impact the measurement of the profit rate, which is the outcome of all expenses and investments. It prohibits, however, the investigation of an important aspect of the dynamics of capitalism: How much was spent on PRM activities? As for the measurement of the efficiency of PRM labor, it is hard to imagine how it could be assessed.

Although we cannot prove it empirically, we believe that the rise of the new technologies of information and communication, which are actually the technology of management, represents a crucial factor (among others) in the restoration of this capability of management to counteract the unfavorable features of technical change during the last two decades. They are, to some extent, responsible for the new underlying trends of technical change and profitability since the early 1980s.

Overall, the role of PRM labor in the history of capitalism, at least since the Civil War in the United States, has been outstanding. The explanatory power of the theory of PRM labor is distinct from that of the labor theory of value, but now equally important.

Notes

1. Duménil (1980), Foley (1982, 1986), Lipietz (1982), and Ehrbar and Glick (1986).
2. From this latter element, follows the divergence with the already old but more recent interpretation which conserves the values of inputs transferred from previous periods independently of the possible alteration of their conditions of production (Freeman and Carchedi 1996; Duménil and Lévy 2000). This divergence is completely alien to the prevalence of equilibrium or disequilibrium in the economy, contrary to what is often stated.
3. 'Besides the actual buying and selling, labour time is spent on book-keeping, which requires pens, ink, paper, desks and other office equipment as well as objectified labour. Thus it is spent in this function both as labour-power and as means of labour. In this connection, the same state of affairs obtains as with buying and selling time' (Marx 1885: 211).
4. Marx (1885: 207).
5. Marx (1867: 1021).
6. Marx (1867: 1025).
7. Marx (1867: 985).
8. Marx (1867: 1021).
9. Marx (1867: 1035).
10. Marx (1867: 482).
11. Marx (1981: 507).
12. Ibid.
13. For example, in the analysis of the tendential features of technological change that command the tendency for the profit rate to fall, technology and wages are at issue. This leads to the selection of a broad measure of profits, such as the total product minus labor compensation, and a physical measure of capital, such as fixed capital or fixed capital plus inventories. When the emphasis is on the consequences of the falling profit rate, a measure closer to the management of firms is more adequate. Taxes and interest can be subtracted from profits, and a financial measure of capital may be used, notably net worth (total assets minus debt).
14. Marx (1867: 1035).
15. Marx (1981: 512).
16. Marx (1981: 512).
17. Marx (1867: 450).
18. Marx (1885: 209).
19. The relationship with the labor theory of value is not straightforward: A noncommodity society (where a labor theory of value is irrelevant) can be a class society in this respect.
20. Obviously, rates of exploitation may differ among firms, industries, and categories of workers. Marx explores, however, structural properties of capitalism that lie beyond such individual traits.

21. Poulantzas (1974), Duménil (1975).
22. Duménil (1975), Duménil and Lévy (1994). Originally, Eric Olin Wright drew on the distinction between discipline and organization to distinguish various components among unproductive salaried workers (Wright 1978). He later abandoned this distinction (Wright 1997).
23. Recent accounts can be found in Duménil, Glick and Lévy (1997), Duménil and Lévy (2001a, 2001b).
24. A classical reference is: Chandler (1977).
25. The extension to other countries is possible, but must take account of the process of catching-up that occurred in the most advanced capitalist countries, in particular after World War II.
26. In this respect, we differ with the thesis put forward in Moseley (1991). This disagreement must be understood in the context of the broad convergence of opinion with Moseley concerning the importance of the profit rate and its decline.

9

Marxian Theory of the Decline of the Rate of Profit in the Postwar US Economy

Fred Moseley

In the US economy between 1950 and 1975, the general rate of profit for the economy as a whole declined approximately by 50 percent. There are different measures of the rate of profit, depending on the precise definition of profit and the capital invested, but all the different measures show approximately the same significant downward trend. According to my estimates, the rate of profit declined from 22 to 12 percent (Figure 9.1).[1,2]

I and other Marxist economists (Weisskopf 1979; Wolff 1986; Shaikh 1992b; Duménil and Lévy 1993; Brenner 1998) have argued that this significant decline in the rate of profit was the main cause of the deterioration of economic performance in the US economy since the 1970s. In the early postwar period, the US economy performed remarkably well. The rate of growth averaged 4–5 percent a year, the rate of unemployment was seldom above 5 percent, inflation was almost non-existent (1–2 percent a year), and the living standards of workers improved substantially (the average real wage, or the purchasing power of wages, roughly doubled over this period). This was the 'golden age' of US capitalism.

However, this 'golden age' ended in the 1970s. Since then, the rate of growth has averaged 2–3 percent, the rate of unemployment and the rate of inflation have both been higher, and the average real wage has not increased at all (and by some measures has even declined 10 percent or so). The 'American dream' of ever rising living standards ceased to be a reality for many workers. For the first time in US history, many young workers fear that they will have a lower standard of living than their parents. It is in this sense that we refer to the 'stagflation' of the US economy in recent decades.

This turn from prosperity to stagflation in the US economy and the consequent decline of real wages was completely unexpected in the 1960s. For example, Herman Kahn, a well-known futurologist, predicted in 1967 that the average real wage in the US economy would more than triple by the year 2000 (Kahn 1967: 176–80). A similar prediction – that real wages would increase 150 percent by the year 2000 – was made in a special issue of

Forbes magazine the same year. From the perspective of the optimism of the 1960s (based on the trends of the early postwar 'golden age'), the last quarter of the twentieth century in the US economy has been a shocking disappointment.

I and other Marxist economists argue that the main cause of both of the 'twin evils' of higher unemployment and higher inflation, and hence also of the lower real wages, of recent decades, was the significant decline in the rate of profit in the preceding decades. As in periods of depression of the past, the decline in the rate of profit resulted in a decline in business investment and higher unemployment. One new factor in the postwar period is that many governments in the 1970s responded to the higher unemployment by adopting Keynesian expansionary policies (more government spending, lower interest rates, etc.) in an attempt to reduce unemployment. However, these government attempts to reduce unemployment generally resulted in higher rates of inflation, as capitalist enterprises responded to the government stimulation of demand by raising their prices at a faster rate in order to reverse the decline in their rate of profit. In the 1980s, financial capitalists revolted against these higher rates of inflation and have generally forced governments to adopt restrictive policies (less government spending, higher interest rates, etc.). The result has been less inflation, but also sharply higher unemployment and sharply reduced living standards. Therefore, government policies have affected the particular combination of unemployment and inflation that has occurred, but the fundamental cause of both of these 'twin evils' has been the decline in the rate of profit.

It is striking that mainstream explanations of the stagflation of recent decades have completely ignored the very significant decline in the rate of profit. These mainstream explanations emphasize 'exogenous shocks' (i.e. accidents), such as government policy mistakes, the Organization of petroleum exporting countries (OPEC) oil price increase, a mysterious slowdown in productivity growth, and so on. According to Marxian theory, these other factors are not 'exogenous shocks,' but are instead those caused by the decline in the rate of profit. By ignoring the rate of profit, mainstream explanations miss this fundamental cause and remain on the level of superficial appearances.

Furthermore, surprising as it may seem, mainstream economics provides no credible theory of the rate of profit which might be used to help explain the decline of the rate of profit in the postwar US economy. Mainstream macroeconomics has no theory of profit at all (profit is not a variable in this theory of a capitalist economy!). In microeconomics, the marginal productivity theory of profit (or interest) is completely static (i.e. provides no theory of trends over time) and is also now in general disrepute, because it has been shown to be logically contradictory (as a result of the 'capital controversy'). This much-maligned theory is being quietly dropped from microeconomic textbooks at both the undergraduate and the graduate levels.

The only economic theory that provides a substantial theory of the rate of profit and its trends over time is Marxian theory. Indeed, the rate of profit and its trends over time is the *main question* of Marxian theory. The rate of profit is the main variable in Marxian theory, in striking contrast to mainstream theories in which profit is not a variable at all.

Therefore, if we want to understand the causes of the decline in the rate of profit and its likely trend in the future, the only economic theory available to us is Marxian theory. It is often said these days that Marxian theory is 'dead' or 'obsolete.' But this assertion is simply false. As this book itself demonstrates, there are many excellent Marxian economists around the world, using Marxian theory to analyze and understand contemporary capitalism, including the current world economic crisis. Indeed, Marxian theory is essential if we want to understand the rate of profit and its trends. There is simply no credible alternative theory of the rate of profit available.

Let us turn now to the explanation offered by Marxian theory of the decline in the rate of profit in the postwar US economy, and of the lack of a full recovery of the rate of profit in recent decades.

Marxian theory of the decline in the rate of profit

The main point of the Marxian theory of profit is that profit is produced by workers, by the surplus labor of workers, because the value added to commodities by the labor of workers is greater than the wages the workers are paid (Profit is equal to the difference between the value produced by workers and the wages they are paid.) This conclusion follows from the labor theory of value, which is usually misinterpreted by mainstream economists as a theory of individual prices, like mainstream microeconomics. But this is a misunderstanding. The Marxian labor theory of value is mainly a macroeconomic theory of the total profit produced in the economy as a whole.

Marxian theory concludes that the rate of profit (the ratio of the total profit to the total capital invested) will decline over time, for two main reasons. The first main cause of the decline in the rate of profit, emphasized by Marx himself, is technological change – an inherent, ever-present feature of capitalist economies – which tends to replace workers with machines, and thus tends to reduce the number of workers employed in relation to the total capital invested in machinery, plant and equipment, and so on. However, since profit is produced by workers, the reduction in the number of workers employed also reduces the amount of profit produced, in relation to the total capital invested. In other words, the rate of profit will decline. Expressed inversely, technological change causes the total capital invested to increase faster than the number of workers employed, or causes the average *capital invested per worker* to increase, which in turn causes the rate of profit to fall.

Marxian theory argues further that the negative effect on the rate of profit of the increase in the capital per worker can be partially offset by increasing the amount of *profit produced by each worker*, which also tends to increase as a result of technological change, which increases the productivity of labor. This positive effect of new technology and higher productivity on the profit produced per worker is also reinforced by other ways to increase the profit per worker, such as wages cuts and increases in the intensity of labor.

However, Marxian theory argues that there are inherent limits to the increase in the profit produced by each worker. The main limit is that there are only so many hours in the working day, and it becomes harder and harder to increase the profit produced by each worker in a given working day. Another limit is the resistance of workers, who usually fight against wage cuts and fight for higher wages and a share of the benefits of the higher productivity. As a result of these limits, Marxian theory concludes that 'labor-saving' technological change will eventually cause the rate of profit to decline. This decline of the rate of profit is no accident or due to 'external causes.' Rather, the decline of the rate of profit is the result of capitalism's own internal dynamics of continual technological change (see Moseley 1991: Chapter 1, for a further discussion of Marx's theory of the falling rate of profit).

The above trends, predicted by Marxian theory, are essentially what happened in the postwar US economy. Technological change increased the capital invested per worker, and also increased the amount of profit produced by each worker. And, as predicted by Marxian theory, the capital invested per worker increased faster than the profit produced per worker, so that the rate of profit declined significantly, as we have seen above.

Another important determinant of the rate of profit, according to Marxian theory, which Marx himself did not emphasize, but which seems to have been important in the postwar US economy, is the proportion between *productive labor and unproductive labor* in the capitalist economy. According to Marxian theory, profit is not produced by all employees in capitalist firms, but only by workers engaged directly or indirectly in production activities (actually making or designing or transporting something), which Marx called 'productive labor.' There are two other main groups of employees who are *not* engaged in production activities, which Marx called 'unproductive labor': 'sales' employees (sales and purchasing, accounting, advertising, finance, etc.) and 'supervisory' employees (managers, supervisors, 'bosses' in general). These two groups of unproductive labor, although entirely necessary within capitalist firms, nonetheless do not themselves produce value and profit for the economy as a whole (see Moseley 1991: Chapter 2, for a further discussion of Marx's concepts of productive and unproductive labor).

According to Marxian theory, if unproductive labor (which does not produce profit) increases faster than productive labor (which does produce profit), this will also cause the rate of profit to fall, because costs are increasing, but profit is not, for the economy as a whole. This is what happened in the postwar US economy: the ratio of unproductive labor to productive labor almost doubled during the 'golden age,' and this very significant increase contributed to the decline in the rate of profit. This increase in the ratio of unproductive labor to productive labor also seems to have been due, in large part, to technological change, which increased the productivity of production workers more rapidly than that of non-production workers, and which therefore required more and more sales workers to sell the more rapidly increasing output of production workers (see Moseley 1991: Chapter 5, for a further discussion of the causes of the relative increase of unproductive labor).

Therefore, according to the Marxian theory presented here, there were two main causes of the decline of the rate of profit in the postwar US economy from the late 1940s to the mid-1970s: an increase in the capital invested per worker, and an increase in the ratio of unproductive labor to productive labor. According to my estimates, these two trends contributed roughly equally to the total decline in the rate of profit during this period (see Moseley 1991: Chapter 4). Both of these causes were themselves the result of technological change, an inherent feature of capitalist economies. Therefore, the decline of the rate of profit in the postwar US economy was not due to accidental, external causes ('exogenous shocks'), but was instead due to the inherent dynamic of technological change. It is an interesting and important question whether this Marxian explanation of the stagflation of recent decades also applies to other advanced countries. My conjecture is that it does.

Failure to increase the rate of profit

Capitalist enterprises have responded to the decline in the rate of profit by attempting to restore the rate of profit in a variety of ways. We have already mentioned the strategy of inflation, that is, of increasing prices at a faster rate. Businesses have also attempted to slow down wage increases, and in some cases even to cut wages. Another strategy to reduce wage costs has been to move their production operations to low-wage areas of the world. This has been the main driving force behind the so-called 'globalization' of recent decades: a world-wide search for lower wages in order to increase the rate of profit.

Another strategy has been to make workers work harder and faster; that is 'speed-up.' Such a 'speed-up' in the intensity of labor increases the value produced by workers and therefore increases profit and the rate of profit. The higher unemployment of this period contributed to this 'speed-up,' as workers have been forced to compete with each other for the fewer jobs available by working harder. One common business strategy has been 'down-sizing,' that is, lay-off 10–20 percent of a firm's employees and then require the remaining employees to do the work of the laid-off employees. This method also generally increases the intensity of labor even before the workers are laid off, as all workers work harder so that they will not be among those who are laid off.

We can see that the strategies of capitalist enterprises to increase their rate of profit in recent decades have, in general, caused suffering for workers – higher unemployment and higher inflation, lower living standards, and increased stress and exhaustion on the job. Marx's 'general law of capitalist accumulation' – that the accumulation of wealth by capitalists is accompanied by the accumulation of misery of workers – has been all too true in recent decades.

However, the startling fact is that, despite the decline in real wages and the 'speed-up' of workers' labor, the rate of profit in the United States has not increased very much since the 1970s (see Figure 9.1). There have been cyclical increases in the rate of profit, especially in the 1990s, but most of these increases have been wiped out in the subsequent downturn, so that overall the rate of profit has recovered only about a third of its previous decline. The rate of profit today (2002) remains about 30 percent below the early postwar peaks. This absence of a full recovery in the rate of profit is the main reason why the US economy has not returned in recent decades to the more prosperous conditions of the 'golden age.' My guess is that the same conclusion also applies to other advanced countries.

The Marxian theory presented above provides an explanation not only of why the rate of profit declined in the early postwar period, but also of why the rate of profit has increased so little in recent decades, despite the stagnant real wages, increased intensity of labor, and so on. According to this Marxian theory, the rate of profit varies directly with the profit per worker,

Figure 9.1 The rate of profit in the postwar US economy.

and also varies inversely with the capital per worker and the ratio of unproductive labor to productive labor. Therefore, there are three main ways to increase the rate of profit: (1) increase the profit per worker, (2) reduce the capital per worker, and (3) reduce the ratio of unproductive labor to productive labor.

Marxian theory suggests further that an increase in the profit produced per worker (by means of wage-cuts, speed-ups, etc.) is not likely by itself to be sufficient to restore the rate of profit to its previous levels, since the prior decline in the rate of profit was not caused by a decline in the profit per worker, but was instead caused by increases in the capital per worker and in the ratio of unproductive labor to productive labor. We have already seen that a significant increase in profit per worker in recent decades has resulted in a relatively small increase in the rate of profit. Marxian theory suggests that what is required to fully restore the rate of profit is to reverse the two trends that caused its decline, that is, to reduce the capital invested per worker and to reduce the ratio of unproductive labor to productive labor.[3]

The main way capital per worker has been reduced in the past has been through the widespread bankruptcies of capitalist firms, which are caused by the combination of falling profits and rising debts. As a result of bankruptcies, surviving firms are able to purchase the productive assets of the bankrupt firms at a very low price, thereby reducing the amount of capital invested per worker and raising their rate of profit. This process of bankruptcies, and so on (which Marx called the 'devaluation of capital') continues until the capital per worker has been reduced enough and the rate of profit increased enough in the economy as a whole for capital investment to resume and for a period of recovery and expansion to begin. Of course, widespread bankruptcies also worsen the economy in the short run, and many times in the past have turned a recession into a depression.

The main way to reduce the ratio of unproductive labor to productive labor would be to lay-off large numbers of non-production employees (sales, managers, etc.). Leaving aside the questions of whether such a large reduction of non-production employees is feasible in the US economy today, and how it would be brought about, such a large displacement of non-production employees would sharply increase the rate of unemployment, especially among these occupations. Thus we can see that all the various ways in which the rate of profit could be increased (wage-cuts, bankruptcies, lay-offs, etc.) involve hardships and declining living standards for workers.

Since the mid-1970s, as discussed above, profit per worker has increased significantly (through wage cuts, etc.) and this has indeed contributed to an increase in the rate of profit (at the same time contributing to an increase in the hardships of workers). However, these other two crucial adjustments necessary to increase the rate of profit have not yet happened in the US economy. The capital invested per worker has remained more or less constant (first decreasing in the 1980s and then increasing in the 1990s) and the ratio of unproductive labor to productive labor has continued to increase (although at a slower rate) and thus has continued to have a negative effect on the rate of profit. This is the main reason why the rate of profit has increased so little since the 1970s, in spite of the significant increase in the profit produced per worker (see Moseley 1997, for a further discussion of the trends in these key variables since the 1970s).

What lies ahead?

What does this Marxian theory imply about the future course of events in the US (and world) economy? In the first place, this theory implies that the future of the US economy, like its past, will depend mainly on the rate of profit. If the rate of profit increases significantly, then perhaps the US economy will return to the more prosperous early postwar 'golden age.' However, if the rate of profit remains at the current low levels, then a return to prosperity is not very likely. Instead, the US economy will continue to experience sub-par growth and higher unemployment, and perhaps even worse.

Furthermore, this theory suggests that the future trend of the rate of profit depends on the three main factors discussed above: the profit produced per worker, the capital invested per worker, and the ratio of unproductive labor to productive labor. Profit per worker will probably continue to increase as in recent years (as slow growth and higher unemployment continues to put downward pressure on wages), which will continue to have a positive effect on the rate of profit. Further, if the economy continues to expand (although slowly), then the capital per worker will probably also increase slowly, which will have a negative effect on the rate of profit. And the ratio of unproductive labor to productive labor will probably continue to increase, which would continue to have a negative effect on the rate of profit. The net effect of these opposing trends is difficult to predict with precision, but extrapolating from the recent past, it does not appear very likely that there will be a significant increase in the rate of profit in the foreseeable future. In the absence of such an increase in the rate of profit, the US economy will at best remain stuck in the stagnation of recent decades (see Moseley 1997, for a further discussion of the likely future trends in these key variables).

In addition, according to Marxian theory, there is not much the government can do to avoid this gloomy prospect, because there is not much government economic policies can do to increase the rate of profit. Expansionary fiscal and monetary policies do not increase the profit produced per worker, nor reduce the capital invested per worker, nor reduce the relative proportion of unproductive labor. Therefore, even though expansionary and monetary policies may provide a temporary boost for the economy, they are not able to achieve the necessary precondition for a return to a new era of prosperity: a significant increase in the rate of profit.

As this is written (September 2002), the brief 'recovery' from the recession of 2001 appears to be stalling, and the economy appears to be falling back again into recession, which threatens to be a severe one. This 'double-dip' recession has not been caused by the September 11 attacks, but rather by a rapid decline in the rate of profit since 1997 (see Figure 9.1), which has led to a sharp reduction in capital investment since 2000. Also, capitalist firms borrowed record amounts of debt in recent years in order to finance the 'investment boom' of the late 1990s (and also to help finance the stock market boom of the late 90s, as firms used about half of the money they borrowed to repurchase their own stock!). This combination of low profits and high debt makes the risk of defaults and bankruptcies today the highest in the postwar period. Also, households have taken on record levels of debt to finance their 'consumer spending spree' of the late 90s, and they too face a higher danger than ever before of defaults and bankruptcies, which would further worsen the recession.

Such a deepening recession in the United States would have a devastating effect on the rest of the world, especially Asia and Latin America. The main hope of these countries for recovery from their current economic difficulties is to increase their exports to the United States. But if the US economy falls back into recession, then this hope will disappear and these economies will likely remain in depressed conditions for years to come.

Whether this global recession turns into global depression cannot be predicted with precision. But if Marx's theory (and history) is any guide, the postwar period of declining profitability and increasing debt will eventually be followed by a period of prolonged depression, characterized by significant and widespread bankruptcies of capitalist firms, which will eventually raise the rate of profit for surviving firms and eliminate much of the existing debt, thereby creating the conditions for another period of expansion and prosperity. In other words, a return to prosperity requires a prior depression. It may be possible to continue to avoid such a depression for a few more years; but without such a depression, Marxian theory suggests that a return to the more prosperous conditions of the early postwar 'golden age' is not very likely.

Such a worsening crisis of global capitalism would inflict great suffering – loss of jobs, lower incomes, greater hunger and poverty, greater anxiety and desperation, etc. – on the world's working population, especially in developing countries. How would workers in the United States and around the world respond to this widespread and increasing misery? It seems likely that in the next few years, workers all over the world will be forced to choose between passively accepting higher unemployment and lower living standards and actively resisting these hardships and striving to defend their economic livelihood. It is possible that, as economic conditions deteriorate, these struggles by workers to maintain their living standards within a capitalism in crisis will lead more and more of them to call into question capitalism itself, and the adequacy of capitalism to meet their basic economic needs. If capitalism requires these attacks on our economic livelihood, then perhaps there is a better economic system that does not require such attacks and which could better satisfy our economic needs and wants.

Notes

1. My estimates of the rate of profit are for the Business sector as a whole. Estimates for the Non-Financial Corporate Business Sector are also frequently used and these estimates show essentially the same downward trend; for example see Weisskopf (1979).
2. This significant decline in the rate of profit appears to have been part of a general world-wide trend during this period, affecting all major capitalist economies.
3. Japan has been in a prolonged slump for the entire decade of the 1990s, and has fallen again this year (2001) into even deeper recession. According to Marxian theory, the main reasons for this prolonged slump are: a significant decline in the rate of profit and the unwillingness (or inability) of Japanese banks to force money-losing firms into bankruptcy. The Japanese experience seems to suggest, in support of Marxian theory, that these bankruptcies cannot be avoided.

Part IV

Revisiting the Theory of Value

10
Some Critical Reflections on Marx's Theory of Value

Ajit Sinha

Introduction

What is *value*? What makes a thing valuable? An old family picture or a gift from a loved one could have great value for an individual, but no one else may be willing to give anything in exchange for these items. Such items, as we all know, have 'sentimental value' but no 'economic value.' Value in its economic sense is a *social measure* of the 'worth' of a thing. It is an *objective measure* in the sense that a thing's worth is not measured by individual subjectivity but by the objective measure of how much of something else that can be obtained for it in exchange. If exchange between two commodities is sporadic, then the measure of the worth of the two commodities may still reflect idiosyncratic subjectivity. When exchange becomes regular, however, the relationship between the two commodities in exchange takes an objective form such as twenty-five goats for an ounce of silver. The problem of value is to answer this question: *What determines such objective measures like twenty-five goats for an ounce of silver*? This is essentially a static problem in the sense that the question relates to a particular point in time. Sometimes the problem of value gets mixed up with an entirely different question that seeks to inquire into the reasons for the changes in the exchange ratios of the commodities over a period of time. Of course, the correct answer to the first question is the prerequisite for a satisfactory answer to the second.

But before we can discuss the question of how the exchange ratios of commodities or the prices of commodities are determined, we first need to ask a more fundamental question. It is obvious that if we were interested in understanding black holes or the beginning of the universe and so on, we would not need to be bothered by the question, why many things have 'value'? The question of value must arise within a theoretical problematic, and thus the mystery of 'value' can only be resolved by investigating the theoretical problematic that gives rise to the problem.

With the advent of capitalism as a historical mode of reproducing human material life, economics slowly separated itself from being a part of ethical philosophy (e.g. the problem of fair price) and developed its own independent personality. There are two, or rather three, fundamental aspects to the capitalist organization of society. First there is extensive social division of labor, that is, fulfillment of human needs requires exchanges of the things produced. Second, the society is divided into two or three classes of capitalists, wage laborers and landlords. And third, there is competition among the capitalists. These aspects give rise to two fundamental questions: (1) how is the exchange of commodities determined? (2) how is the income of the three classes determined, such that they are reproduced from one period of time to another?

In this chapter, we concentrate our analysis on the problematic of value, particularly its relation to the problem of finding a measure of value, in the writings of Marx. In my opinion, Ricardo's theory of value looms large in the background and thus needs to be taken into account in developing an understanding of Marx's problematic of value. Keeping this in mind, the following section is devoted to a brief discussion of Ricardo's problematic and his labor theory of value. After noting Ricardo's problems with the labor theory of value, we discuss in a subsequent section two aspects of Marx's theory of value. First, we show that the non-Ricardian ways of relating labor to value in Marx's analysis are simply untenable. Secondly, we show that Marx's transformation of values to prices of production was designed to achieve a conceptual result similar to Ricardo's. But unfortunately Marx also did not succeed. A final section contains brief concluding remarks.

Ricardo's theory of value

In the Preface to the *Principles of Political Economy and Taxation* (1817–21), the only book Ricardo produced in his lifetime, he set the problematic of political economy in these terms:

> To determine the laws which regulate this distribution, is the principal problem in Political Economy: much as the science has been improved by the writings of Turgot, Stuart, Smith, Say, Sismondi, and others, they afford very little satisfactory information respecting the natural course of rent, profit, and wages (Ricardo [1821] 1951: 5).

Here the problem of the distribution of income has been put at the center of the problematic of political economy. One should also note that the question of the distribution of income is posed both in the static (i.e. 'to determine the laws which regulate this distribution') as well as the dynamic (i.e. '[the] information respecting the natural course of rent, profit, and wages') contexts. The book, however, begins with a long chapter 'On Value,' and only then moves to the analysis of the distributional categories. Sraffa, in collaboration with Maurice Dobb (1951), in his famous general introduction to *The Works and Correspondence of David Ricardo*, gives a cogent and highly persuasive story concerning Ricardo having to come to terms with a theory of value before he could discuss the laws regulating the distribution of income.

According to Sraffa, prior to the writing of the *Principles*, Ricardo was working with an implicit 'corn-profit model.' In this model, given the theory of differential rents established by Malthus and Edward West, the marginal land did not pay any rent, and both the inputs and the output of the land consisted of the same commodity, corn, as seed and corn wages as well as corn output. In this case, the rate of profits could be derived by dividing the physical net corn output by the seed plus the corn wage capital investment. This rate of profits, given the competitive nature of the capitalist economy, would have to prevail in all sectors of the economy. Moreover, a fundamental law of distribution, suggesting that the real wages and the rate of profits are inversely and proportionately related to each other, is established by changing the corn wages and tracing out its effect on the rate of profits.

This simple model had to be given up by Ricardo because of his friend Malthus's consistent protestation that real wages, apart from corn or agricultural goods in general, also contain manufacturing goods. Thus the rate of profits could not be determined in the agricultural sector alone. The one good 'corn-profit model' had to be given up and capital consisting of a bundle of heterogeneous goods had to be taken up. Now one could no longer determine the rate of profits by simply dividing the physical net output by the physical capital investment since the ratio, in all probability, would be a ratio of heterogeneous goods. Ricardo needed to homogenize the ratio of heterogeneous goods in order to derive the rate of profits, and this could only be done with the aid of a *theory of value*. A theory of value would give a theoretical basis for representing or measuring all commodities in terms of one chosen as the 'money commodity.'

The pure labor theory of value seemed to meet the bill at the first blush, as long as it could be assumed that the ratio of direct to indirect labor content in all the sectors were the same. This also proved triumphant in demolishing Adam Smith's incorrect argument that the pure labor theory of value becomes invalid once the surplus income categories such as profits and rents emerge. It was not the emergence of profits and rents that invalidated the labor theory of value as a correct theory of value or prices in a capitalist system, argued Ricardo. The assumption of an equal ratio of direct to indirect labor in all the sectors, however, was too restrictive. And once this restriction was removed, the pure labor theory of value had to be 'modified' to insure an equal rate of profits across the sectors.

This 'modification' of the labor theory of value as such did not bother Ricardo. As we shall see, Marx found it highly objectionable. Ricardo apparently changed gears when faced with the problem of the determination of exchange ratios of commodities and argued in terms of locating the *cause* that *changes* the established exchange ratios.[1] But once such a modification in the exchange ratios is accepted, a rise or fall in real wages would affect the value of all the commodities, including the chosen money commodity, in all sorts of ways. This had one positive and one negative implication for Ricardo.

On the positive side, he could demolish Adam Smith's dictum that a rise in wages would raise all prices. Adam Smith in his *Wealth of Nations* had suggested that the *natural price* of a commodity is determined by adding up *natural wages, natural profits* and *natural rent*, where these natural rates are determined independently of each other. Hence a rise in wages would lead to a rise in all prices. Ricardo argued that Adam Smith was wrong in taking all the distributional variables as independent of each other, since they must be bound by the net output. By showing that a rise in wages could lead to many prices falling (given the composition of the 'money commodity'), Ricardo could demolish the idea that profits could emerge by adding to prices.

On the negative side, however, he found that the effect on the 'money commodity' of a change in wages implies that even if the net output has been kept constant in physical terms a change in its distribution between wages and profits could very well change its size when measured in value or money terms. The *measuring rod* does not remain *invariant* to the distribution of income, and thus no precise laws about the distribution of income could be established.[2] Ricardo remained worried and busy trying to solve this theoretical problem until the end of his life, but did not succeed in finding his invariable measure of value.[3] Notwithstanding this, Ricardo remained convinced that the laws of distribution of income were independent of the determination of prices. In a letter to McCulloch, dated 16 November 1820, Ricardo wrote: '[a]fter all, the great question of Rent, Wages and Profits must be explained by the proportions in which the whole produce is divided between landlords, capitalists, and labourers, and which are not essentially connected with the doctrine of value' (quoted in Sraffa 1951: xxxiii).

Marx's theory of value

Though Marx was highly appreciative of Ricardo's scientific achievements such as the demolition of Smith's additive theory of value and the highlighting of labor as both the determinant of prices and the main cause of their changes, he was quite critical of what he called Ricardo's theoretical 'architectonics.' He considered Ricardo's search for an invariable measure of value to be a 'secondary' problem, and criticized Ricardo for not paying adequate attention to the more fundamental problem of the divergence of price ratios from labor-value ratios when the rate of profits is equalized across sectors.

As I have mentioned above, a capitalist economy has three major aspects in it. Ricardo highlighted the analysis of the second aspect as the central problem of political economy and merged the third aspect into the second in his analysis. His theoretical contention was that the analysis of the second aspect of capitalism was independent of the analysis of the first aspect. It appears that Marx did not fully understand Ricardo's concern in regard to the theoretical separation between the laws regulating distribution of income and the doctrine of value (unfortunately he did not have Sraffa's Ricardo available to him!). Notwithstanding this, as we shall see below, Marx too was concerned about the theoretical separation between the laws of distribution and price determination. His critique of Ricardo shows that he did not fully appreciate that Ricardo was working with the idea of a physical surplus at the back of his analysis.[4] He maintained that Ricardo's theoretical problems originated from two sources. As he put it:

> Ricardo starts out from the determination of the relative values (or exchangable values) of commodities by 'the *quantity of labour*'.... But *Ricardo does not examine* the form – the peculiar characteristic of labour that creates exchange-value or manifests itself in exchange-values – the *nature* of this labour. Hence he does not grasp the connection of *this labour* with *money* or that it must assume the form of *money* (Marx 1968: 164).
>
> Ricardo's method is as follows: He begins with the determination of the magnitude of the value of the commodity by labour-time and then *examines* whether the other economic relations and categories *contradict* this determination of value or to what extent they modify it.... [Its scientific inadequacy] not only shows itself in the method of presentation (in a formal sense) but leads to erroneous results because it omits some essential links and *directly* seeks to prove the congruity of the economic categories with one another (Marx 1968: 164–65).

Below, I argue that Marx did not succeed on either count. I begin by taking up the issue of the relation of labor to exchange ratios of commodities. There are several arguments scattered in Marx's writings on this issue and they are generally invoked by the anti-Sraffian Marxists as proofs of the difference of Marx's analysis from Ricardo's as well as the correctness of Marx's value analysis.

In the Preface to the first edition of *Capital*, Volume 1, Marx presents the subject matter of his work: '[w]hat I have to examine in this work is the capitalist mode of production, and the relations of production and forms of intercourse that correspond to it' (Marx 1977: 90). And in Volume 1 of *Theories of Surplus Value*, Marx writes, '[t]he [Physiocrats'] method of exposition is necessarily governed by their general view of the nature of value, *which to them is not a definite social mode of existence of human activity (labour)*, but consists of material things – land, nature, and the various modifications of these material things' (Marx 1963: 46, emphases added). If we follow this idea consistently, it appears that for Marx the subject matter of political economy is not an analysis of the laws governing the distribution of income; rather it is an analysis of human activity devoted to reproducing its material life in a capitalist mode of production. Thus, the argument follows, labor becomes the *substance* of analysis. *Value* is the mode of existence of this substance in a commodity-producing society, and exchange-value is the *form* of appearance that value, the substance, takes.

The productive activity, however, has two elements. One is the active laboring activity and the other is the means of production on which the laboring activity is performed. Thus the substance of value, which is labor, must have two elements. One is the direct laboring activity that is involved in transforming the means of production into a commodity and the other is the laboring activity that is needed to replace the means of production used up in the process of production. In other words, Marx's value measure must conceive of the means of production as a gift of labor given to the present by its past. Thus the value of a commodity is made up of the direct laboring activity plus the indirect laboring activity – the laboring activity that would have been needed to replace the means of production provided by past labor.

Value, so defined, by no means gives us any clue to the exchange-values of commodities, however. Since exchange-values are ratios, they can be measured by taking any arbitrary commodity as the unit of measurement. In this case, a relationship between exchange-values and labor-values cannot be established, as they have different units of measurement. However, since exchange-values are ratios between commodities, there is a room for introducing a unit of measurement from outside the universe of commodities. If the condition that the total exchange-values of commodities measured in terms of any arbitrary commodity must be equal to the total labor-values in the system is imposed, then all the exchange-values can be interpreted as the commodity's proportional *command* over the total labor-values of the system. In this case, the unit of measurement of exchange-value would be labor time. However, we still cannot say what would be the exchange-value of a given commodity. If the labor-value and the exchange-value coincide then one could say that the exchange-value is the form that value takes in a commodity-producing society, that is, values represent themselves as mirror images in terms of some other commodity. On the other hand, if the labor-values do not coincide with the exchange-values, which is the general case in the competitive capitalist system, then it is not clear what meaning could be assigned to exchange-value as defined above.

Here the introduction of money goes some way toward solving this problem. Marx argues that money is not an arbitrary commodity chosen as a measuring rod for theoretical purposes. It is a historical outcome of a commodity-producing economy, and thus represents abstract labor pure and simple. In this case, the price of a commodity in terms of the money commodity can be directly converted into its command over the total abstract labor and defined as its value, where the value of one unit of the money commodity is determined by dividing the total direct and indirect labor time by the total prices of all the commodities produced. In this case, if two commodities have the same price, they must by definition have equal values.[5]

Value so defined, however, is analytically vacuous. All this exercise does is to take the prices of commodities given in the market and simply multiply those prices by the ratio of total direct and indirect labor time to total prices in the system. It is similar, or rather parallel, to the exercise of peeling off a price given in terms of Francs and sticking on Euro value instead. No analytical insight about commodity relations or about capitalist economy is gained by this exercise. This is because we still do not have a theory of value, in the sense of what is it that determines the prices in the first place?

Furthermore, defining values in this way contradicts Marx's 'law of value.' Marx, along with Smith and Ricardo, had argued that values or prices of production are centers of gravitation around which market prices fluctuate. The values or the prices of production were, however, susceptible of being determined independently of the market prices. In the above given scenario, values must, however, be derived from the given market prices. There is no scope for the idea of center of gravitation in this formulation.

Another strategy of relating labor to commodity exchange ratios is provided in Marx's famous letter of 11 July 1868, to Ludwig Kugelmann. In this letter Marx writes:

> ...All that palaver about the necessity of proving the concept of value comes from complete ignorance both of the subject dealt with and of scientific method. Every child knows that a nation which ceased to work, I will not say for a year, but even for a few weeks, would perish. Every child knows, too, that the volume of products corresponding to the different needs require different and quantitatively determined amounts of the total labour of society. That this *necessity* of the *distribution* of social labour in definite proportions cannot possibly be done away with by a *particular form* of social production but can only change the *mode* of *its appearance*, is self-evident. Natural laws cannot be abolished at all. What can change in historically different circumstances is only the *form* in which these laws assert themselves. And the form in which this proportional distribution of labour asserts itself, in a social system where the interconnection of social labour manifests itself through the *private exchange* of individual products of labour, is precisely the *exchange value* of these products (Marx and Engels 1982: 196).

This letter has been invoked most frequently in the defense of Marx's 'labor theory of value.' Unfortunately the meaning of the passage quoted above is not 'self-evident.' Leaving aside what every child might or might not know, let us analyze the statement: '[a]nd the form in which this proportional distribution of labour asserts itself, in a social system where the interconnection of social labour manifests itself through the *private exchange* of individual products of labour, is precisely the *exchange value* of these products.' Does this mean that in a commodity-producing economy the exchange ratios between commodities are determined by taking the ratios of total labor employed in various sectors? This interpretation will work only in a situation where there are no means of production in the system. In that case, the ratios of total labor spent in various sectors of the economy will be the same as the embodied labor ratios of commodities. This case, however, is not interesting; not only because it is universally agreed that the so-called simple labor theory of value is valid in such cases, but more importantly, a capitalist mode of production is inconceivable without means of production. Once we introduce means of production in the above given interpretation, we find that the above proposition comes to naught.

For example, let us assume there are only two sectors in the economy producing two commodities x and y, and the system of production is given by:

$$10x + 10y + 10\lambda \rightarrow 30x \qquad (10.1)$$

$$10x + 5y + 10\lambda \rightarrow 30y \qquad (10.2),$$

where λ represents simple homogeneous direct labor measured in terms of hours of labor. By the usual embodied labor measure, it can be easily verified that in this system of production the value of x is equal to 7/8 hours of labor and the value of y is equal to 3/4 hours of labor. Thus 1x should exchange for 7/6y according to the simple labor theory of value.

Now, let us interpret Marx's above statement in the light of our given production system. Here 10 hours of labor in total is distributed to the production of 10 units of net output of x. Thus the value of x should be equal to 1 hour of labor. Similarly, 10 hours of total labor is distributed to producing 15 units of net output of y. Thus the value of y should be equal to 2/3 hours of labor. And the exchange-value of the two commodities turns out to be 1x for 3/2y. When we impute these values of x and y so determined to our means of production in the system, it turns out to be:

$$10\lambda_x + 20/3\lambda_y + 10\lambda \rightarrow 30\lambda_x \qquad (10.1')$$

$$10\lambda_x + 5\lambda_y + 10\lambda \rightarrow 30\lambda_y \qquad (10.2'),$$

where λ_x and λ_y represent values of x and y respectively. Since all the λs are simple homogeneous labor time, they can all be added up and the arrows should be replaced by the = sign. However, as it is quite clear from (10.1′) and (10.2′), in this case the left-hand side of the equation will not be equal to the right-hand side of the equation. Hence defining the labor-values and the exchange-values on the basis of distribution of total labor not only gives a measure different from Marx's own practice but, more importantly, leads to contradiction when means of production are measured consistently on their basis. Thus any attempt to erect a defense of labor-values on this basis must lead to a dead end, and can only create verbal confusion.

The third strategy of relating labor with exchange ratios of commodities can be found in the early pages of *Capital*, Volume 1. Here Marx *deduced* 'abstract' labor as the substance of commodity value from the commodity exchange relation itself. He asserts that a commodity-exchange relation represents an equality relation between the two commodities such as 'one quarter of corn = x cwt. of iron.' Therefore, a common substance must be present in the same amount in both the commodities. He rejects the use-value or the useful aspects of the commodities as the substance represented in the exchange relation on the ground that usefulness is a qualitative aspect of a commodity and is not quantifiable. This leaves him with only one other common aspect between the two commodities, 'that of being products of labour.' But then, labors performed in producing two commodities, say corn and iron, are of completely different nature and cannot be accepted as the common substance of the two commodities. Here Marx makes a distinction between *concrete* and *abstract* labor. He argues that the concrete labors such as specific labor of a smith or a corn-farmer produce the use-values of the specific commodities. Since the use-values of commodities are not reflected in the exchange relations being qualitative in nature, on the same account, the concrete labor must disappear from the commodity-exchange relation. The disappearance of the concrete labor, however, does not mean the disappearance of labor altogether, argues Marx. It only means the disappearance of the particular form that the expenditure of human energy takes. The pure expenditure of human energy with complete disregard to the form in which it is spent is what Marx calls abstract labor.[6] Abstract labor is purely quantitative in character and is measured on the scale of time. It is Marx's contention that in a commodity exchange relation, such as 'one quarter of corn = x cwt. of iron,' what is reflected in the equality relation is the equality of abstract labor. In other words, equal amount of human energy is embodied or congealed in one quarter of corn and x cwt. of iron.

Whether Marx's argument is based on Aristotelian metaphysics or Hegelian dialectics is another question. To a modern reader, Marx's method of argumentation above does not sound compelling. It is well known that Böhm-Bawerk famously protested against Marx's argumentation by asking, but what about 'abstract use-value'?:

> Labor and value in use have a qualitative side and a quantitative side. As the value in use is different qualitatively in a table, house, or yarn, so is labor in carpentry, masonry, or spinning. And just as one can compare different kinds of labor according to their quantity, so one can compare values in

> use of different kinds according to the amount of the value in use. It is quite impossible to understand why the very same evidence should result in the one competitor being excluded and in the other getting the crown and the prize ([1896] 1984: 76–77).

In my opinion, Böhm-Bawerk's objection stems from his misinterpretation of Marx's concept of *use-value*. For Marx, the use-value of a commodity stands for those aspects of the commodity that make it useful to human beings in a given culture. These characteristics are *objective* and belong to the commodity. In this case, it is hard to imagine what could be an 'abstract use-value.' And, even if one could imagine such a thing, it is not clear how it could be quantified and what would be its unit of measure. Böhm-Bawerk appears to interpret use-value in the same vein as *utility*. Utility, however, is a different concept from use-value. When we talk about utility we are dealing with a *subjective* relation between a consumer and the commodity. Marx had posed the problem of exchange in a purely objective context.[7]

Notwithstanding this, it is not clear on what grounds Marx could assert that a commodity exchange relation must be conceived as a relation of equality. The Utilitarians could legitimately argue, as far as the formal structure of the argument is concerned, that a commodity exchange relation is in effect a relation of *inequality*. For a person A parts with a commodity x for another commodity y because the utility she/he derives from the commodity y is greater than the utility she/he derives from the commodity x; and vice versa for person B who parts with y for x.

Furthermore, as Böhm-Bawerk had pointed out, Marx himself later on (in Volume 3 of *Capital*) reveals that in a capitalist society exchange relations between commodities do not, in general, represent equality of abstract labor. And this is not due to some accidental reasons but rather due to reasons intrinsic to capitalist production. If this is so, then the above deduction by Marx is invalid for commodity-exchange relations in a capitalist system.

As a matter of fact, Marx appears to suggest that his above proposition about the equality of value in exchange is made in the context of 'simple commodity production,' that is, in a system of production where the means of productions are privately controlled but have still not taken the form of capital. In other words, the workers still own their means of production.[8] In this context, if we go back to our system of production in (10.1) and (10.2), we can easily verify that the exchange ratio of 1x for 7/6y will restore the original distribution of x and y on the assumption that the returns to labor in both the sectors are equal. And this is nothing but the equality of labor-values in exchange when measured by the usual method of adding direct and indirect labor time. Thus Marx's proposition is not mathematically invalid as long as it is applied only to simple commodity production. We should, however, keep in mind that this result is obtained because we take the original distribution of means of production as 'given' or unproblematic.

Once we begin to ask the question, how the person A or the person B acquired the initial means of production, then some sort of a notion of 'capital' begins to rear its head and threatens to invalidate the result.

This brings us to Marx's second criticism of Ricardo: that Ricardo did not follow the step-by-step method of analysis. Marx's strategy in *Capital* appears to be as follows. First the general formula for commodity exchange as exchange of equal values is established in a simple commodity-producing society. Then the specificity of capitalist commodity production is introduced by introducing labor-power as a specific commodity. Labor-power is defined as worker's capacity to work. It is a sort of stored-up energy in a human body that is released during the process of laboring activity. Given the general formula for commodity exchange, the exchange-value of this specific commodity is established on the basis of the same formula. On the other hand, the use-value of this specific commodity happens to be the laboring activity, which in the sphere of production results in the production of value. Thus, in this specific case, the use-value is quantifiable and comparable to the exchange-value as both of them are measured on the same scale of labor time. As the general analysis of the commodity had revealed that the two aspects of a commodity are completely independent of each other, there is no reason to think that the two aspects of the specific commodity labor-power would coincide. Marx's contention is that the origin of surplus value and the existence of surplus income categories such as profits, interest, and so on, in a capitalist economy can be located in the divergence of the use-value and exchange-value of this specific commodity. The use-value of labor-power happens to be larger than its exchange-value, which explains the existence of surplus value in the system. In other words, if the value of the means of production used up in the production process is given by c and the simple labor time spent by the worker is λ, then the value of the commodity is given by '$c+\lambda$.' Marx's contention is that λ can be further decomposed into '$v+s$,' where v represents the variable capital, that is, the labor time spent in the production of the real wage basket, and s is equal to '$\lambda - v$,' which is positive.

As the last step in the analysis, Marx argues that the appropriation of surplus value, given the competitive nature of capitalism, must follow a rule that insures an equal rate of profits on capital investments in all sectors. If commodities are exchanged in proportion to their values, then the rate of profit appropriated in each sector would be equal to $s_i/(c_i+v_i)$, where i stands for the ith sector. Given labor mobility, it is reasonable to assume that the rate of surplus value s_i/v_i would be uniform for all the sectors. Thus, the rate of profits can be equal across the sectors only if the organic compositions of capital c_i/v_i were equal across the sectors as well. But, in general, there is no reason to assume that the organic compositions of capital will be uniform in the system (it is similar to the differences in turnover time for capitals in Ricardo). Thus the condition of the equalization of the rate of profits implies that commodities must not exchange in proportion to their labor-values.

Marx's solution to this problem was simple. He aggregated the total surplus value produced in the economy (S), and divided it by the aggregate of constant plus variable capital ($C+V$). He declared the ratio $S/(C+V)$ as the uniform rate of profits (r) for the system and calculated the prices of production of any commodity *i* by simply marking up the capital investment calculated in terms of value, that is, c_i+v_i, by its average share in the total surplus value, namely $p_i=(1+r)\ (c_i+v_i)$. His method of calculating the uniform rate of profits insured the equality of total values and total prices of production on the one hand, and total surplus value and total profits on the other. On the basis of these results, Marx could argue that prices of production represent bourgeois accounting in the sense that, as far as the distribution of the values between workers and the capitalists is concerned, it remains unaffected. The deviation of prices of production from values only account for the redistribution of the surplus value among the capitalists, such that their share in total surplus value is in proportion to their capital investments.[9]

Since Bortkiewicz, it is well known that Marx's procedure of deriving the prices of production was faulty. Once it is admitted that prices of production diverge from values, it is no longer legitimate to measure capital investment in terms of values. Thus Marx's uniform rate of profits is not necessarily correct. Marx was aware of this problem but did not explore its significance to the end.[10] This is not the place to get into the long controversy on the *transformation problem*. My positions on this issue can be found in Sinha (1997, 1999, 2000a, 2001b,c). For our present purpose, the question that we need to ask is: what theoretical significance do prices of production have in Marx's scheme? As we have seen, its formation was designed to show that the equalization of the rate of profits does not affect the distribution of value between the two classes. But this result was crucially dependent on the incorrect measure of capital investment. Once this is rectified, we find that, in general, the uniform rate of profits diverges from Marx's rate of profits and his two equality results can no longer be maintained. We are back with Ricardo's problem with full force.[11] The problem with Marx's procedure is that it inadvertently misinterprets the nature of the rate of profits in a capitalist system. The profits on capital investments must accrue to the capitalists on a compound interest basis. Any attempt to reduce the measure of capital to simple labor-values assumes that profits accrue on a simple interest basis. Sraffa (1960) has proven that any attempt to measure capital independently of the rate of profits will end up in contradiction.[12]

Marx, however, needed a theory of value at an earlier stage of analysis as well. The production of surplus value was explained on the basis of exchange of equal values in the case of labor-power. If labor-power is a commodity, then its value must be determined by the labor time needed to reproduce this particular commodity. This formulation implies that real wages in Marx's theory must be interpreted as 'subsistence wages.' Several Marx scholars reject the claim that Marx had a subsistence wage theory (see Mandel 1968;

Rosdolsky 1977; Baumol 1983). They seem to argue that the value of labor-power is equal to the value of whatever real wages happen to be. This proposition severs the essential connection between socially necessary labor time and the measure of value of a commodity; thus weakening the theoretical status of labor-power as a commodity if not completely destroying it. In my opinion, Marx does keep close to the notion of the subsistence wage in his theory of wages. His repeated remarks that labor of higher intensity or longer hours must receive higher wages to replenish greater wear and tear of labor-power do point in that direction (see Marx 1971: 308ff., 1977: 687ff.). On the other hand, he also maintained that there was a secular tendency for real wages to decline. Thus real wages must be higher than subsistence wages to have the possibility of a secular decline. The resolution of this apparent contradiction could be found in his notion of a 'moral and historical' element as part of real wages. It seems Marx believed that in established capitalist countries, the traditional standard of living of the masses that turned into the class of proletariat was higher than the minimum subsistence at that historical juncture.[13] This caused real wages to be higher than the minimum subsistence, which gave a margin for the real wages to decline with the progress of capitalism.[14] Thus, on the side of the exchange-value of labor-power, Marx seems to keep close to the notion of labor-power as a commodity.

On the other hand, when it comes to the notion of use-value of labor-power, we find that he progressively moves away from the notion of a commodity. Elsewhere (Sinha 1996) I have argued in detail, and thus the argument will not be repeated here, that with the concept of labor-power as a commodity Marx had tried to bridge the problematics of the social division of labor on the one hand and the production of a surplus on the other. The problematic of the social division of labor is concerned with *scarcity and human needs* and is essentially rooted in a single individual, such as Robinson Crusoe, whereas the problematic of *surplus production* is rooted in *class relations* and can in no way be reduced to the problematic of a Robinson Crusoe. These two problematics are separate and cannot be submerged under one grand problematic, as Marx attempted in *Capital*. That is why we find that a tension begins to develop in his writing on this crucial concept, where he ends up rejecting the notion of labor-power as a commodity in the *Resultate*[15] and *Theories of Surplus Value*, Volume 3:

> This destroys the last vestiges of the *illusion*, so typical of the relationship when considered superficially, that in the circulation process, in the marketplace, two equally matched *commodity owners* confront each other, and that they, like all other *commodity owners*, are distinguishable only by the material content of their goods, by the specific use-value of the goods they desire to sell each other. Or in other words, the *original* relation remains intact, but survives only as the *illusory* reflection of the *capitalist* relation underlying it (Marx 1981: 1062–63).

> However, the sale and purchase of labour-power, as the constant result of the capitalist process of production, implies that the worker must constantly *buy back* a portion of his own produce in exchange for his living labour. This *dispels* the illusion that we are concerned here merely with *relations with commodity owners* (Marx 1981: 1063).

> there are those who regard this superficial relation, this *essential formality*, this *deceptive appearance* of capitalist relations as its true *essence*. They therefore imagine that they can give a true account of those relations by classifying both workers and capitalists as *commodity owners*. They thereby gloss over the essential nature of the relationship, extinguishing its *differentia specifica* (Marx 1981: 1064).

> Profit (or rather surplus-value) does not result from the exchange of an amount of materialised labour for an equivalent amount of living labour, but from the portion of living labour which is appropriated in this exchange without an equivalent payment in return, that is, from unpaid labour which capital appropriates in this *pseudo-exchange* (Marx 1971: 15, emphasis added).

Once the notion of labor-power as a commodity is rejected, the need for a 'labor theory of value' loses its remaining relevance in Marx's scheme.

Conclusion

In this chapter, we have argued that Ricardo's theory of value was designed to show that the laws governing the distribution of income are independent of the doctrine of value. Ricardo did not succeed in establishing this crucial theoretical proposition. Marx attempted to solve Ricardo's problem and more by developing an overarching theoretical problematic that subsumed the problems of social division of labor and exchange on the one hand and income distribution on the other. Our discussion above has led us to the conclusion that Marx did not succeed in this endeavor. His overarching problematic breaks down as he finds himself unable to maintain consistently the concept of labor-power as a commodity in a capitalist system. His several strategies of drawing a direct relation between social division of labor and commodity exchange on the one hand and labor-values on the other only led to dead ends and blind alleys! The failure of a successful transformation of values into prices of production further reveals that he did not succeed in establishing Ricardo's proposition that the division of values between workers and capitalists is independent of prices of production. After Sraffa's (1960) contribution it has become evident, at least to those who care to see it, that although the central Ricardian and Marxian proposition about distribution being independent of prices is robust, any search for an ultimate *cause* of value is futile. Prices are simply implicated in a given structure of production and distribution and *nothing is hidden behind them.*[16]

This is not to say that Marx's analysis of capitalism is irrelevant. On the contrary, his analyses of the labor process and technical change are quite relevant for understanding the dynamics of modern capitalism. Unfortunately a disproportionately large part of scholarship on Marx has for a long time been bogged down by the controversy over the 'labor theory of value.' Sraffa (1960) should be read as an attempt to liberate Marxist scholarship from this dead end path so that it could concentrate on more fruitful endeavors.

Notes

I wish to thank Geoff Harcourt, John King and Paul Zarembka for comments on the earlier draft of this chapter. The usual caveat applies.

1. Stigler (1965) has created confusion in the literature by misinterpreting Ricardo's position as a 93 percent labor theory of value. What he suggests is that according to Ricardo the price ratios obtained by simple labor theory of value will not be more than 6–7 percent off the mark. But this was not Ricardo's argument. His argument was that a change in wages would not explain any more than 6–7 percent of changes in prices (36ff.).
2. Ricardo could nevertheless argue that the relationship between wages and profits is at least an inverse one. Sraffa (1960) has shown that Ricardo was right in the case of singly produced commodities. However, in the case of joint production even this claim cannot be established without the use of Sraffa's Standard commodity as the measuring rod.
3. As I have suggested above, Ricardo was also interested in finding the laws that regulate income distribution in the dynamic context. Thus he was also interested in finding an invariable measure of value that would remain invariant to changes in methods of production, given diminishing returns in agriculture. From Sraffa (1960) we have learnt that Ricardo's first problem of the invariable measure of value in the context of changes in income distribution without any change in the methods of production has a logical solution (i.e. Sraffa's standard commodity). His second problem has no logical solution. Some Ricardo scholars such as Ong (1983), Caravale and Tosato (1980), and to some extent Blaug (1987b, 1999) have challenged Sraffa's reading of Ricardo by highlighting his second problem and denying any concern for the first. This, however, does not stand up to the evidence (see Sinha 2000b).
4. In *Theories of Surplus Value*, Part II, Marx criticizes Ricardo for '[smuggling] in the proposition of a general rate of profit' and argues that, without a notion of absolute value, 'the average profit is the average of nothing, pure fancy' (190).
5. The so-called 'New Solution' to the transformation problem defines the value of money as the ratio of total direct labor-time to the total prices of the net output. This does not make any difference to our argument above. For my critique of the 'New Solution' see Sinha (1997).
6. Marx defines abstract labor as 'productive expenditure of human brains, muscles, nerves, hands, etc.' (1977: 134). This definition of abstract labor differs from the earlier one we have encountered as definable only at the aggregate level as a pool of total labor in the system. Faccarello (1998) has discovered four different definitions of

abstract labor in Marx's writings. He argues that these definitions end up in contradictions. In my opinion, only the above definition of abstract labor is throughout consistent with Marx's theory.

7. Faccarello (1998) points out that Hegel in his *Philosophy of Rights* had also argued that exchange must represent equality. But he had resolved it in favor of *abstract need*. Marx's complete silence on the Hegelian notion of abstract need in this context suggests that he did make a conceptual distinction between subjective notions such as needs or utility on the one hand and use-value on the other.
8. In *Capital*, Volume 1, the categories of wage labor and capital are first introduced in Chapter 6. There Marx writes: 'The appearance of products as commodities requires a level of development of the division of labour within society such that the separation of use-value from exchange-value, a separation which first begins with barter, has already been completed. But such a degree of development is common to many economic formations of society, with the most diverse historical characteristics' (273). And in *Theories of Surplus Value*, Volume 2, we read: '[t]hus we can see that in Chapter 6 [i.e. Ricardo's *Principles*] not only are *commodities* assumed to exist – *and when considering value as such, nothing further is required...*' (168, second italics added).
9. 'The various different capitals here are in the position of shareholders in a joint stock company, in which the dividends are evenly distributed for each 100 units, and hence are distinguished, as far as the individual capitalists are concerned, only according to the size of the capital that each of them has put into the common enterprise, according to the number of his shares' (Marx 1991: 258).
10. 'As the price of production of a commodity can diverge from its value, so the cost price of a commodity, in which the price of production of other commodities is involved, can also stand above or below the portion of its total value that is formed by the value of the means of production going into it. It is necessary to bear in mind this modified significance of the cost price, and therefore to bear in mind too that if the cost price of a commodity is equated with the value of the means of production used up in producing it, it is always possible to go wrong' (Marx 1991: 265).
11. Garegnani (1991) has argued that in the absence of Sraffa-type simultaneous equation method Marx had no better way of arriving at the uniform rate of profits than the procedure he followed. His recommendation is that now we should accept Sraffa's procedure and give up Marx's unsatisfactory procedure of determining the uniform rate of profits and the prices of production.
12. Recently, Laibman (2002) has argued that one need not derive prices of production from values but rather derive values from Sraffa's prices of production. His prescription amounts to taking Sraffa's prices in money terms and multiplying it with the ratio of total direct labor-time to money prices of the net output, which he calls 'implicit value content of the money unit.' This is similar to the 'New Solution' except that the 'New Solution' takes national income accounting data for the total prices of the net output rather than Sraffa's theoretical prices. Thus my criticism to the 'New Solution' (see Sinha 1997) applies to Laibman as well. Furthermore, it is not clear what is the purpose of such a derivation, Laibman's rhetoric about 'the general wage share' notwithstanding. One can understand class struggle for a higher standard of living or better working conditions and lower working hours, and so on, but not a 'general wage share,' which can only be an ex post result of the whole economic process (I am indebted to Ian Steedman for this idea.). Prior to Laibman, Wolff, Callari and Roberts (1984) had also attempted

to derive values from Sraffian prices of production. In their formulation value is determined by the constant capital measured in terms of prices of production plus the direct labor-time needed to produce the commodity. Though it is not clear how prices are converted to labor-time units in the case of constant capital, it is easy to show that their formulation nevertheless ends up in contradiction. Since constant capital is nothing but commodities, we have two contradictory determinations of commodity value in one scheme. When commodity value is measured in its function as constant capital, it is equated with its price of production, and when it is measured as an output, it is equated with the prices of production of its constant capital plus direct labor-time. For example, let us assume that 1/2 ton of corn and L hours of labor are used to produce 1 ton of corn. Now by the usual 'embodied' value measure, the value of 1 ton of corn would come out to be 2L hours of labor. Let us further suppose that price of production of corn happens to be yL hours of labor, where yL is *not* equal to 2L, since, in general, prices of production deviate from 'embodied' values. Now, according to Wolff *et al.*'s method of calculating value, the value of 1 ton of corn should be equal to $(yL/2+L)$ or $L/2(y+2)$ hours of labor. For consistency $L/2(y+2)$ must be equal to yL, since $L/2(y+2)$ is nothing but value of 1 ton of corn measured by Wolff *et al.*'s method and yL is the value of 1 ton of corn when measured as constant capital. This implies that $y+2=2y$ or $y=2$. Therefore, $yL=2L$, contradicting Marx's basic proposition that prices of production in general deviate from values.
13. In the case of new colonies such as America and Australia, Marx believed that the conditions for the historical and moral element were still under preparation.
14. Marx's theory of wages is a highly controversial issue. Apart from Baumol, Mandel and Rosdolsky mentioned above, also see Cottrell and Darity Jr (1988), Green (1991a, 1991b), Hollander (1984, 1986), Lebowitz (1992), Ramirez (1986), Rowthorn (1980), and Sinha (1998, 2001a).
15. The *Resultate* seems to have been written between June 1863 and December 1866. It was originally intended to be Part Seven of Volume 1 of *Capital* but for unknown reasons did not find a place in the published version. It was first published simultaneously in Russian and German in 1933, and for the first time in English as appendix to Volume 1 of *Capital* by Vintage Books in 1977. See Mandel's 'Introduction' to the appendix for detail.
16. See Sinha (2002) for a detailed exposition of the nature of Sraffa's contribution.

11
What Do We Learn from Value Theory?

Thomas T. Sekine

Value theory, as I understand it in this chapter, is that part of Marxian economic theory which explains how the *micro* activities of individual capitals find themselves integrated into a systematic whole, that of a general equilibrium in the capitalist economy. It is only in this state, I do wish to emphasize that the social relations that constitute capitalism emerge unambiguously to full view.

Value theory, however, is not closed by itself, as it can only determine the values of commodities *given (i.e. presupposing) the value of labor-power*. For the determination of this latter variable, we must fall back on another theory that explains the *macro* dynamics of the aggregate-social capital, that is, on what may be called the theory of cyclical accumulation.[1] Marxian economic theory too, like others, consists of the micro and the macro component. This derives from the nature of capitalism itself as the institution that organizes the *real economic life* of society by the *commodity-economic principle* of the market. Since capitalism thus possesses and displays both its micro and macro features, economic theory must perforce reflect this fact. The difference between the bourgeois and the Marxian approach lies only in that the latter can easily account for the relationship between the two components of economic theory, which the former entirely fails to do.

I

In value theory, we simply posit that the underlying technology is productive enough to yield a surplus, and that the labor that produces the surplus gets enough wage-goods to survive on. But capitalism does not directly tell us what assortment of wage-goods would insure an adequate livelihood for the existing class of productive workers. We must find that out in the actual process of capital accumulation, which is bound to be cyclical. It is in the depth of depression, when competition among capitals proves to be the harshest, that they tend to adopt new technology by trial and error. Once this is done, an *extensive* capital accumulation can begin in the 'widening' phase of prosperity. But not all industries are expected to grow at the same pace from the beginning, at which point average profits cannot as yet be earned by all capitals. Only when the sub-phase of recovery leads into what Marx named the *period of average activity* do we begin to observe an approximation to the state of balanced growth, in which average profits tend to be earned at the margin of all industries. It is also in this sub-phase that we observe a situation in which the demand for labor-power more or less corresponds with its supply, so that something like an equilibrium wage-rate may be said to prevail under the technology that capital has adopted for the present process of accumulation. A general equilibrium is an idealization of the capitalist market in this sub-phase; or, to put it otherwise, the existence of such a sub-phase in the course of the actual accumulation of capital assures us the *ontological foundation* of a general equilibrium of the capitalist economy. This is so, even though, in the course of accumulation, the period of average activity soon turns into the following sub-phase of precipitancy (or overheating), which foreshadows a periodic crisis (Figure 11.1).

This crucially important connection is forgotten in many Marxist treatments of value theory, which conceive the reproduction of labor-power to be a mere technological datum as in von Neumann's model, that is, to be analogous to the reproduction of ordinary products (animate and inanimate).[2] With such treatments, the micro value theory is irrevocably severed from the macro accumulation theory, and the relationship between the two components of economic theory becomes as blurred and arbitrary as in bourgeois economics. Actually, far too many Marxists have been insensitive to the methodological distinctiveness of Marx's approach, as they apply mathematical skills (just

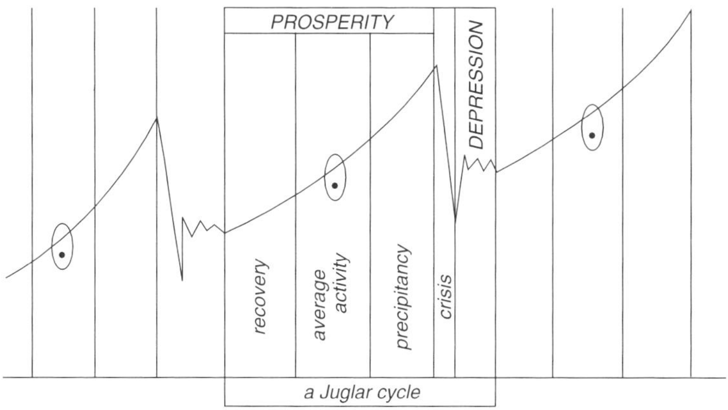

Figure 11.1

as uncritically as bourgeois economists do) to the formulation of their 'social' theories. The result is an incongruous union of the ideological allegiance to Marxism on the one hand and the unconscionable flourish of bourgeois economics on the other. This error is avoided most unambiguously in Uno's treatment of Marxian economic theory.

To Uno, Marxian economic theory is nothing other than the *dialectic of capital*[3] or, in other words, a *definition of capitalism by capital itself*. With its micro and macro theories, based on the *law of value* and the *law of (relative surplus) population* respectively, the dialectic of capital lays bare the 'software' or the inner program, as it were, of capitalism. For 'defining capitalism' boils down to showing how it is 'programmed' to operate. Only in the light of such a referent, which is 'objective' in the sense of not depending on our 'subjective' judgment, may we evaluate how capitalist or non-capitalist our present economic regime is. This evaluation, in its turn, does involve judgment or subjective interpretation on our part of what we observe and experience. That must be admitted, for, in such exercises, we cannot by the nature of things do away with subjective elements in our interpretation.[4]

It is on that basis then that I wish to claim here that, in the light of the unmistakable 'withering away' of value substance in recent times, contemporary economy has definitely entered the final phase of the process of ex-capitalist transition. The next three sections will be devoted to a review of the methodological peculiarities of the Unoist approach. They will be followed by three more sections aimed at clarifying the grounds for my evaluation of the contemporary trends. I will then conclude with a recapitulation of my basic understanding of the concept of value.

II

The Unoist approach is founded on a rather peculiar scientific method which is not shared by others, be they Marxist or bourgeois, in social science of which economics constitutes the core. It unambiguously refuses to import into its field of investigation the empiricist, positivist and instrumentalist methods, commonly adopted by the natural scientists, and often eagerly imitated by bourgeois economists. For instance, it does not construct arbitrary economic *models* purporting to represent 'the real world,' from the analysis of which one may draw wishful conclusions, such as a strategy to liberate the working classes. Even though in ideological stance, Marxists are diametrically opposed to the bourgeois economists, they are often in perfect agreement with each other as far as their *scientific method* is concerned.

To them 'theory,' in one way or another, abstracts from reality certain of its essential features into a 'model' or an 'ideal type,' so as to enable us to conceptualize it in a duly simplified form. Thus, it is like a map which helps to guide us in the real geographical space. Though economic reality is chaotic and confusing to the untrained eye, the theorist is supposed to be able to put an order to the apparent jumble of misleading bits and pieces, and to explain their internal connections in a persuasive fashion. They can detect, as the mechanic does, where the machine fails to function and can advise how to remove the trouble; they can diagnose, as the doctor does, what illness the patient suffers from and suggests appropriate treatments for its cure. In other words, a theory is like special eyeglasses available only to the specialist, enabling him to see what lay persons cannot see. This kind of myth is often uncritically accepted by the practicing scientist, who in most cases, does not stop to think further of the process in which their models or eyeglasses were acquired by their predecessors. That, however, should not cause any problem so long as these instruments do 'work.' They have to rethink only when they prove to be inadequate for the purpose.

To study a natural phenomenon, one begins with a hypothesis that an event x occurs when conditions $a, b, c, \ldots$ are fulfilled: $(a, b, c, \ldots) \rightarrow x$. This type of 'predictive' proposition must be empirically tested before it is accepted, or not accepted, as valid. Operational rules must, therefore, be agreed upon in advance as to what sort of tests the proposition must undergo in order to prove its validity. Normally, a proposition is accepted unless counter-evidence is produced by the test. A scientific theory is made up of propositions which have so far withstood counter evidence; that is to say, it consists of so-far-so-good hypotheses. Such a procedure is perfectly valid and legitimate with regard to our (necessarily) partial knowledge of nature.[5] We thus learn certain regularities (or repetitiveness) in what nature does, which enables us, to some extent, to predict its future course of actions. It is, moreover, for that reason that our knowledge of nature lends itself to technical applications. But it is clear, at the same time, that with this kind of knowledge we cannot 'revolutionize' nature from time to time to make it suit our radically renewed perspective. All we can do is to 'conform' to the natural forces and to 'piggyback' on them in order to protect ourselves from harm. This comes from the fact that we are not ourselves the creator of nature, and that it is given to us irrevocably from the outside.

In contrast, society is that which we ourselves make up: we are ourselves its creator. That is to say, we are (or ought to be) fully privy to its internal working, to its structural program. For no society is irrevocably given to us from the outside as 'natural' order to conform to; no society, in other words, retains a *thing-in-itself* that would for ever remain unknowable to us. It would be hypocritical to claim that it is something beyond us, whose regularities must be detected only from the outside by repeated observation and experiment. Why do we need to hypothesize its laws which deep down we already know very well, and then pretend to test them empirically? With that sort of pretense we would be inviting an unsound 'conformism' to the established order, which would make us renounce responsibility to improve upon the working of our society. Instead of conjuring up such a fantasy, we should ask ourselves a much simpler and more straightforward question: what we have been, are, and will be, doing here in the framework of this society. Yet our attention is deliberately diverted from this obvious truth. Why? The reason is that it suits the ruling classes of any society to make believe that the existing social order is either an extension of the natural order or ordained by divine wisdom. The neo-liberal idolatry of the market and the old doctrine of the divine right of kings are like the ideology of the ruling classes, amounting in effect to a smokescreen put up to protect their private interests from objective investigations of social science.

This is what Uno meant, when he demanded a sharp separation of science from ideology,[6] even though, unfortunately, many misunderstood his word 'science' to mean 'objective' knowledge as exemplified by natural science. From what has been said, however, it should be clear, on the contrary, that *a natural-scientific approach to the study of capitalism, such as is promoted by bourgeois economics, amounts to a 'sell-out' to the capitalist ideology*. The acceptance of such an ideology disables any objective critique of capitalism from being accomplished, no matter how strident the accompanying war cries may be against some of capitalism's obvious failures. Of all the lessons that one can learn from Marx, nothing is more valuable *and powerful* than the *dialectical method* which he struggled to apply, if only with partial success, to his economic theory in *Capital*.

III

We may interpret Marx's 'law of motion of modern society' in the sense of *that which makes capitalism what it is*, that is, capitalism's inner program or its 'software.' Since we cannot continue forever to be duped by the capitalist ideology and to believe capitalism to be a harmonious social order as immutable as nature itself, we must seek to 'lay bare' the inner logic that objectively synthesizes capitalism. Clearly, we cannot accomplish this specific task with a facile method borrowed from the natural sciences; we must instead follow Marx's lead and construct a dialectical (i.e. a non-naturalistic)[7] theory of capitalism. For, failing it, we would never really know what to abolish or suspend in order to surmount capitalism and to make a decisive step forward to humanity's liberation.[8] Among generations of Marxists who employed themselves in various 'creative' exegeses of *Capital*, no one, it seems to me, has been more alert to this crucial task than Uno.

Uno's dialectic of capital is not a model (or an ideal type) of capitalism, which we may construct arbitrarily by observing it from the outside. It is, as I mentioned already, a definition of capitalism *by capital itself*. This means that capital is here the dialectical subject which *recounts its own story*. As in Hegel's absolute, the dialectical subject must be 'infinite,' in the sense of transcending human finiteness. Elsewhere,[9] I explain the procedure whereby one may obtain capital by rendering our 'economic motive' (our propensity to maximize gains and minimize losses) infinite, in much the same way as Feuerbach once obtained the *Absolute* by rendering human virtues infinite. Once this is done, we only need provide capital with a *pure space* within which it can complete its solipsistic monologue, just as, in Hegel's Logic, the absolute exposes himself 'in the realm of pure thought' which existed 'before the creation of nature and a finite spirit.'[10]

But what to make of the 'pure space' in question is where the difficulty lies. It has to represent something of a concrete use-value space in which the real economic life of human society occurs. Yet, it also has to be the space which is wholly 'subsumable' under the logic of capital. Real capitalism is always *an uncertain union of the pure logic of capital and a use-value space*, such that, if the former entirely fails to subsume the latter, it cannot exist. On the other hand, if the use-value space were literally completely 'subsumable,' there would exist no *real* capitalism. Thus, the pure space that we must presuppose as the theater in which capital is made to complete its long solipsistic monologue must be an *idealized* use-value space which does not exist in reality, a 'frictionless' space of the mathematical economist in which all use-values are house-broken into a mere set (x_1, x_2, x_3, . . . , x_n) of just so many different products. Only in such a space, a pale shadow of the real use-value space, would capital reveal its full agenda.

Uno has often been criticized for his 'pure' theory of capitalism by the Marxists who erroneously take any pure theory as belonging to the neo-classical approach. They fail to distinguish between that which is pure in the Hegelian sense and that which is so in the Walrasian sense. They, in other words, confuse Hegelian-pure theory (dialectic) with Walrasian-pure theory (axiomatic). From what has been said above, however, it should be patent that a Hegelian-pure theory simply means the one which provides the dialectical subject with a full chance to recount its own story, and has nothing to do with a Walrasian-pure theory, which simply insures that it consists of mutually tautological propositions.[11] In economics, the former gives capital a fair chance to speak out its case, while the latter simply shuts off reality from the models. The enemies of capital who are ideologically determined to hang it even before hearing its story out have so little patience as even to distinguish between the two entirely different methods. With such a muddle, how could they ever hope to grasp the objective logic that synthesizes capitalism? The fact that the space within which the dialectic of capital is made to unfold is 'pure,' and not 'real,' does not in any way prevent it from constituting the referent of 'materialist' investigations. It only confirms the fact that the dialectic of capital is 'software' (inner logic) without a hard body. By being so, it makes all the more clear (1) that not all the use-value spaces are amenable to management by the logic of capital, and (2) that even those that are so amenable contain 'externalities' that must be 'internalized' by the economic policies of the bourgeois state.

IV

The first point amounts to a reconfirmation, from the point of view of economics, of the fundamental thesis of historical materialism that capitalism is a transient institution. If the use-value space is not yet suitable for overall commodification,[12] capitalism does not come into being; if the use-value space no longer fits overall commodification, capitalism simply withers away with or without a proletarian revolution. This implies that there is a particular set of use-value spaces that can be run capitalistically, the one that can embody the dialectic of capital, the 'software' as it were of capitalism. In Figure 11.2, all conceivable use-value spaces are represented by coordinates of the Cartesian system, in which the zero corresponds to the infinitely commodifiable 'pure space,' and in which real use-value spaces are placed the closer to the origin the more capitalistically commodifiable they are. A circle is inserted with its center falling on the origin to show that all use-value spaces inside it are the capitalistically operable ones. In this fashion, we can imagine a path of evolution of human society as entering the circle at one point and exiting from it at another, while inside the circle the path comes at one stage ever closer to the zero yet never actually traverses it.

The second point bears on the path of evolution of society. Once inside the circle, a capitalist society becomes possible, but this does not mean that its real use-value space is entirely subsumable under the logic of capital. On the contrary, there always remain elements which would resist the embracement of capital, and which we call 'externalities.' This is where we need to invoke the *bourgeois state*, whose role it is to insure the 'internalization'

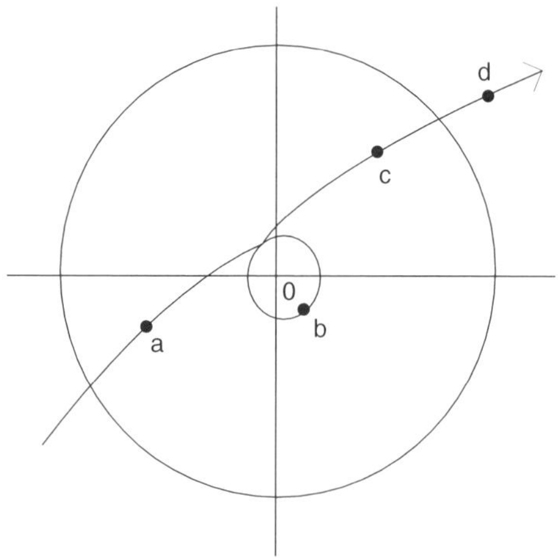

Figure 11.2

of such externalities by means of its economic policies. Uno identified three types of economic policies of the bourgeois state, depending on the nature of the use-value space: the mercantilist, the liberal and the imperialist.

It was moreover on this basis that Uno introduced his stages-theory of capitalist development, in such a way that each of the three stages is characterized by a typical use-value space. The latter is a space in which all use-values are like the *wool* produced by the domestic industry of the mercantilist period, like the *cotton* produced by small capitalist factories in atomistic competition, as in the British cotton industry of the mid-nineteenth century, or like the *steel* produced by the organized German monopolies of the imperialist era, whose heavy investment of fixed capital was financed by the system of joint-stock companies. A typical use-value space is thus an idealized type but one that is based on human history actually lived through.[13] This is as far as we can go in theorizing a use-value space without reducing it to its shadow. It is for that reason that the stages-theory of capitalist development situates itself 'mid-range' between the ethereal-pure theory, in which use-values are reduced to mere labels, *and* the concrete-empirical history, in which millions of naked use-values are just rampant and out of control. That is, between the theorist's pure space and the historian's concrete-empirical space there remains a large gap that must be filled. By inventing the stages-theory and giving it the mediating role between the two antipathetic spaces, Uno has skillfully solved the problem, though with subtlety well beyond the ken of the die-hard adherents of the logical-historical method.

This mediation between theory and reality holds good for capitalist societies, that is, for societies whose use-value space is capitalistically commodifiable and is therefore situated close enough to the zero of the above-mentioned coordinate system. In various places, however, I have claimed that the present world economy is in the *process of ex-capitalist transition* and can no longer be viewed as embodying a stage of development of capitalism proper.[14] This thought originated in Uno who regarded the world economy after World War I as having entered a transitional phase out of capitalism into socialism. To him, the War of 1914–18 had put an end to the world-historic stage of imperialism, and subsequently no recognizable new stage of development of capitalism evolved. He certainly did not subscribe to the popular conception of state-monopoly capitalism. But since he elaborated little on this matter, it devolves on us to work out our own perspectives on the 'contemporary economy.' Elsewhere,[15] I stated that the process of ex-capitalist transition could itself be periodized into the interwar, the Fordist and the post-Fordist periods. While little dissension seems to exist in this tripartite division of the post-World War I history, my thesis of ex-capitalist transition has so far been universally and categorically rejected even by many Unoists. The rest of this chapter will, therefore, be devoted to its vindication.

V

For capitalism proper to exist, both the law of value and the law of population should enforce themselves fully. If in our *judgment* they do not, yet we continued to claim that capitalism proper survives, then we would disqualify ourselves as Unoists by contradicting the dialectic of capital, the definition of capitalism by capital itself. Now, the law of value is not just a rule stipulating the terms of exchange of commodities; it insures that all commodities tend to be produced in appropriate (socially necessary) quantities, that is, that they tend to be neither overproduced nor underproduced relative to the existing social demand. In other words, the law of value sees to it that a capitalist economy automatically tends toward a state of general equilibrium under which society's productive resources will be optimally allocated (i.e. allocated in the least wasteful fashion). By productive resources of society, we mean elements, or factors, of production that cost the society (not the individual capitalist). However, since the natural means of production, generically represented by land, do not, apart from their routine maintenance, cost anything at all to society as a whole, the productive resources for which society pays real cost consist of labor-power (an original element of production) and produced means of production (intermediate products) only. Since, moreover, the intermediate goods are themselves produced by labor-power and other intermediate goods, it can be concluded that all goods are ultimately produced by productive labor alone, the exertion or use-value of labor-power. This comes to the same thing as to say that, given the state of arts, the capitalist economy tends to allocate productive labor of society optimally (i.e. in the least wasteful fashion) to all branches of production. So allocated productive labor is called 'socially necessary labor' and constitutes the *substance of commodity values*. The labor theory of value thus involves only very straightforward economics which is understandable to anyone, Marxist or bourgeois.

Yet many Marxists seem to believe that accepting such plain economics would constitute an irrevocable concession to their ideological enemies, and would expose themselves to a mortal onslaught of the neo-classical school. In order not to compromise their position, they feel compelled to resort, in various ways, to what Myrdal once termed 'the attractive Anglo-Saxon kind of unnecessary originality'[16] and invent highly creative (mis)interpretations of Marx's economics, of which the most remarkable and recent example is the so-called 'non-equilibrium value theory.'[17] Whatever its merit may be, there is no such thing as non-equilibrium value, which, to me, is a pure oxymoron. Yet, if its claim to legitimacy derives from the initial observation that the contemporary economy no longer possesses the much touted 'automatic tendency' toward a general equilibrium and optimal allocation of resources, that observation *per se* can be fully defended. Indeed, the absence of such a tendency is a telltale sign of the non-working of the law of value and hence of the process of ex-capitalist transition. It is precisely for that reason that the economic policies of the bourgeois state did prove inadequate for the stabilization of national economies after World War I, which in due course led to the demise of the bourgeois state.

The social-democratic *welfare state* which replaced it has significantly expanded the public sector economy, while resorting to macro-policies whose role has no longer been confined to mere 'internalization of the externalities.' The US Employment Act of 1946 symbolized the establishment of the welfare state which was emerging during the interwar period. The commitment to full employment and price stability, which meant the management of the aggregate demand and the currency, could not be expected from a bourgeois state. Not only did it mean that the monetary role of gold was radically restricted if not abolished, but also that the labor market was no longer to be left to its self-regulation. Thus, money and labor, two of Polanyi's fictitious commodities, have since been de-commodified to mitigate the severity of industrial crises that periodically devastated nineteenth-century capitalism. As for the third fictitious commodity, land, the declining importance of the agricultural sector coupled with the series of farm and food related programs have radically changed its character.[18] All these circumstances point to the fact that the system of self-regulating markets on which capitalism proper stood has been seriously undermined, as the social-democratic welfare state supplanted the bourgeois state.

But by far the most important of all these trends has been the increasing de-commodification of labor-power since the depression of the 1930s. This, it seems to me, has been demonstrated most cogently by the vanishing of the decennial Juglar cycles, which so strikingly characterized the cyclical accumulation of capital in the nineteenth century. For, these cycles do reflect the law of relative surplus population peculiar to capitalism, the working of which determines the value of labor-power. Indeed, the only 'business cycles' that the pure theory of capitalism considers as reflections of the cyclical accumulation of capital are of this type.

VI

Only after World War II was it widely recognized that the typical shape of business cycles had changed. Not only did cycles become shorter and milder, but they were also largely superposed on a growth trend free from punctuation by cataclysmic crises. This was no doubt due in part to the application of macroeconomic policies by the state. But it also meant that the cyclical accumulation of capital which, by alternating the processes of 'widening' and 'deepening,' rhythmically regulated the supply of labor-power by means of technical innovation was no longer at work. In other words, the *market principle of capital* did not remain solely in charge of the adoption of new industrial technology, but that there also intervened the *planning principle of the state*. That further meant that the state, too, took part in the determination of the value of labor-power. Indeed, in one way or another, the development of industrial technology has become a policy issue along with the pursuit of industrial peace in all social-democratic welfare states. Even the United States, to which 'industrial policy' was an ideological anathema, heavily subsidized progress in military technology during the Fordist period, the result of which was subsequently passed on to US civilian industries to reaffirm their international competitiveness. After the Trade Act of 1988, it thus became even more unambiguous that labor policy and technology policy are the two sides of the same coin. With the value of labor-power thus partly becoming an 'administered price,' the law of value had let slip its anchorage.[19]

Although at its inception, capitalism required a far-reaching transformation of agriculture, it soon developed a capacity to regulate its own supply of labor-power by way of creating relative surplus population, at which point industrial capital could leave agriculture behind without necessarily modernizing it. This tendency appeared most strikingly in Germany, which could import industrial capitalism in its fully developed form in the nineteenth century. There the Junker farmers were at first free traders, but later demanded protection from cheap agricultural imports which made their lives difficult. But the protection of home agriculture would raise the cost of manufactured products and would contravene the interests of finance capital, which then faced an antinomy between the economic rationality of resorting to cheap agricultural imports and the social and political need to placate fellow farmers. This then was the *Agrarfrage* which pestered Imperial Germany. Overall, however, the traditional, international division of labor between the industrial and the agricultural nations held good during the era of imperialism. It was after World War I that this uncertain compromise became untenable, as nationalistic politics dictated agricultural protection in industrialized countries. Due, moreover, to the vigorous expansion of cash-crop farming that had occurred during the European War, the world economy was saddled with chronic overproduction of agricultural produce, which in turn led to debt crises and eventually to the world depression of the 1930s. As nations struggled to survive, each trying to redress its internal, at the sacrifice of external, equilibrium, the gold standard had to be abandoned, and official management of both the currency and the macroeconomy could no longer be avoided. These were indeed the tasks that exceeded by far the confines of a bourgeois state.

But the full establishment of the welfare state had to wait for the age of Fordism and Consumerism, which, because of the timely advent of petroleum-based technology, could nicely solve the old agricultural problem. It is true that a whole series of farm support programs were still needed, but the rapid transfer of population from the agricultural to the industrial sector, made possible by the outburst of Fordist mass production fueled as it was by petro-technology and abetted by the high consumption of the urban masses, was surely much more effective. The unprecedented economic prosperity of 'the thirty glorious years' could then be realized, in which the old Juglar cycles left no trace. But that was only to be expected, since the decennial cycles were the manifestation of the actual process of accumulation, in which capital by itself controlled both the innovation of industry and the value of labor-power. The change in the modality of business cycles indicated nothing but the fact that the accumulation of wealth was no longer the exclusive business of capital, or, to put it another way, the fact that the use-value space exceeded the full control of capital.

In the absence of the Juglar cycles, it is impossible to relate each business upswing with a particular set of techniques which capital has chosen for its accumulation. Neither can a 'period of average activity' be identified, which backs up ontologically the tendency of the capitalist economy to move toward a general equilibrium, nor can the 'value of labor-power' be determined unambiguously. Such circumstances should have a corrosive effect on the working of the law of value which, through the price mechanism of the market, is supposed to achieve an optimal allocation of resources available to society to all branches of production.[20] For a long time, economics has taught the virtue of competitive pricing which would realize Pareto optimality, miraculously harmonizing the conflicting interests of all parties. But this providential message sounds distinctly less convincing in the age of post-Fordism, which constitutes the last phase of ex-capitalist transition. The reason, it seems to me, is twofold: (1) the pricing of commodities has become *strategic* instead of remaining objective (in the sense of responding to market parameters), as industries characterized by *increasing returns* have become important, and (2) the economy has become more *service-oriented* and less dependent on the production of material wealth.

VII

The incompatibility of increasing returns and general equilibrium had been known for some time,[21] but that hardly bothered bourgeois economics for so long as it could treat increasing returns as exceptional cases. It was only in the 1980s, when the international competitiveness of the United States in traditional industries was put into grave doubt, that a new thought suddenly arose to the effect that the Americans should strive to seek their 'dynamic' comparative advantage in the field of high-technology industries, which were more likely to be subject to increasing returns to scale. This more or less capped the stealthy change which had been going on for some time in microeconomic theories, shifting their analytical tools from calculus to game-theory. Correspondingly, general equilibrium models of the Walras–Lagrange type were displaced by partial equilibrium ones of the Cournot–Nash type, while Pareto-optimality was abandoned in favor of Prisoners' Dilemma. The latter no longer implied an optimal allocation of resources blessed by angels, but the least desirable misallocation of resources consequent upon anti-social dis-co-operation of the devils. The stress was most acutely felt in international economics in which the old-fashioned liberals still sought unilateral free trade, while the younger-generation turks of 'fair trade' insisted on 'strategic trade policies' which would benefit the United States at the expense of their foreign rivals.[22]

Even prior to this paradigmatic re-orientation in economics, many traditional industries were already engaged in oligopolistic competition in which leading firms operated *strategically* not only in the pricing of their products but also in colluding with the 'technostructure of the new industrial state.'[23] As closer ties were built between large oligopolistic firms and governments, the price mechanism of the market no longer functioned as it was supposed to in mediating an optimal allocation of resources, but embodied more and more government-regulatory and firm-strategic elements. Yet economics as a profession needed to stick to its time-old ideology of exalting the virtue of the free enterprise system, and thus adapted slowly to the newly emerging reality. The increasing vitiation of the free-market price mechanism, not only as it pertained to such key variables as wages, interests, public utility and farm prices, and so on, but also as it affected the prices of key industrial commodities, was the trend at work since the Great Depression of the 1930s. This would mean that the basic presuppositions of value theory as understood in the Marxian context gradually ceased to apply from then on, until it became a complete shambles in the post-Fordist economy of today.

What is even more striking and decisive is the tendency for developed economies to become increasingly more *service-oriented*, in the last phase of the process of ex-capitalist transition, both in terms of the share in GDP and in terms of the proportion of employment. This well documented tendency is surely in reflection of the fact that society has become more knowledge-intensive and less muscle-intensive, and that the provision of software (especially information) has become more important than the production of hardware (material wealth). Just as capitalism proper once tended to substitute the import of cheap agricultural products for the modernization of domestic agriculture, developed nations today tend to prefer importing manufactured goods from abroad rather than to produce them at home to meet the domestic demand. With the constant shifting of production bases abroad, manufacturing industries in developed nations have become increasingly 'hollowed out.' This tendency will no doubt be reinforced by further development of information technology.

In order for a society to survive by mostly importing cheaper foreign products without itself being engaged in their production, it has to be able to export advanced services and intellectual property rights abroad, in addition to catering for increasing domestic demand for services. Some services are easily exportable (finance, distribution, information services, etc.), while others are more likely to be targeted for domestic needs (education, health care, police, garbage collection, etc.). So far no single country has achieved the status of total dependence on services (software), which would mean importing all goods (hardware) it requires from abroad. But one can observe signs that the United States *tend toward* such a status, whether it be in fact achievable or not. This is not the place to analyze such a tendency in detail, but what is relevant here is the implication of a society that manifests such a tendency.

A society which is no longer interested in the production of use-values as such is obviously exempt from the requirement to maintain an adequate mechanism whereby to insure the commodification of labor-power, human capacity to produce use-values. Such a society should also be exempt from the working of the law of value, there being no further need to maximize the production of material wealth by way of optimizing the use of productive resources available to society.

VIII

What remains is to review the concept and significance of value in economics to clinch the above argument. Value, above all, is the form of indifference to specific use-values. It represents the abstract-general (mercantile/commodity-economic) side of wealth as opposed to its concrete-specific (material) side. The pursuit of wealth as value can go on indefinitely, whereas the pursuit of wealth as use-value sooner or later reaches a limit, as the human wants are satiated. Thus, capitalism can come into being only when wealth acquires this abstract-general quality of value. But what does it mean for material wealth to acquire this quality, to become a commodity (value-object), and thus to take on the form of indifference to use-values? It means that capital, as the form of value-augmentation, may produce *any* use-value that promises it maximum returns. To earn maximum returns, capital moves from one branch of industry to another without a hitch or qualm, while allocating society's productive resources optimally (i.e. most efficiently) for the maximum possible production of material wealth in society. In other words, the capitalist method of production is the most rational and efficient way for human society to maximize the production of material wealth.

This method of production clearly did not fit a predominantly agricultural society, for agricultural production depended on, and was constrained by, the natural cycles beside the fact that, as Adam Smith once remarked, maximizing the produce beyond 'the narrow capacity of the human stomach' had little meaning.[24] This was the reason why capitalism began only when manufacturing gradually dis-embedded itself from agriculture, and reached its full development in the subsequent age of machinery, during which the demand for manufactured goods appeared boundless, that is, while produced goods were conceived 'scarce.' Indeed, throughout the age of capitalism proper, this *condition of scarcity* pertaining to material wealth was maintained as industry continued to be run by technology based on the burning of coal. But this situation changed radically, during the process of ex-capitalist transition, with the advent of petroleum which revolutionized industrial technology. The age of Fordism (mass production) and Affluent Society (mass consumption) materialized, which the old industrial technology based on coal had never dreamed of. The production of material wealth which had always occupied the top priority of any human society for its survival suddenly became a relatively easy matter, liberating human society for the first time in history from the burden of productive labor.

This tendency has since been vastly reinforced with the evolution of information and communication technology in the present age of post-Fordism, the last phase of ex-capitalist transition. Production of things (material wealth) as such no longer occupies the central place in human society if its administration, finance, management and control still do. This view seems to be supported by the industrial hollowing out of developed countries and the shift of production bases to peripheral areas. Recent trends reviewed above in this chapter seem to me to demonstrate the fact that today we are rapidly growing out of capitalism, *the last of the production-centered societies.* True, there still remain many vestiges of capitalist society, some more long lasting than others. But the mechanism of the law of value, which constituted the lifeblood of capitalism, has definitely ceased to operate in the contemporary economy for precisely no other reason than that its sophisticated function is no longer called for.

Notes

1. Descriptions in the following two paragraphs are based upon work in Sekine (1997).
2. The long paragraph in Marx (1967a: 167–68) which begins with 'The value of labor-power is determined, as in the case of every other commodity, by the labor-time necessary for the production ... of this special article' and ends with: '[n]evertheless, in a given country, at a given period, the average quantity of the means of subsistence necessary for the laborer is practically known,' is well known. It has been quoted and re-quoted, in part or in whole, a great many times by Marxists as the final word on the 'value of labor-power.' But this gives a false impression that, in our theoretical investigations, we can arbitrarily dictate an appropriate assortment of wages-goods *as a datum* as constituting the real basis of the value of labor-power. That is precisely where lies the danger of the 'quotationist' approach to economic theory, which Marxists are so reputedly fond of. What did Marx mean, or should have meant, by 'at a given period'? To my knowledge Uno (1980) has been the only one to pose that question and to answer it satisfactorily.
3. The 'dialectic of capital' means the logic of capital which coincides with economic theory, in much the same sense as Hegel's logic of the Absolute coincided with metaphysics. See Wallace (1975: 36), Hegel (1991: 56). On the close parallel between the dialectic of capital and Hegel's logic, see Sekine (1997 Vol. 1: 5–7), Sekine (1998).
4. It is, however, important to recognize that there is a vast difference between an 'educated guess' based on a firm grasp of the objective referent, the dialectic of

capital, and a wishful thinking inspired only by an arbitrary ideology. Marxists have frequently erred by substituting self-righteous ideology for a rigorous study of the dialectic of capital.

5. The reason that our knowledge of nature must remain partial is demonstrated as follows: Suppose that by verifying a hypothesis $(a, b, c, \ldots) \rightarrow x$, we could establish $a, b, c, \ldots$ to be the proximate causes of x, we will then need to explain the event, say, a by verifying a similar statement such as $(a_1, a_2, a_3, \ldots)$ a. But once that is done, we will then have to explain, say, a_2 by verifying yet another statement such as $(a_{21}, a_{22}, a_{23}, \ldots) \rightarrow a_2$, and so on, ad infinitum. The same applies to causes $b, c, \ldots$ Consequently, this kind of inquiry can have no end, which means that the knowledge acquired on such a basis is necessarily 'divergent' and never conclusive. Since nature can be known to us only in this way, its knowledge can never be total.
6. On Uno's idiosyncratic approach to Marxism in the background of modern Japanese social science see, for example, Barshay (1999).
7. By a 'non-naturalistic' theory, I do not mean a 'non-objective,' 'voluntaristic' or 'subjective (ideologically motivated)' theory. A dialectical theory is objective, but not in the natural scientific sense. Nature is objective because it is outside us and beyond us, in the sense that we never took part in its creation. No society is objective in that sense. But the logic of capital, which synthesizes a purely capitalist society, is objective because it is the logic of the homo economicus, which is a being transcending an ordinary human being. See references cited in note 9.
8. This precisely is the lesson that we must learn from the tragic failures of many so-called 'real' socialisms which were experimented with during the twentieth century.
9. See Sekine (1998: 436), Sekine (1997 Vol. 1: 6).
10. 'Accordingly, logic is to be understood as the system of pure reason, as the realm of pure thought. This realm is truth as it is without veil and in its own absolute nature. It can therefore be said that this content is the exposition of God as he is in his eternal essence before the creation of nature and a finite spirit' (Miller 1969: 50).
11. See Ayer (1974: 21–22).
12. By 'overall commodification' I mean the commodification of all important use-values as well as of labor-power, land and funds (money).
13. An 'idealized type' may be a contorted expression asking for troubles. Earlier in this chapter, I said that a purely capitalist society is not a 'model' or an 'ideal type,' and now I say that a developmental stage of capitalism is an 'idealized type.' Elsewhere (Sekine 1975), I once used the term 'material type' for that. A 'model,' as explained in section I, is a theoretical (logical) construct that the natural scientist (or the neo-classical economist) uses for analysis, and an 'ideal type' is a generalized picture of the situation that the historian builds. Clearly, Uno's theory of a purely capitalist society has nothing to do with either of them, for it is capital's own logical definition of capitalism, which transcends us. But between the logic that belongs to capital and the history that belongs to us, we need the developmental stage as an intermediate term. This one looks somewhat like a 'model' or an 'ideal type.' But it is, in my view, not a 'model' because it is not an arbitrary construct of the theorist; it is not an 'ideal type' because it is not just a product of *histoire raisonnée*. It has a link with objective theory on the one hand and with actually lived history on the other.
14. I use the term capitalism, here as elsewhere in this chapter, in the narrower sense of capitalist society. The term 'capitalism' can also mean more broadly 'acting like

a capitalist' in the sense of 'being engaged in profit-seeking activities' (Sekine 1997 Vol. 1: 17).

15. Bell and Sekine (2001).
16. Myrdal (1939: 8). The term 'Anglo-Saxon' in the quote, which referred specifically to Keynes as the author of *A Treatise on Money*, should today be replaced by 'Anglophone' and be applied to the galaxy of Marxist economists publishing in English.
17. See Freeman and Carchedi (1996). The impact of Sraffianism was devastating on the Anglophone studies in Marxian economics, whose subsequent development has been seriously distorted. In order to avoid its venom, some have gone so far as to repudiate the very concept of equilibrium in Marxian economics. But a non-equilibrium theory is often a hoax, meaning that it is only a metaphor and not a theory. For 'disequilibrium' or 'non-equilibrium' means 'out of equilibrium' or 'not in equilibrium,' so that we would not know what we are really talking about short of having a prior theory of equilibrium. Besides, to criticize capitalism in its failure (to achieve equilibrium, for instance) is quite cheap. For capitalism never denies the fact that it often, or most of the time, falls short of perfection. In order to adequately criticize capitalism, we must show that, even in its perfect functioning, it is upside down, de-humanizing or otherwise unsatisfactory. This, I believe, was what Marx intended to do.
18. Polanyi (1957: 71ff.).
19. The phase of Fordism-Consumerism, of course, did not last for more than 'the thirty glorious years,' since the uncontrolled application of petro-technology soon led to an exhaustion of non-renewable resources and a widespread destruction of the living environment. But the subsequent phase of post-Fordism has not restored capitalism proper. The regime of social democracy and welfare state persists, if on the defensive, despite the increasingly strident call for neo-liberalism and the adoration of the market. For otherwise why does capital need to so eagerly 'go global'?
20. If innovations occur and the economy adopts a new technology at any time, it makes no sense to presuppose what I called a 'technological complex T' (Sekine 1997 Vol. 2: 12ff.) for the determination of values and equilibrium prices. These can be meaningfully determined only when T is stable for ten years or so, once it is adopted in the depression phase of business cycles. The vanishing of the Juglar cycles thus renders not only the value (and equilibrium price) of labor-power but also the values (and equilibrium prices) of produced commodities suspicious concepts.
21. Sraffa (1926).
22. See for example, Krugman (1986).
23. Galbraith (1967).
24. Smith (1976).

12
Marx's Value Theory and Subjectivity

Robert Albritton

One reason often given for dismissing Marx's theory of value as presented in the three volumes of *Capital* is its seeming failure to directly address issues of subjectivity (Barrett 1991: 110). This failure becomes all the more glaring in light of current preoccupations with theories of subjectivity usually informed by some combination of psychoanalytic, phenomenological, or poststructuralist currents of thought. The reading of Marx's *Capital* is neglected these days, and when it is read, it is assumed to be a more or less structural or abstract theory of economics, far removed from the formation of subjectivities. And those who do try to address subjectivities in direct connection with Marx's theory of capital's inner logic tend to be drawn by the mere abstract structural character of the theory into class reductionism.[1] Yet others propose theoretically unsustainable balancing acts between structure and agency, or between the abstract laws of motion of capital and historical class struggle without taking into account the mediations that must be developed between any theory of capital's inner logic and historical analysis.[2]

Indeed, in my view, Marx's *Capital* is a theory of capital in the abstract and in general, or, in other words, a theory of the necessary inner connections amongst the most fundamental social forms assumed by economic practice in capitalism. The gap between such a theory and subjectivities that are contextually and concretely conditioned might seem to be insurmountable. In this chapter, I shall argue on the contrary that *at the present time no single theory has greater potential for advancing the theory of subjectivity than Marx's value theory*. I do not for a moment believe that we can derive any kind of 'complete' theory of subjectivity from value theory, but rather, given the relative neglect of value theory's possible contributions compared to say psychoanalytic theory or discourse analysis, the unrealized potential contributions of value theory are truly exciting. Comparatively so little work has been done on this, that I will only be able to trace out certain general directions in this chapter.

Following in the footsteps of Japanese Political Economists Kozo Uno and Tom Sekine, I shall use levels of analysis as a means to develop mediations between more abstract and dialectical levels of theorizing and more concrete and historical levels (Sekine 1997). The theory of pure capitalism reveals the necessary inner connections amongst the fundamental socio-economic forms such as commodity, money, price, wage, profit, rent and interest. Mid-range or stage theory explores the configurations that result when these forms are articulated with stage specific economic, political, legal, and ideological patterns. Finally historical analysis explores actual contexts of historical process and change. My focus in this chapter will be on the implications of the capitalist value-form for theorizing subjectivity at the level of pure capitalism, at the level of the stage of consumerism (post-World War II), and at the level of American dominated global capitalism at the start of the twenty-first century.

In order to delimit and structure an otherwise unwieldy topic, I shall deal with three topics at each level of analysis. First is the issue of the relationship between value and use-value, with emphasis on value's indifference to use-value. Second, is the tendency for value to homogenize and shrink space by subsuming it to a time bent on an unlimited increase in the speed of production and consumption. And third is a tendency to hollow out moral, political, and rational subjectivity and subsume them to legal subjectivity. The latter two are really more specific forms of value's indifference to use-value.

Pure capitalism

In Volume 3 of *Capital* Marx writes:

> And even though the equalization of wages and working hours between one sphere of production and another, or between different capitals invested in the same sphere of production, comes up against all kinds of local obstacles, the advance of capitalist production and the progressive subordination of all economic relations to this mode of production tends nevertheless to bring this process to fruition. Important as the study of frictions of this kind is for any specialist work on wages, they are still accidental and inessential as far as the general investigation of capitalist production is concerned and can therefore be ignored. In a general analysis of the present kind, it is assumed throughout that actual conditions correspond to their concept, or, and this amounts to the same thing, actual conditions are depicted only in so far as they express their own general type (1981 Vol. 3: 241–42).

And later in the same volume, Marx writes: 'The constant equalization of ever-renewed inequalities is accomplished more quickly, (1) the more mobile capital is... (2) the more rapidly labor-power can be moved from one sphere to another and from one local point of production to another' (Vol. 3: 298).

Marx goes on to claim that capital mobility depends on (1) free trade and competition; (2) a credit system to mobilize social savings for capital; (3) all spheres of production being subordinated to capitalists; (4) a high population density (ibid.). Labor mobility depends on: (1) abolition of all laws preventing the movement of workers; (2) indifference of the worker to the use-value character of the production process; (3) the maximum reduction of skilled to unskilled labor; (4) disappearance of prejudices of trade and craft amongst workers; (5) the subjection of workers to capital (ibid.).

A careful reading of *Capital* demonstrates that throughout Marx assumes 'that actual conditions correspond to their concept' and that among other things this implies for Marx the unimpeded mobility of capital and labor, or in other words a fully competitive capitalism. Indeed, value theory in *Capital* Volume 1 which is conceived as a relation between homogeneous labor and homogeneous capital, necessarily assumes unimpeded mobility since otherwise homogeneity could not be achieved. While Marx is fully aware that such an economy can never exist in history, Marx shows that it can exist in theory, and furthermore, that such a theory is justified by the fact that up to a point the laws of motion of capital in history do increasingly approximate their inner logic. In short, Marx's theory of capital reveals precisely what capital is when it operates unimpeded according to its own principles. This theory of unimpeded competitive capital that Marx introduces and Sekine refines, is what I refer to, following Sekine, as 'the theory of pure capitalism.'

It is clear that Marx believed that the law of value operates only to the extent that labor is mobile, but if we look at the history of capitalism, the law of value is continually compromised by the relative immobility of labor both within nation states and between them. This must be taken into account in any quantitative application of the law of value, and it would seem to make such applications difficult to make because no purely quantitative economic theory can grasp the political interventions that swirl around the mobility/immobility of labor-power.

Marx begins *Capital* with an analysis of the commodity form because this is the most simple and abstract social form of a capitalist economy.[3] For this reason, the inner logic of capital can also accurately be called a 'commodity-economic logic.' The dialectical logic that unfolds the motion of value in a capitalist economy does so by continually overcoming obstacles that have a qualitative/material character, or, in Marx's language, the character of use-value. It follows that the basic contradiction of the dialectic of capital is between value and use-value.[4]

Indifference to use-value

As something exchangeable, a commodity is pure quantity, but in order to be exchangeable it must have distinct material properties differentiating it qualitatively from other commodities. As values all commodities are qualitatively the same, differing only quantitatively, and as use-values every commodity differs qualitatively from every other commodity. From the point of view of capitalists in a purely capitalist society, commodities create a homogenous social world. All that matters to capital are prices and profits such that all commodities might as well be the same except for these numerical differences.

Capital is fundamentally the use of money to make more money. In order to maximize profits, a capitalist must be prepared to shift production from a less profitable commodity to a more profitable one, and this implies a stance of indifference to use-value. Whatever his personal attachment to vanilla ice cream, a capitalist will produce less vanilla and more chocolate ice cream if it is profitable to do so. Similarly because labor-power is commodified, capitalists hire or fire labor-power as required to maximize profits with total indifference to the human suffering that this may cause.

Indifference to use-value is also indifference to human values and human beings. Thus capitalists, if not constrained by outside forces, will have no concern for the working conditions of their workers or their lives. Unless constrained by law or by worker organization, capitalists will always try to get the most work from workers for the least pay.

In principle, capitalists will engage in any activity that will yield a higher profit unless constrained by outside forces. Indifference to use-value implies indifference to the possible destructiveness of both the production process and the commodity output to humans or to the environment. If it is profitable to adopt a production process that spews mercury into the environment or that exposes workers to toxic substances, then capitalists will do so. Were it legal to produce and market heroin, then a capitalist would do so. Were it profitable to clear-cut all of the world's forests, capitalists would do this as well. The profitability of marketing foods that are addictive because of being high in fats and sugars would certainly be pursued by capitalists despite creating unhealthy and obese populations.

It is apparent that an unimpeded capitalism would be a highly destructive economic system, and that capitalism is only tolerable because it is constrained in many ways. Thus, while pure capitalism with its total indifference to use-value would be inconsistent with the continuation of human life on this planet, we need to carry out a thought experiment, imagining that it does exist in order to explore *in principle* the impact of the purest forms of capital on the construction of subjectivities. This will help us to understand the impact less pure forms of capital have on subject formation.

The quantification of temporality and the homogenization of space

Capital is only interested in linear-sequential temporality, or, in other words, in quantitative time. Qualitative time implies being immersed in some activity to the extent that we ignore the passage of quantitative time. What is today called 'quality time' is usually time squeezed out of the passage of quantitative time, but such bits of squeezed time must be subsumed to quantitative time and hence their qualitative character is compromised. Similarly it is difficult even for leisure time to take on qualitative characteristics if it is rushed by an ever-increasing pace of life.

Marx makes it clear that if it could, capital would reduce both the production time of commodities and their circulation time to zero because this would maximize profits. This would imply that commodities were instantaneously both produced and consumed, an impossibility given the use-value constraints associated with the producing and consuming of use-values. Capital does, however, always strive in this direction with the result that the pace of production and consumption continually speeds up and with them the pace of life. Postone (1996: 289–91) refers to a 'treadmill-effect' such that the faster we go, the faster yet we must go in order to maintain profit rates. Over the long run, this means that without outside constraints, capital will speed up the pace of life until the stress levels become impossible to sustain. Speed, then, becomes a crucial consideration in considering the impact of capital's laws of motion of value on the formation of modern subjectivities.

From the point of view of time as speed up, space is reduced to nothing but distance that must be traversed more and more quickly or to resources that must be processed more and more quickly. In other words, indifference to use-value is also indifference to space except as potential resistance to speed up. Capital as self-expanding value would love to achieve a stance of indifference to space by subordinating its qualitativeness to an expanded reproduction machine that continually accelerates. The earth itself is commodified and indifferently fed into the giant maws of an ever-hungrier capital. Every global resource is reduced to a potential input into a profit-making production process or marketing scheme.

Abstract value and subjectivities

Hegel (1971: 40–46) begins his *Philosophy of Right* with the legal subject understood as the externalization of the will into private property. This is followed by theorizing the moral subject, who through a process of internalization develops a soul and conscience. Finally the ethical or political subject synthesizes the external and internal into institutions appropriate to the full development of both the legal and moral subjects. The synthesis of the legal, moral, and political subject can be called the rational subject.

While this is no doubt a powerful dialectical way of proceeding, his efforts fall short because he fails to understand the extent to which the legal subject is not only specific to capitalism but also as the dominant subject form in capitalism subsumes both the moral and the political subjects. Further, far from being universal, his moral subject is an idealized Christian subject, and his political/ethical subject depends on a capitalism constrained by 'organic' feudal institutions (supposedly to counter the atomizing tendencies of civil society) that were already passing away as Hegel wrote his book in the early years of the emergence of capitalism in Prussia.

From the point of view of capital in a purely capitalist society, only the legal subject must be recognized (Pashukanis 1978). Moreover, capital's indifference to use-value implies a non-recognition of moral, political, or rational subjectivity. In a purely capitalist society all that is required is subjects capable of owning commodities, selling or buying commodities, or making contracts involving exchange transactions or transfer of ownership. Capital needs subjects who are totally free to enter contracts to produce or exchange commodities and who can both embody and recognize property rights involving exclusive control over pieces of materiality. These legal subjects can have absolute rights over things and rights over the productive use of bodies limited by the rights of contract and exit that those bodies must have in order to be legal subjects. From this point of view, the capital/labor relation is a relation between legal subjects who own and control the means of production and legal subjects that 'freely' (insofar as they are single-mindedly thought of as legal subjects as does capital in a purely capitalist society) sell their labor-power for the use of capital in return for a wage. From the point of view of capital, the only kind of subjectivity that exists is free legal subjectivity: there are no moral subjects, political subjects, rational subjects and certainly no class subjects.

The reason that I started this section with reference to Hegel is that I believe that he deftly theorizes the basic forms of legal subjectivity. Hegel's legal subject is the most abstract, formal, and externalized subject form. It is basically the will of a person manifested in that person's private property. As the most shallow and contentless subject, for Hegel, it must be filled in by the dialectical unfolding of the moral and political subject. But capital in its inner logic cannot do this and has no interest in doing this. Indeed, were we to imagine that a purely capitalist society actually came into historical existence, the result would be a general hollowing out of the soul and an extreme externalization of the self into a commodity world. Selves would be nothing but differently appearing bodies plus the commodity accouterment that they possess. They would be only differentiated from commodities by their capacity for self-movement, by their capacity for exclusive property rights against one another, and by their particular commodity equipage and consumption patterns.

I say 'rights against one another' because a purely capitalist society is essentially atomistic and competitive, pitting individual against individual in the pursuit of profits or wages. Strictly speaking, other legal subjects are only of interest insofar as they can be used to improve one's economic position. It follows that legal subjects would gain recognition mainly by being productive or by capturing the outputs of other's productivity. 'Disabled' subjects or subjects considered unproductive for whatever reason would have no standing to be recognized in such a society. For capital, existence is either the production of wealth or the possession of wealth.

An externalized subject is inherently decentered, since having a center has always implied some kind of inner core whether called 'ego,' 'soul,' or something else. The legal subject of pure capitalism is radically decentered since such a subject is simply a collection of profit-making capacities without any center or inner connectedness. In this case, the subject writ large is capital and individuals are only recognized as subjects insofar as they are useful to capital. It is the commodity form (and its variations) that provides the basic social connection, and it is the movement of commodities that ultimately determines the basic socio-economic outcomes. Thus the movements of legal subjects are ultimately determined by the movement of commodities in markets that through the quantitative movement of wages, prices, and profits provide the signals that determine their actions.

In his influential essay 'Ideology and Ideological State Apparatuses,' Althusser (1971) argues that the most fundamental category of all ideology is the category 'subject.' He treats religion as the paradigm case of ideology since it is fundamentally through God as Subject writ large each individual is called upon to be a subject. It is interesting to reflect that where Marx eschews theorizing 'production in general' in favor of historically specific modes of production, in contrast Althusser theorizes 'ideology in general' but not historically specific modes of ideology. Lacan also tries to develop a general or universal theory of subjectivity (1977: 1–7). While they use a mirror metaphor somewhat differently, in both cases it plays a fundamental role in identity formation. It may well be that we spend our whole lives either believing that we are whole or striving to become whole, but the important thing about the mirror is that we first see an image of wholeness reflected in a capitalistically produced commodity and this produces the misrecognition that wholeness can be achieved through the possession of commodities or commodity-like persons. This suggests that the best starting point for understanding the human psyche under capitalism is not some imagined universal family structure or universal interpolation, but rather the historically specific capitalist commodity form.

Where capital in a purely capitalist society may be considered in some sense a Subject writ large, it is a different kind of Subject writ large than Althusser's god or Lacan's father. Capital as subject has some distinct differences from Gods and Fathers or from God the Father. Capital collectivizes and quantifies individual actions sometimes pushing them along and sometimes blocking them, but in all cases it produces outcomes that no one intended and that can only be altered by powerful collectivist interventions. Capital is us, as we are objectified in the course of acting through the commodity form. It cannot act without our actions, but at the same time it adds up our actions into resultant prices and profits that drive the economy in directions that no one intended. Thus at the level of the individual, we are all supposedly free to engage in any exchange transactions that we wish, while at the level of the whole most people experience sharp constraints relative to their positioning in the economy. This freedom of the individual and tyranny of the whole is specific to capitalism and heavily impacts on the main tendencies of capitalist ideology. Capitalist ideologues always play on the fact that for individuals in capitalist society it is much easier for them to think of themselves as free than it is for them to understand capital's logic that can make a travesty of their freedom. Ideologically capitalism always celebrates the individual freedom that it presumably promotes while ignoring the determinism that in a purely capitalist society totally trumps all individual actions with the overriding laws of motion of capital.

To summarize, the basic subject form of capitalism is the legal subject. Legal subjects always relate to others instrumentally or simply as bodies that may be useful for self-promotion. There is no process of othering since others are always already simply other. Legal subject as other has no being except as a body with a will that may be manipulated to advance the self's profits. The externalization of selves implies that all selves are simply collections of external appearances without a soul. Such hollowed-out souls are indifferent to persons as quality, but instead relate to them as quantities or potential quantities. Time and space are purely quantitative resulting in a flattening out of the social world, such that time as speed increasingly nullifies rootedness in the qualitative and nullifies care for nature and for other human beings.

The stage of consumerism

It is beyond the scope of this chapter to discuss in detail how both the theory of pure capitalism and historical analysis can be utilized to construct mid-range theory.[5] I refer to the current stage of capitalist development as the stage of consumerism and locate its golden age spatially in the United States and temporally between 1950 and 1970.[6] I call it 'consumerism' because of the elevated role of the consumer in the dominant economy of this stage of capitalist development. Elsewhere, I argue that the dominant modes of accumulation theorized as articulations of the economic, ideological, legal, and political are qualitatively distinct as between different stages even though they articulate the same underlying law of value. This is because value is externalized in different use-value or institutional contexts requiring it to be rethought as it articulates with certain forms specific to capital accumulation over a particular stage. These qualitative distinct articulations involve specific resistances, supports, and compromises.

A fundamental issue to theorize in connection with stages of capitalist development is the type and range of use-values capitalistically produced and how capital itself is organized in order to successfully carry out accumulation in connection with such use-values. When we consider the history of capitalist manufacturing, we find that the first important use-value to be extensively subsumed to capital's dynamism is cottage wool production.

This was followed by light industry typified by cotton factory production. Next came the predominance of monopolistic heavy industry typified by steel production. And in the stage that I refer to as consumerism the mass production of consumer durables, most typically the automobile, is carried out by 'multinational' capital.

From the point of view of the stage of consumerism, I shall argue first that the mass production of consumer goods has subsumed an unprecedented array and quantity of use-values to the motion of value, and that the resulting elevation of the consumer has necessitated strong ideological, legal, and political supports in order for capital accumulation to proceed smoothly. Second, in order to maintain profit rates and high rates of consumption capital ranges throughout the globe seeking cheaper inputs and markets for outputs. To some extent, capital has always done this, only now it has the technological means and ever-expanding array of use-value outputs that results in a more thoroughgoing search for control. In other words, commodification is now penetrating every nook and cranny of the earth and of human life in search of new profit possibilities. Space is increasingly shrunk and homogenized by the commodity form. A part of this shrinkage is the speeding up of the pace of life and of consumption, again made more possible than ever before by new technologies. Thus time is increasingly reduced to pure quantity for the sake of being sped up. Third, capital would like legal subjects to identify themselves primarily as relatively passive and gullible consumers. To the extent desires can be directed toward the commodity world this world can seem to offer endless pleasures, and the more disruptive potentials of desire can be distracted and absorbed into consumerism. Every stage of capitalism needs to rely either on means of coercion or means of subject formation that create relatively docile subjects. Today relative docility is achieved by fostering mass addiction to commodities some of which are inherently addictive like tobacco, alcohol, crack, fats, and sugar; some of which, we are indoctrinated into believing, we need for status or other reasons; and some of which we do need because alternatives are not sufficiently available (e.g. private car versus public transportation). Of course, this docility is only relative given renewed signs of resistance to capital worldwide.

Massive commodification

The strength of the working class in the West and of the so-called socialism in the East after World War II fueled a cold war that stimulated the development of a welfare/warfare state. At the same time, the shear number and range of commodities increased astronomically as capitalism attempted to buy off the working class in the West with an incredible array of commodities, the most important of which were the automobile, the television, and the single-family dwelling. These were the rewards for the soldiers returning from World War II and their continuing loyalty was insured by indoctrinating them with a fear of communism that generated an insatiable need for security that not only prevented American politics from moving to the left, but also justified the continuation of a huge military establishment.

Western capitalism was able to flood working people with commodities because of a radically increasing inequality and productivity on a global scale. Low wages and low costs in the Third World and in First World sweat shops made for affordable commodities in the rich world. Consumption was further stimulated by debt expansion and by an advertising regime that more and more channeled human desires toward the consumption of commodities as the path to happiness. Shopping became the number one 'leisure' activity in the First World.

In terms of its impact on human life, the automobile and the television are perhaps the most revolutionary commodities ever produced.[7] Both of them represent the increasing mechanization and chemicalization of human life, particularly the automobile whose production requires a vast array of chemicals and whose use produces a vast array of chemical pollutants. It was not foreordained that transportation would take such an individualized and environmentally destructive form, though once off the ground, the auto industry developed around it deeply entrenched and immensely powerful vested interests. And of course, television helps to convince consumers that the automobile is a must-have commodity.

The elevation of consumer identities in the stage of consumerism tended to push class identities into the background. Trade unions all too often helped this along by maintaining a disciplined work force in return for increases in standard of living. Yet the threat of socialism and trade union militancy coupled with an expanding capital accumulation both pushed and enabled the capitalist state to expand the welfare state and the accompanying 'social wage.' Large funds were channeled toward health, education, and welfare as the caring professions that humanize capitalism also grew. The cold war fueled a military Keynesianism that helped to maintain economic growth and stability. These trends led to rapidly growing indebtedness both for the state and the individual. At the same time, capitalism's inherent indifference to use-value seemed to be constrained by the welfare state and the growth of caring professions.

Shrinking space and homogenizing time

While in principle, capital should not be committed to any spatial location since to be so would impede the mobility required to opportunistically pursue profit; in history, the spatial development of capital is very uneven and the nation state develops in part to defend and promote the gains of one location at the expense of others. This uneven development along with capital's inherent expansiveness has produced throughout history a variety of colonialisms and imperialisms. Where the emphasis on quantity over quality reduces persons to numbers, thus essentially atomizing society, nationalisms, ethnicities, racisms and/or various religions convert numbers back into qualitative groupings. Capitalism cannot and would not always get rid of these qualitative groupings, so whenever possible it manipulates them for its own advantage. By creating or sustaining boundaried spatial arrangements ruled by states, various groups can be either oppressed or mobilized as needed by profit-making activity. Nationalist identifications have played a particularly important role in suppressing class conflict and mobilizing masses for war.

The atomizing character of capitalism sometimes generates reaction in the form of emotionally based groupings whether families, religions, cultures, nations, or races. These reactionary groupings, as for example, the American 'moral majority,' can sometimes be mobilized to support capitalism, but, if this is not possible, they can always be vilified and turned into evil enemies (as in the case of Islamic fundamentalism) thus supporting the more of less endless development of a capitalist military establishment.

In history, capital has been far less spatially indifferent than it would be were it able to fully realize a commodity-economic logic. It may well be that indifference to location accords with capital's self concept, but because of its historical uneven development and the development of the nation-state, more often than not it has set location against location generating either preparation for war or war. Furthermore, while the development of capital has fostered the increasing global mobility of capital, it has often placed obstacles in the way of the global mobility of labor. The result is an apartheid world characterized both by almost continual war or preparation for war and by reactionary groupings that are often labeled as 'good' or 'evil.'

After World War II, the global inequality associated with the uneven development of capitalism resulted in a three-world stratification that revolved around a superpower cold war. The cold war played a fundamental role in maintaining strong nationalist ideologies in face of a growing threat of internationalism. Mass media were used to instill deep fears and insecurities, requiring a strong military state able to contain or even roll back communism on every front. Hysterical anti-communist ideology often fed fear of all that was different (or other) including a vast array of racisms, ethnocentricisms, sexisms, and homophobia. The need for security became increasingly the primary need and it justified not only Central Intelligence Agency (CIA) and military interventions around the world, but also domestic policies that vilified the left. The narrow calculations of capitalist profit-making were accompanied by reactionary emotion-based groupings ('moral majority') with a boundless hunger for enemies to crush. America increasingly became the world's policeman with the power to ignore international law.

While capitalism has an inherent impulse to speed up the rate of production and consumption, it is in the stage of consumerism that transportation and communication technologies become available that both drastically shrink space and homogenize time as pure quantity. Henceforth, the entire globe is converted into potential raw material for profit-making. If trade unions are too strong in one place, capital will move to places where workers are cheaper and more docile. If environmental protection laws are too strongly enforced in one jurisdiction, capital will move to another where it can freely pollute. One might think that this increased mobility of capital would generate global equality, and while it has broken down the three worlds, they have been replaced by a global hierarchy of even greater inequality. One reason for this is that the speed up of capital mobility around the world has not been accompanied by the same mobility for labor.

The speed of life has increased enormously with faster transportation and communication technologies.[8] By and large this increased speed has not enriched the quality of human life, but has instead increased a 'treadmill-effect' that causes us to become more exhausted without getting anywhere. The increased speed serves primarily to maintain profit rates against their tendency to fall by squeezing more productivity and intensity of work out of people without significantly adding to their time for free creativity or for rest and relaxation. The impact of increased speed on the earth is similar, since the earth also needs recovery time without which environmental degradation will increase. Indebtedness, then, extends from consumer debt and state debt to sleep debt and ecological debt. And what is debt but present pleasure at the cost of future pain. Capitalism by its very nature encourages a short-term profit orientation, and by its very commitment to the market, long range planning is anathema.

The swelling of debt in every dimension of life has huge consequences for the future. First, it places enormous power in the hands of those who hold the debt and who decide who is creditworthy. Second, the debtors to a large extent have given the creditors control over their futures. The debtors must work hard on terms dictated largely by creditors, and many people and institutions remain deeply in debt for life. It is not uncommon for individuals to hold two and three jobs just to make enough money to pay existing debt payments and have a little to live on. And people are encouraged to go into debt by easy credit and by media that convince them that happiness is to be achieved by spending more money on present consumption. The slogan of the age becomes: 'Buy now, pay later.' And when it comes to ecological issues, it will be future generations that will have to pay the price of a planet increasingly out of balance – poisoned and lacking recovery time. The relation of capitalism to time means that it simply cannot achieve the orientation that would be required to deal with long-term ecological questions. In the stage of consumerism, time waits for no person as it becomes a linear-sequential treadmill exhausting both humans and nature.

Consuming subjects

The capitalist equivalent of Lacan's (1977: Chapter 3) passage from the imaginary to the symbolic is the passage from relatively protected family life to the tough-minded world of competitive capitalist accumulation. Those who do not successfully maneuver through this transition, will end up among the unproductive refuse of capitalist society, and, of course this is much more likely for the people in the third world, for poor people, for people of color, for women, or for disabled people. Lacan's so-called 'mirror stage' is simply the effort to try to center oneself in the radically decentering world of selves externalized into the evanescent speediness of commodities whose value is their price that continually changes with the movement of competitive pressures. The transition is not from a mother-centric imaginary to a father-centric symbolic, instead it is from the caringness of family life (where it exists) to the strict profit orientation of pure capitalism. And where the force of capitalist accumulation penetrates family life, it will have a dissolving effect on care and tend to turn the family itself into a cash nexus.

Consider the 'captain of industry' as a capitalist ego-ideal or as a subjective type that would be favored by capitalism. Capitalism implies preoccupation with quantity and detachment from the qualitative such that decisions must be made strictly in accord with prices and profits. But this kind of quantitative thinking is abstract; it shuts out the concrete particular which is always qualitative. If fixation on abstract quantitative thinking does violence to the qualitative, that violence is ignored from the point of view of capital. If it is profitable to shut down the single significant enterprise in a company town, thus destroying the livelihood of all town citizens, then this is what capital would consider 'rational.' It follows that capitalistic 'rationality' implies a certain 'tough-mindedness' that splits reason off from the emotions. It is a calculating manipulative way of thinking that can never give in to sentimentality if it is to succeed capitalistically. Indeed from the point of view of a captain of industry, those who would impede his production processes because they damage the environment are likely to be viewed precisely as bleeding-heart sentimentalists. Thus the split between quantity and quality and the privileging of quantity over quality is also a split between reason and emotion, between mind and body, and ultimately between male and female. Classically all captains of industry were male and their world of cold, tough, calculating reason would by itself be intolerable. Hence the need for a so-called 'private realm' where female nurturing and emotionality could heal the wounds of capitalist battle and nurture over-controlled and stifled emotions.

But the splitting off and belittling of the private realm of the family meant that this realm became sentimentalized and romanticized, and along with it the women who were identified with this realm. The ideal of femininity found its location in the realm of the family; hence there is a convergence between the implications of capital's logic and Freudian object-relations theory which emphasizes the absent father as part of the dynamic of gender differentiation. Indeed, the 'abstract masculinity' referred to by Hartsock (1998: Chapter 6) is precisely what is required for 'captains of industry' with their detachment from all that is qualitative. I believe that the most important underlying cause of 'abstract masculinity' is capitalism with its ideal family of the single bread-winning father and its need to split off reason from emotion.[9]

In a capitalist society, it follows that men would tend to be the tough-minded profit-makers, and women the caring and nurturing back-up. Strictly speaking, this division cannot be logically derived from the law of value, but given that patriarchy already existed in history, once we see the split between quantity and quality, we can begin to see a capitalist patriarchy shaped along these lines.

The externalization of self characteristic of legal subjects in pure capitalism takes on particular forms in the stage of consumerism. The relationships between Hegel's legal subject, moral subject, and political subject assume a certain constellation typical of the stage of consumerism. The legal subject becomes more powerful than ever before with 'consumer sovereignty' lending its support to a certain kind of democracy, where presumably consumers' economic sovereignty consists in casting dollar ballots for commodities that they are confronted with and their political sovereignty consists in casting ballots for candidates that they are confronted with. The aim of the moral subject is the happiness achieved by maximizing want-satisfaction through the judicious spending of income. It follows that the moral subject and political subject tend to be absorbed into the consuming legal subject. This leaves a vacuum in the moral and political arenas that is inviting to emotionally based fundamentalisms.

Hegel's property-owning subject primarily owned land, and in his theory this has the effect of giving the individual and family a rootedness or stable grounding. In the case of the modern consuming subject, the property in question is more like fashion with a high rate of turnover. What is 'in' one year may be 'out' the next. We can say that for Hegel the ideal was a landed property that was the stable basis of family life through generations, while for the current requirements of consumerist speed, the ideal is a continually changing fashion.

Capitalism makes it seem as though all legal subjects as legal subjects are equal. Thus consuming legal subjects are free to spend their income as they please, producing legal subjects are free to offer their labor-power for sale to any taker, moral legal subjects can maximize marginal utilities, and political legal subjects can vote as they please. All legal subjects are free and equal. In practice this enables the well-off legal subjects of the stage of consumerism to feel comfortable with monstrous inequalities that from another point of view might be totally unacceptable. This ideology that takes in only one narrow dimension of human existence becomes so hegemonic, that in the stage of consumerism it is difficult for 'common sense' to see behind this many-layered curtain. Rapidly growing inequalities sometimes become the basis for organization and struggle, but it is always against an immensely powerful ideology of legal subjecthood and triumphant 'free' enterprise.

Hegemonic legal subjecthood can stomach the fight for rights more than class struggle. Many struggles for rights have been very important and they offer greater possibilities for success in the short-run since they can be recognized more easily and dealt with by the dominant ideology. The most typical form of resistance in this stage of capitalism is the new social movement or Non-Governmental Organization (NGO) fighting to extend rights or to relieve the suffering associated with particular inequalities.

The consuming subject and the legal subject are mutually reinforcing. Since the legal subject is fundamentally a property-owning subject, the consuming subject is perhaps the most obvious appearance that the legal subject takes on. Strictly speaking, the identity of a consumer amongst other consumers is formed by a certain packaging and accouterment of commodities. One's self is essentially externalized through one's commodities and through other persons related to as commodified selves. Desires are channeled through commodities converting needs into wants for specific commodities and commodified persons. Status in such a world is recognition by commodified others of the want-value of one's commodified world. It is in this way that one becomes valued. Thus needs are converted into desires and wants are channeled toward certain commodities or commodified life-styles by the mass media. Indeed, to a certain extent, advertising both creates and directs desire in a world where meaning and recognition are to be discovered through commodities. The consuming subject and the legal subject, thus appear, as simply two different sides of the property-owning subject.

Capitalism today: approaching its limits?

At the level of historical analysis, I use the theory of capital's inner logic and the mid-range theory of consumerism to inform my analysis of current trends of capitalist development and resistance to those trends. The analysis that I have presented indicates that capitalism may be approaching its limits, though projecting trends into the future must always be speculative to the extent that it depends on how people organize to transform a seriously compromised capitalism. When I claim that capitalism may be approaching its limits, I mean to call attention to fundamental structural contradictions that do not seem resolvable within capitalism in the sense that any structural change that would remain consistent with the continuation of capitalism could not successfully deal with these problems.

The revenge of use-value

Today the global economy is addicted increasingly to high levels of mass consumption in the richer countries. Many economic pundits have emphasized this point by claiming that high growth rates in the 1990s depended heavily on high rates of spending by the American consumer, and that the future well being of the global economy will also depend on this. At the same time, at least a fair portion of this high American consumption has been based on debt expansion, government subsidies, artificially high stock and bond earnings, an artificially high American dollar, and artificially low costs created by scouring the world for cheap and unprotected natural and human production inputs. The artificiality and limitedness of all this suggests that the American growth of the 1990s was largely a fools paradise. Debt expansion and government subsidies are clearly limited, while world sourcing is also limited by political instabilities and the possibilities of organized resistance. The financialization of the global economy that has resulted in a considerable flow of world savings to the United States, and hence a huge growth of US financial markets, is speculative and ultimately destabilizing. Thus the same economic force that has fueled the rise of the American financial markets and kept the American dollar strong could in another time send both the financial markets and the value of the currency tumbling.

Furthermore, the kinds of use-values being produced are increasingly destructive to human life. For example, the chemicalization of the environment has been a major cause of the exponential growth of cancer.[10] While the richer countries may have some success in enforcing controls on the more extreme forms of chemical pollution, the careful study of long-term environmental impacts of various chemicals has barely begun. Comparatively few resources are directed toward this problem, the solution of which would probably entail a radical shift in research priorities which in turn would lead to altering what is produced and how it is produced.

Chemicals in the form of pharmaceuticals are produced to treat the illnesses such as cancer, mental illness, and asthma caused largely by other chemicals. By and large, it is only the rich of the world that have access to these prescription drugs, and as a result health has become a commodity that increasingly is only affordable to the rich. This is compounded by the fact the pharmaceutical corporations cannot make a profit from drugs that may cure the illnesses of the poor such as tuberculosis; hence, no research money goes in these directions.

Other chemicals in the forms of quasi-foods or drugs are ingested as escapes from stressful and painful lives or as fillers in empty lives. The full story of crack cocaine in the United States is yet to be told, but it appeared to radically demoralize the poor, while making them subject to incarceration. The stresses resulting from the increased pace of life are dealt with by different classes in different ways. For the well-off the way is often the purchase of expensive but legal psychotropic drugs, while the drugs of choice of the poor are often illegal and addictive.

Given its short-run profit orientation, capitalism always prefers to find profitable ways to treat symptoms as opposed to dealing with long-term underlying causes. It would rather discover new expensive chemicals to treat cancer, than to explore in depth the environmental causes of it. It would rather sell new diet drugs rather than reduce its production of foods loaded with empty calories. The trend of the age is the production of more and more expensive commodities to relieve us of the sufferings caused by the previous production of commodities. To put it differently, the trend of the age is for value to become more and more out of touch with use-value, and quantity out of touch with quality. As value spins through the world at a more frantic pace, it becomes both more destructive of life and more indifferent to that destruction. Neo-liberals as the keepers of the budget have to make the 'tough' decisions to cut to the quick those humanizing innovations that had made capital seem to be more caring during the prosperous phases of consumerism. Thus the 'caring professions' are being cut back at precisely the time when capitalism is increasing the number of casualties that need care.

Hyper-speed as exhaustion

The enormous transfer of wealth from the public to the private sector associated with neo-liberalism coupled with the need to speed up both production and consumption has resulted in a massive commercialization of public space. The amount of space and time given over to advertising increases as an impoverished public sector attempts to gain funding from the private sector, or struggling sports franchises attempt to cash in on their captive audiences. This commercialization of space is often also a homogenization of space as the larger cities of the world come increasingly to resemble each other as their public spaces fill up with the same brand names.

Just as the advertising sector attempts to permanently mobilize consumers, the military-industrial complex permanently mobilizes support by instilling the population with deep seated and permanent insecurities. These insecurities are then mobilized to support wars against vague and boundless enemies. The war on drugs or on terrorism leave enormous discretionary power in the hands of those with the authority to pursue these wars. Since the enemy is vague and boundless, such wars can be more or less permanent and can always be utilized to mobilize citizens against imagined enemies either to stimulate the economy or win elections. Since pure capitalism cannot directly generate its own emotion-based communities, such mobilizing becomes particularly important against various 'fundamentalisms.' These are spawned as reactions against capitalism, but must also be controlled by or subsumed to the very capitalism that spawns them.

As speed shrinks the world and increases the possibilities of rapid movement through space of the privileged few and of capital, the boundaries of the richer nation-states are becoming less permeable to immigration, and thus the majority of the world's working people find themselves increasingly imprisoned in the country of their birth. As a result the world is transformed into a hierarchy of ghettos, where the rich live in 'secure' gated communities and gated nation-states – gated against an inequality that has reached truly obscene proportions.

Hi-tech, which could in principle reduce working time, has had the opposite effect. In order to buy all of the commodities that consumers have been led to believe will make them happy, they must either go deeper in debt or work longer hours. Leisure time itself becomes increasingly intensified as a time of continued consumption either of mind-dulling escapism or commercialism. High stress levels lead to ever-greater social malaise that in turn generates every kind of social dysfunction.

Subjectivity and resistance

If capital is fundamentally indifferent to use-value, including human beings and nature, then all of the caring dimensions of capitalism must have ultimately stemmed not from capital but from socialized human beings often resisting the tendencies of capital. But it must be understood that capitalism's reifying force always makes resistance difficult. Furthermore, it is moral and political subjects that are more capable of agency than legal subjects, who are hollowed out or externalized; and yet, capitalism has no inherent tendency to develop moral or political subjects. It follows that to effect change, such subjects must be developed within capitalism despite capital's indifference. For this reason class formations are always heterogeneous and tenuous coming together with varying degrees of solidarity, organization, and radicalness.

In the past 20 years, the class capacities within the most advanced industrial countries have been seriously undermined. No doubt a combination of factors played a role, but surely among the most important would be the downfall of the USSR, the globalization of capital, and the relative impoverishment of the public sector. As a result, neo-liberal policies that have weakened the welfare state and all the caring professions have not been met with much resistance. Through the power of modern advertising, it is relatively easy for capital to promote consumerist identities, whereas class identities, which clearly go against the grain of hegemonic neo-liberal ideologies, have to be born out of the hard struggle and dangerous work of resistance and opposition. The building of morally and politically informed subjectivities to counter the hollowed out legal subjects of pure capitalism is not easy. In this, Gramsci, who advocated a socialist culture to counter the atomizing and demoralizing nature of capitalist culture, was surely thinking in the right direction. In the current setting, the anti-globalization movement is perhaps the beginning of a new oppositional force that, as it grows, will be able to at first challenge and eventually transform capitalism.

Conclusions

The fundamental categories of this chapter are value and use-value since it is my claim that it is value's indifference to use-value that is crucial to clarifying some of the most important dimensions of subjectivity in our era. Because the chapter is very condensed and contains many assertions that I could not back up with extensive argumentation, it may at times seem dogmatic or perhaps claiming too much causal efficacy for capital as self-expanding value. In fact I do not think that modern subjectivities are simply a function of capital, rather in this chapter I emphasize the role of capital because it has been neglected in the past. Ultimately a much more fine-grained analysis is needed. My aim here has been to present configurations of connections that seem to be mutually supporting, though in many cases it would no doubt be possible to bring in other important causal factors.

On the one hand, Foucault is probably correct in a general way when he argues that our identities are largely constructed by the discursive formations that we engage with. On the other hand, Foucault tends to neglect the political economic discursive formations associated with capitalism. And this is probably one of the main reasons that most of his followers who write about discursive formations neglect political economy. It is not enough to analyze local political economic discursive formations when we have a powerful theory of capital's inner logic that can shed so much light on capitalism as an epochal global force. And it is not a question of deducing the particular from the general, but of using the general to inform our understanding of particulars that also have to be understood on their own terms.

Thus the way in which we attempt to rebuild moral and political subjectivities as part of a general resistance to capital will have international-collective as well as local-collective dimensions. We stand at a historical juncture when either our very biology will be increasingly degraded or we will find a way to work ourselves out of capitalism and toward some form of democratic socialism.

Notes

I would like to thank Stefanos Kourkoulakos for his helpful comments.

1. Class reductionism and class voluntarism are particularly characteristic of the school of thought that has labeled itself 'Open Marxism.' See for example, the two volumes edited by Bonefeld *et al.* (1992) and the volume edited by Bonefeld *et al.* (1995).
2. I have argued elsewhere that the lack of attention to levels of analysis in Marxian political economy is the most fundamental problem that needs dealing with (Albritton 1991).
3. See Albritton (2003) for a discussion of the strengths and weaknesses of Lukacs' treatment of the commodity form.
4. See Albritton (1999) for a fuller account of the importance of the contradiction between value and use-value for the dialectic of capital.
5. See Albritton (1991) for more on the nature of stage theory.
6. See Albritton (2001) for an argument that the stage of consumerism is likely to be the final stage of capitalism.

7. In our fractal and mirrored world it is perhaps not surprising that auto + mobile (self-movement) ironically mirrors the self-movement of capital. This was pointed out to me by Michael Marder.
8. While I do not agree with many of Virilio's (1977) specific positions, his emphasis on speed has informed by thought.
9. Such splitting off would tend to make reason itself 'irrational.'
10. See McMurtry (1999).

Bibliography and Select Readings

Afanasyev, V. (1976) *Bourgeois Economic Thought, 1930s–70s* (Moscow: Progress).

Aglietta, M. (1979) *A Theory of Capitalist Regulation, the US Experience* (London: New Left Books).

Albritton, R. (1986) *A Japanese Reconstruction of Marxist Theory* (Basingstoke: Macmillan).

Albritton, R. (1991) *A Japanese Approach to Stages of Capitalist Development* (London: Macmillan).

Albritton, R. (1999) *Dialectics and Deconstruction in Political Economy* (London: Macmillan).

Albritton, R. (2001) 'Capitalism in the future perfect tense', in Albritton, Itoh, Westra and Zuege, eds.

Albritton, R. (2003) 'Superseding Lukacs: A Contribution to the Theory of Subjectivity', in R. Albritton and J. Simoulidis, eds, *New Dialectics and Political Economy* (Basingstoke: Palgrave Macmillan).

Albritton, R., Itoh, M., Westra, R. and Zuege, A., eds (2001) *Phases of Capitalist Development: Booms, Crises and Globalizations* (Basingstoke: Palgrave Macmillan).

Albritton, R. and Simoulidis, J., eds (2003) *New Dialectics and Political Economy* (Basingstoke: Palgrave Macmillan).

Althusser, L. (1971) *Lenin and Philosophy and other Essays* (London: New Left Books).

Altvater, E. (1993) *The Future of the Market* (London: Verso).

Amin, S. (1976a) *Unequal Development* (New York: Monthly Review Press).

Amin, S. (1976b) *Imperialism and Unequal Development* (New York: Monthly Review Press).

Anderson, P. (1979) *Lineages of the Absolutist State* (London: Verso).

Angelo, R. (1994) 'New developments on structural change and the labor theory of value: review article', *Review of Radical Political Economics*, **26**, 4.

Arestis, P., Palma, G. and Sawyer, M., eds (1997) *Capital Controversy, Post-Keynesian Economics and the History of Economics: Essays in Honour of Geoff Harcourt*, Volume 1 (London: Routledge).

Armstrong, P., Glyn, A. and Harrison, J. (1978) 'In defence of value', *Capital & Class*, **5**, Reprinted in Mohun (1994a).

Arnon, A. (1984) 'Marx's theory of money: the formative years', *History of Political Economy*, **16**, 4.

Arrighi, G. (1994) *The Long Twentieth Century* (London: Verso).

Arrow, K.J. (1981) 'Real and nominal magnitudes', in D. Bell and I. Kristol, eds, *The Crisis of Economic Theory* (New York: Basic Books).

Arthur, C.J. and Reuten, G., eds (1998) *The Circulation of Capital: Essays on Volume Two of Marx's Capital* (London: Macmillan).

Arthur, C.J. (1979) 'Dialectic of the value-form', in Elson, ed.

Arthur, C.J. (1998) 'Systematic dialectic', *Science & Society*, **62**, 3.

Arthur, C.J. (2001) 'Value, labour and negativity', *Capital & Class*, **73**.

Arthur, C.J. (2002) *The New Dialectic and Marx's Capital* (Leiden: Brill Academic).

Ayer, A.J. (1974) *Language, Truth and Logic* (London: Penguin Books).

Backhaus, H.-G. (1980) 'On the dialectics of the value-form', *Thesis Eleven*, **1**.

Backhaus, H.-G. (1992) *'Between Philosophy and Science: Marxian Social Economy as Critical Theory'*, in Bonefeld, Gunn and Psychopedis, eds, Volume 2.

Backhouse, R. (1985) *History of Modern Economic Analysis* (New York: Basil Blackwell).

Bailey, S. (1967) *A Critical Dissertation on the Nature, Measures, and Causes of Value* (New York: A.M. Kelley).
Banaji, J. (1979) 'From the commodity to capital, Hegel's Dialectic in Marx's "Capital"', in Elson, ed.
Bank for International Settlements (BIS) (2001) 'Central Bank Survey of Foreign Exchange and Derivatives Market Activity in April 2001: Preliminary Global Data', Press release 31/2001/E, 9 October.
Barber, W.J. (1967) *A History of Economic Thought* (New York: Praeger).
Barratt Brown, M. (1995) *Models of Political Economy*, Second Edition (New York: Penguin).
Barrett, M. (1991) *The Politics of Truth* (Standford: Standford University Press).
Barshay, A.E. (1999) 'Thinking through *Capital*: Uno Kozo and marxian political economy in Japan', *Osaka City University Economic Review*, **35**, 1.
Baumol, W. (1974) 'The transformation of values: what Marx "really" meant (an interpretation)', *Journal of Economic Literature*, **12**.
Baumol, W. (1983) 'Marx and the iron law of wages', *American Economic Review-AEA Papers and Proceedings*, May.
Becker, J. (1977) *Marxian Political Economy: An Outline* (New York: Cambridge University Press).
Bell, J. and Sekine, T. (2001) 'The disintegration of capitalism: a phase of ex-capitalist transition', in Albritton, Itoh, Westra and Zuege, eds.
Bellamy Foster, J. (1986) *The Theory of Monopoly Capitalism* (New York: Monthly Review).
Bellofiore, R. (1989) 'A monetary labor theory of value', *Review of Radical Political Economics*, **21**.
Bellofiore, R., ed. (1998) *Marxian Economics: A Reappraisal*, 2 Volumes (London: Macmillan).
Bellofiore, R., ed. (1999) *Global Money, Capital Restructuring, and the Changing Patterns of Production* (Cheltenham: Edward Elgar).
Berger, S. and Dore, R., eds (1996) *National Diversity and Global Capitalism* (Ithaca: Cornell University Press).
Blaug, M. (1987a) *Economic Theory in Retrospect*, Fifth Edition (Cambridge: Cambridge University Press).
Blaug, M. (1987b) 'Classical economics', in Eatwell, Milgate and Newman, eds (1987).
Blaug, M. (1999) 'Misunderstanding classical economics: the sraffian interpretation of the surplus approach', *History of Political Economy*, **31**, 2.
Block, F. (1990) *Postindustrial Possibilities: A Critique of Economic Discourse* (Berkeley: University of California Press).
Böhm-Bawerk, E. von (1984) [1896] 'Karl Marx and the close of his system', in Sweezy, ed.
Bonefeld, W., Gunn, R. and Psychopedis, K., eds (1992) *Open Marxism*, 3 Volumes (London: Pluto).
Bonefeld, W., Gunn, R., Holloway, J. and Psychopedis, K., eds (1995) *Open Marxism*, Volume 3 (London: Pluto press).
Bonefeld, W. and Holloway, J. (1991) *Post-Fordism and Social Form* (London: Macmillan).
Bortkiewicz, L. von (1952) 'Value and price in the marxian system', *International Economic Papers*, **2**.
Bottomore, T., ed. (1991) *A Dictionary of Marxist Thought*, Second Edition (London: Blackwell).
Botwinick, H. (1993) *Persistent Inequalities: Wage Disparities under Capitalist Competition* (Princeton: Princeton University Press).
Brenner, R. (1998) 'The economics of global turbulence', *New Left Review*, **229**.
Brenner, R. (2002) *The Boom and the Bubble: The US in the World Economy* (London: Verso).

Bridel, P. (1997) *Money and General Equilibrium Theory: From Walras to Pareto (1870–1923)* (Cheltenham: Edward Elgar).
Brown, A., Fleetwood, S. and Roberts, J.M., eds (2002) *Critical Realism and Marxism* (London: Routledge).
Brunhoff, S. de (1973) 'Marx as a-ricardian: value, money and price at the beginning of "capital" ', *Economy & Society*, **2**, 3.
Brunhoff, S. de (1976) *Marx on Money* (New York: Urizen Books).
Brunhoff, S. de (1978) *The State, Capital and Economic Policy* (London: Pluto).
Bryan, D. (1985) 'Monopoly in marxist method', *Capital & Class*, **26**.
Bryan, D. (1986) 'Competition and monopoly: a reply', *Capital & Class*, **30**.
Bryan, D. (1987) 'The state and the internationalisation of capital: an approach to analysis', *Journal of Contemporary Asia*, **17**, 3.
Bryan, D. (1995a) *The Chase Across the Globe: International Accumulation and the Contradictions for Nation States* (Boulder: Westview).
Bryan, D. (1995b) 'The internationalisation of capital and marxian value theory', *Cambridge Journal of Economics*, **19**.
Bryan, D. (1997) 'International capital and the valuing of labour', *Journal of Contemporary Asia*, **27**, 4.
Burns, T. and Fraser, I. (2000) *The Hegel-Marx Connection* (Basingstoke: Macmillan).
Callari, A., Roberts, B. and Wolff, R. (1998) 'The transformation trinity: value, value form and price', in Bellofiore, ed., Volume 2.
Caparaso, J. and Levine, D. (1992) *Theories of Political Economy* (New York: Cambridge University Press).
Caravale, G.A. and Tosato, D. (1980) *Ricardo and the Theory of Value, Distribution and Growth* (London: Routledge and Kegan Paul).
Caravale, G.A., ed. (1991) *Marx and Modern Economic Analysis* (Aldershot: Edward Elgar).
Carchedi, G. (1984) 'The logic of prices as values', *Economy and Society*, **13**, 4.
Carchedi, G. (1987) *Class Analysis and Social Research* (Oxford: Basil Blackwell).
Carchedi, G. (1991) *Frontiers of Political Economy* (London: Verso).
Carchedi, G. (2001) 'On temporality, simultaneity and TSS: reply to Laibman', *Science & Society*, **65**, 4.
Carnoy, M. (1984) *The State and Political Theory* (Princeton, NJ: Princeton University Press).
Carver, T., ed. (1975) *Karl Marx: Texts on Method* (Oxford: Blackwell).
Chandler A.D. (1977) *The Visible Hand: The Managerial Revolution in American Business* (Cambridge: Harvard University Press).
Chaudhury, A. (1998) 'Toward closing a century-old debate: transformation of values into prices in a world of heterogeneous labors', *Rethinking Marxism*, **10**, 1.
Clarke, S. (1979) 'The value of value', *Capital & Class*, **10**, reprinted in Mohun (1994a).
Clarke, S. (1983) 'State, class struggle, and the reproduction of capital', *Kapitalistate*, **10/11**.
Clarke, S. (1988) *Keynesianism, Monetarism and the Crisis of the State* (Cheltenham: Edward Elgar).
Clarke, S. (1989) 'The basic theory of capitalism: a critical review of Itoh and the Uno school', *Capital & Class*, **37**.
Clarke, S. (1991) *Marx, Marginalism and Modern Sociology: From Adam Smith to Max Weber*, Second Edition (Basingstoke: Macmillan).
Clarke, S. (1994) *Marx's Theory of Crisis* (Harmondsworth: Macmillan).
Cleaver, H. (1979) *Reading 'Capital' Politically* (Brighton: Harvester).
Clifton, J. (1977) 'Competition and the evolution of the capitalist mode of production', *Cambridge Journal of Economics*, **1**.

Coates, D. (2000) *Models of Capitalism: Growth and Stagnation in the Modern Era* (Cambridge: Polity Press).

Cockshott, P. and Cottrell, A. (1997) 'Labour time versus alternative value bases: a research note', *Cambridge Journal of Economics*, **21**.

Cockshott, P. and Cottrell, A. (1998) 'Does Marx need to transform', in Bellofiore, ed., Volume 2.

Cockshott, P., Cottrell, A. and Michaelson, G. (1995) 'Testing Marx: some new results from UK data', *Capital & Class*, **55**.

Cockshott, P., Cottrell, A. and Michaelson, G. (1996) 'Reply to Maniatis', *Capital & Class*, **59**.

Cohen, G.A. (1981) 'The labour theory of value and the concept of exploitation', in Steedman, ed.

Cole, K., Cameron, J. and Edwards, C., eds (1991) *Why Economists Disagree: The Political Economy of Economics*, Second Edition (London: Longman).

Colletti, L. (1973) *Marxism and Hegel* (London: New Left Books).

Colletti, L. (1977) 'Some comments on Marx's theory of value', in Schwartz, ed.

Colletti, L. (1978) 'Value and dialectic in Marx', *International Journal of Political Economy*, **28**, 3.

Cottrell, A. and Darity, W.A. Jr (1988) 'Marx, Malthus, and wages', *History of Political Economy*, **20**, 2.

Cullenberg, S. (1994) *The Falling Rate of Profit* (London: Pluto).

Cutler, A., Hindess, B., Hirst, P. and Hussain, A. (1977) *Marx's 'Capital' and Capitalism Today*, 2 Volumes (London: Routledge and Kegan Paul).

Dasgupta, A.K. (1985) *Epochs of Economic Theory* (London: Basil Blackwell).

Davis, J.B., ed. (1992) *The Economic Surplus in Advanced Economics* (Brookfield: Edward Elgar).

Deane, P. (1977) *Evolution of Economic Ideas* (Cambridge: Cambridge University Press).

Deane, P. (1989) *The State and the Economic System: An Introduction to the History of Political Economy* (Oxford: Oxford University Press).

Deleplace, G. (1999) *Histoire de la Pensée Economique* (Paris: Dunod).

Desai, M. (1979) *Marxian Economics* (Oxford: Basil Blackwell).

Devine, J. (1989) 'What is "simple labor"? A re-examination of the value-creating capacity of skilled labor', *Capital & Class*, **39**.

Devine, J. (1990) 'The utility of value: the "new solution", unequal exchange, and crisis', *Research in Political Economy*, **12**.

Devine, J. (1993) 'Microfoundations and methodology in modeling capitalism', *Review of Radical Political Economics*, **25**, 3.

Dicken, P. (1998) *Global Shift: Transforming the World Economy* (London: The Guilford Press).

Dixon, W. and Kay, G. (1994) 'Marx's theories of value: a response', *Cambridge Journal of Economics*, **19**, 4.

Dmitriev, V.K. (1974) *Economic Essays on Value, Competition and Utility* (Cambridge: Cambridge University Press).

Dobb, M. (1940) *Political Economy and Capitalism* (London: Routledge and Kegan Paul).

Dobb, M. (1973) *Theories of Value and Distribution since Adam Smith* (Cambridge: Cambridge University Press).

Dos Santos, T. (1970) 'The structure of dependence', *American Economic Review*, **60**, 2.

Dragsted, A., ed. (1976) *Value: Studies by Marx* (London: New Park).

Duménil, G. (1975) *La position de classe des cadres et employés. La fonction capitaliste parcellaire* (Grenoble: Presses Universitaires de Grenoble).

Duménil, G. (1980) *De la valeur aux prix de production* (Paris: Économica).

Duménil G., Glick M. and Lévy D. (1997) 'The history of competition policy as economic history', *The Antitrust Bulletin*, **42**, 2.

Duménil, G. and Lévy, D. (1991) 'Szumski's validation of the labour theory of value: a comment', *Cambridge Journal of Economics*, **15**, 3.

Duménil, G. and Lévy, D. (1993) *The Economics of the Profit Rate: Competition, Crises, and Historical Tendencies in Capitalism* (Aldershot: Edward Elgar).

Duménil, G. and Lévy D. (1994) 'The emergence and functions of managerial and clerical personnel in Marx's capital', in N. Garston, ed., *Bureaucracy: Three Paradigms* (Boston: Kluwer Academic).

Duménil, G. and Lévy D. (2000) 'The conservation of value: a rejoinder to Alan Freeman', *Review of Radical Political Economy*, **32**, 1.

Duménil, G. and Lévy D. (2001a) 'Periodizing capitalism: technology, institutions and relations of production', in Albritton, Itoh, Westra and Zuege, eds (2001).

Duménil, G. and Lévy D. (2001b) 'Costs and benefits of neoliberalism: a class analysis', *Review of International Political Economy*, **8**, 4.

Dunayevskaya, R. (1989) *Marxism and Freedom: From 1776 until Today* (New York: Columbia University Press).

Dunayevskaya, R. (1991) *Rosa Luxemburg, Women's Liberation, and Marx's Philosophy of Revolution* (Urbana and Chicago: University of Illinois Press).

Dunn, P., ed. (1991) *Quantitative Marxism* (Cambridge: Polity Press).

Dunn, P. (2000) *'Labour-Power and the Value-Form'*, Paper presented to the 2000 mini-conference of the IWGVT at the Eastern Economic Association, Washington, D.C., March (available at www.gre.ac.uk/~fa03/iwgvt).

Dunn, P. (2002) *'On the Identity of Value and Labour: A Defence of Intrinsic Value'*, Paper presented to the 2002 mini-conference of the IWGVT at the Eastern Economic Association, Boston, March (available at www.gre.ac.uk/~fa03/iwgvt).

Dussel, E. (2001) *Towards an Unknown Marx* (London: Routledge).

Eatwell, J., Milgate, M. and Newman, P., eds (1987) *The New Palgrave: Marxian Economics* (London: Macmillan).

Economist (2002) *Special Report Wall Street*, June 8, 63–66.

Edwards, C. (1985) *The Fragmented World: Competing Perspectives on Trade, Money and Crisis* (London: Methuen).

Ehrbar H. and Glick M. (1986) 'The labor theory of value and its critics', *Science & Society*, **50**, 4.

Ehrbar, H.G. (1989) 'Mathematics and the labor theory of value', *Review of Radical Political Economics*, **21**, 3.

Ehrbar, H.G. (2002) *'Critical Realist Arguments in Marx's Capital'*, in Brown, Fleetwood and Roberts, eds.

Eldred, M. and Roth, M. (1978) *Guide to Marx's 'Capital'* (London: CSE Books).

Eldred, M. and Roth, M. (1980) 'Introduction to H.-G. Backhaus', *Thesis Eleven*, **1**.

Eldred, M. and Hanlon, M. (1981) 'Reconstructing value-form analysis', *Capital & Class*, **13**.

Eldred, M. (1984a) 'A reply to Gleicher', *Capital & Class*, **23**, reprinted in Mohun (1998).

Eldred, M. (1984b) 'Japanese marxism: Uno and Itoh', *Thesis Eleven*, **8**.

Elson, D., ed. (1979a) *Value: The Representation of Labor in Capitalism* (London: CSE Books).

Elson, D. (1979b) 'The value theory of labour', in Elson ed. (1979a).

Emmanuel, A. (1972) *Unequal Exchange* (London: New Left Books).

Ernst, J. (1982) 'Simultaneous valuation extirpated: a contribution to the critique of the neo-ricardian concept of value', *Review of Radical Political Economics*, **14**, 2.

Evans, T. (2003) 'Marxian and post-keynesian theories of finance and the business cycle', *Capital & Class*, forthcoming.

Faccarello, G. (1998) 'Some reflections on Marx's theory of value', in Bellofiore, ed., Volume 1.

Farjoun, E. and Machover, E. (1983) *Laws of Chaos: A Probabilistic Approach to Political Economy* (London: Verso).

Fine, B. (1980) *Economic Theory and Ideology* (London: Edward Arnold).

Fine, B. (1982) *Theories of the Capitalist Economy* (London: Edward Arnold).

Fine, B. (1985/6) 'Banking capital and the theory of interest', *Science & Society*, **49**, 4.

Fine, B. ed. (1986) *The Value Dimension: Marx versus Ricardo and Sraffa* (London: Routledge and Kegan Paul).

Fine, B. (1988) 'From capital in production to capital in exchange', *Science & Society*, **52**, 3.

Fine, B. (1989) *Marx's 'Capital'*, Third Edition (London: Macmillan).

Fine, B. (1990) *The Coal Question: Political Economy and Industrial Change from the Nineteenth Century to the Present Day* (London: Routledge).

Fine, B. (1992) *Women's Employment and the Capitalist Family* (London: Routledge).

Fine, B. (1994) 'Coal, diamonds and Oil: towards a comparative theory of mining', *Review of Political Economy*, **6**, 3.

Fine, B. (1995) 'Flexible production and flexible theory: the case of South Africa', *Geoforum*, **26**, 2.

Fine, B. (1997) 'The new revolution in economics', *Capital & Class*, **61**.

Fine, B. (1998a) *Labor Market Theory: A Constructive Reassessment* (London: Routledge).

Fine, B. (1998b) *The Political Economy of Diet, Health and Food Policy* (London: Routledge).

Fine, B. (1998c) 'Value theory: a personal account', Translated into Greek, *Utopia*, **28**.

Fine, B. (2000) 'Endogenous growth theory: a critical assessment', *Cambridge Journal of Economics*, **24**, 2.

Fine, B. (2001a) *Social Capital versus Social Theory: Political Economy and Social Science at the Turn of the Millennium* (London: Routledge).

Fine, B. (2001b) 'The continuing imperative of value theory', *Capital & Class*, **75**.

Fine, B. (2002a) *The World of Consumption: The Material and Cultural Revisited* (London: Routledge).

Fine, B. (2002b) 'Globalization and development: the imperative of political economy', Paper presented to the conference, *Towards a New Political Economy of Development: Globalization and Governance*, Sheffield, July.

Fine, B. and Harris, L. (1979) *Rereading 'Capital'* (London: Macmillan).

Fine, B., Heasman, M. and Wright, J. (1996) *Consumption in the Age of Affluence: The World of Food* (London: Routledge).

Fine, B. and Lapavitsas, C. (2000) 'Markets and money in social theory: what role for economics?', *Economic and Society*, **29**, 3.

Fine, B. and Leopold, E. (1993) *The World of Consumption* (London: Routledge).

Fine, B. and Rustomjee, Z. (1997) *South Africa's Political Economy: From Minerals-Energy Complex to Industrialization* (London: Hurst).

Fine, B. *et al.* (2001) *'Transforming the Transformation Problem: Why the "New Solution" is a Wrong Turning'*, mimeo.

Fleetwood, S., ed. (1999) *Critical Realism in Economics: Development and Debate* (London: Routledge).

Foley, D. (1982) 'Value of money, the value of labor power and the marxian transformation problem', *Review of Radical Political Economics*, **14**.

Foley, D. (1986) *Understanding Capital: Marx's Economic Theory* (Cambridge: Harvard University Press).
Foley, D. (1989) 'Roemer on Marx on exploitation', *Economics and Politics*, **1**, 2.
Foley, D. (1997) 'Review of Marx and Non-equilibrium economics', *Eastern Economic Journal*, **23**, 4.
Foley, D. (2000a) 'Recent developments in the labor theory of value', *Review of Radical Political Economy*, **32**, 1.
Foley, D. (2000b) 'Response to Freeman and Kliman', *Research in Political Economy*, **18**.
Freeman, A. (1995a) 'Marx without equilibrium', *Capital & Class*, **56**.
Freeman, A. (1995b) 'Price, value and profit – a continuous, general, treatment', in Freeman and Carchedi, eds (1995).
Freeman, A. (1997a) 'If They're So Rich, Why Ain't They Smart?: Another Prelude to the Critique of Economic Theory', in International Working Group on Value Theory, 1997 Mini-Conference Working Papers (available at www.gre.ac.uk/~fa03/iwgvt).
Freeman, A. (1997b) 'Time, the Value of Money and the Quantification of Value', Paper presented to the 1997 mini-conference of the IWGVT at the Eastern Economic Association, Washington, D.C., April (available at www.gre.ac.uk/~fa03/iwgvt).
Freeman, A. (2001a) 'Money: What it is and what it Represents', Paper presented to 2001 IWGVT Summer Symposium, Greenwich, London, July (available at http://www.gre.ac.uk/~fa03/symposium/2001/programme.html).
Freeman, A. (2001b) 'Value from Nowhere: A Response to Duménil and Lévy', Working Paper.
Freeman, A. and Carchedi, G., eds (1995) *Marx and Non-Equilibrium Economics* (Cheltenham: Edward Elgar).
Freeman, A., Kliman, A. and Wells, P.J., eds (2003) *The New Value Controversy* (Cheltenham: Edward Elgar).
Galbraith, J.K. (1967) *The New Industrial State* (Boston: Houghton Mifflin).
Garcia De LA Sienra, A. (1992) *Logical Foundations of the Marxian Theory of Value* (Boston: Kluwer).
Garegnani, P. (1991) 'The labour theory of value: "detour" or technical advance?', in Caravale, ed.
Gerstein, I. (1986) 'Production, circulation and value: the significance of the "transformation problem"' in Fine, *Marx's Critique of Political Economy*. ed.
Giussani, P. (1991) 'The determination of prices of production', *International Journal of Political Economy*, **21**, Winter.
Giussani, P. (1996) 'Empirical evidence for trends toward globalization: the discovery of hot air', *International Journal of Political Economy*, **26**, 3.
Gleicher, D. (1984) 'A historical approach to the question of abstract labour', *Capital & Class*, **21**, reprinted in Mohun (1994a).
Gleicher, D. (1985a) 'Abstract labor, the Rubin school and the marxist theory of value', *Capital & Class*, **24**, reprinted in Mohun (1994a).
Gleicher, D. (1985b) 'Note: a rejoinder to Eldred', *Capital & Class*, **24**.
Gleicher, D. (1985–86) 'The ontology of labour values', *Science & Society*, **49**, 4.
Glick, D. and Ehrbar, H. (1985) 'The transformation problem: an obituary', *Australian Economic Papers*, **26**, 49.
Glick, M. and Ehrbar, H. (1986–87) 'The labour theory of value and its critics', *Science & Society*, **50**, 4.
Gough, J. (1996a) 'Not flexible accumulation: contradictions of value in contemporary economic geography, Part 1: workplace and inter-firm relations', *Environment and Planning A*, **28**.

Gough, J. (1996b) 'Not flexible accumulation: contradictions of value in contemporary economic geography, Part 2: regional regimes, national regulation and political strategy', *Environment and Planning A*, **28**.

Gowan, P. (1999) *The Global Gamble: Washington's Faustian Bid for World Dominance* (London: Verso).

Green, F. (1991a) 'Marx, Malthus, and wages: a comment on Cottrell and Darity', *History of Political Economy*, **23**, 1.

Green, F. (1991b) 'The relationship of wages to the value of labour-power in Marx's labour market', *Cambridge Journal of Economics*, **2**.

Green, F. and Nore, P., eds (1977) *Economics: An Anti-Text* (London: Macmillan).

Green, F. and Nore, P., eds (1979) *Issues in Political Economy* (London: Macmillan).

Green, F. and Sutcliffe, B. (1987) *The Profit System: The Economics of Capitalism* (Harmondsworth: Penguin).

Greenspan, A. (2000) 'Technology and the Economy', Remarks before the Economic Club of New York, www.internetstockreport.com/reporter/article/0,1785,1941_283491, 00.html.

Grossman, H. (1992) *The Law of Accumulation and the Breakdown of the Capitalist System*, translated and abridged by J. Banaji (London: Pluto).

Gunder-Frank, A. (1969) *Latin America: Underdevelopment or Revolution* (New York: Monthly Review Press).

Hahn, F.H. (1982) *Money and Inflation* (Oxford: Blackwell).

Harcourt, G.C. (1972) *Some Cambridge Controversies in the Theory of Capital* (Cambridge: Cambridge University Press).

Harcourt, G.C. (1976) 'The cambridge controversies: old ways and new horizons – or dead end', *Oxford Economic Papers*, **28**, 1.

Hartsock, C.M. (1998) *The Feminist Standpoint Revisited and Other Essays* (Boulder: Westview Press).

Harvey, D. (1982) *The Limits to Capital* (Chicago: University of Chicago Press).

Harvey, D. (1996) *Justice, Nature and the Geography of Difference* (Oxford: Blackwell).

Hegel, G.W.F. (1971) *Philosophy of Right*, translated by T.M. Knox (Oxford: Oxford University press).

Hegel, G.W.F. (1991) *The Encyclopedia Logic* (Indianapolis: Hacket Publishing).

Held, D., McGrew, A., Goldblatt, D. and Perraton, J. (1999) *Global Transformations: Politics, Economics and Culture* (Stanford, CA: Stanford University Press).

Himmelweit, S. and Mohun, S. (1981) 'Real abstractions and anomalous assumptions', in Steedman, ed.

Hirst, P. and Thompson, G. (1996) *Globalization in Question* (Cambridge: Polity Press).

Hodgson, G. (1982) *Capitalism, Value and Exploitation* (London: Robertson).

Hodgson, G.M. (1997) 'The fate of the Cambridge Capital Controversy', in Arestis, Palma and Sawyer, eds.

Hodgson, G.M. (1991) *After Marx and Sraffa* (Basingstoke: Macmillan).

Hollander, S. (1984) 'Marx and Malthusianism: Marx's secular path of wages', *American Economic Review*, **74**, 1.

Hollander, S. (1986) 'Marx and Malthusianism: reply', *The American Economic Review*, **76**, 3.

Hollingsworth, J.R. and Boyer, R., eds (1998) *Contemporary Capitalism: The Embeddedness of Institutions* (Cambridge: Cambridge University Press).

Holloway, J. (1992) 'Crisis, fetishism and class composition', in Bonefeld, Gunn and Psychopedis, eds, Volume 2.

Howard, M.C. (1983) *Profits in Economic Theory* (London: Macmillan).

Howard, M.C. and King, J.E. (1985) *The Political Economy of Marx*, Second Edition (London: Longman).

Howard, M.C. and King, J.E. (1992) *A History of Marxian Economics*, 2 Volumes (Princeton: Princeton University Press).

Hunt, E.K. (1979) 'Marx as a social economist: the labor theory of value', *Review of Social Economy*, **37**, 3.

Hunt, E.K. (2002) *History of Economic Thought: A Critical Perspective*, Updated Second Edition (Armonk: M.E. Sharpe).

Ietto-Gilles, G. (2002) *Transnational Corporations: Fragmentation amidst Integration* (London: Routledge).

Ilyenkov, E.V. (1982) *The Dialectics of the Abstract and the Concrete in Marx's 'Capital'* (Moscow: Progress).

Itoh, M. (1980) *Value and Crisis* (New York: Monthly Review Press).

Itoh, M. (1988) *The Basic Theory of Capitalism* (London: Macmillan).

Itoh, M. and Lapavitsas, C. (1998) *Political Economy of Money and Finance* (London: Macmillan).

Jessop, B. (1990) *State Theory: Putting the Capitalist State in its Place* (University Park: The Pennsylvania State University Press).

Junankar, P.N. (1982) *Marx's Economics* (London: Philip Allan).

Kahn, H. (1967) *The Year 2000: A Framework for Speculation on the next Thirty-three Years* (New York: Macmillan).

Kant, E. (1933) *The Critique of Pure Reason* (London: Macmillan).

Kay, G. (1979a) *Economic Theory of the Working Class* (London: Macmillan).

Kay, G. (1979b) 'Why labour is the starting point of capital', in Elson, ed. (1979).

Kay, G. (1999) 'Abstract labour and capital', *Historical Materialism*, **5**.

Keen, S. (2001) *Debunking Economics* (London: Pluto).

Keynes, J.M. (1930) *A Treatise on Money*, 2 Volumes (London: Macmillan).

Keynes, J.M. (1936) *The General Theory of Employment, Interest and Money* (London: Macmillan).

King, M. (1993) *'Debt Deflation: Theory and Evidence'*, Presidential Lecture, European Economic Association, 27 August, Helsinki.

Kitschelt, H., Lange, P., Marks, G. and Stephens, J.D., eds (1999) *Continuity and Change in Contemporary Capitalism* (Cambridge: Cambridge University Press).

Kliman, A. (1988) 'The Profit Rate Under Continuous Technological Change', *Review of Radical Political Economics*, **20**, 2&3.

Kliman, A. (1993) 'Value in process: a reply to Naples', *Capital & Class*, **51**.

Kliman, A. (1996) 'A value-theoretic critique of the Okishio Theorem', in Freeman and Carchedi, eds.

Kliman, A. (1997) 'A Contribution to the Ongoing Inquiry into the Existence of Marx's Marxism', in International Working Group on Value Theory, 1997 Mini-Conference Working Papers (available at www.gre.ac.uk/~fa03/iwgvt).

Kliman, A. (2000) 'Marx's concept of intrinsic value', *Historical Materialism*, **6**.

Kliman, A. (2001) 'Simultaneous valuation vs. the exploitation theory of profit', *Capital & Class*, **73**.

Kliman, A. (2002a) 'Stigler and Barkai on Ricardo's Profit Rate Theory: Some Methodological Considerations 35 Years Later', Paper presented to the 2002 mini-conference of the IWGVT at the Eastern Economic Association, Boston, March (available at www.gre.ac.uk/~fa03/iwgvt).

Kliman, A. (2002b) 'The law of value and laws of statistics: sectoral values and prices in the US economy, 1977–97', *Cambridge Journal of Economics*, **26**.

Kliman, A. and Freeman, A. (2000) 'Rejoinder to Duncan Foley and David Laibman', *Research in Political Economy*, **18**.

Kliman, A. and McGlone, T. (1988) 'The transformation non-problem and the non-transformation problem', *Capital & Class*, **35**.

Knafo, S. (2002) 'The fetishizing subject in Marx's *Capital*', *Capital & Class*, **76**.

Kobrin, S.J. (1999) 'Back to the future: neomedievalism and the postmodern digital world economy', in A. Prakash and J.A. Hart, eds, *Globalization and Governance* (London: Routledge).

Krause, U. (1982) *Money and Abstract Labour* (London: Verso).

Krugman, P., ed. (1986) *Strategic Trade Policy and the New International Economics* (Cambridge, MA: MIT Press).

Kuhn, T.S. (1962) *The Structure of Scientific Revolutions* (Chicago: University of Chicago Press).

Kühne, K. (1979) *Economics and Marxism*, 2 Volumes (London: Macmillan).

Lacan, J. (1977) *Ecrits: A Selection* (New York: Norton).

Laibman, D. (1991) *Value, Technical Change, and Crisis* (New York: M.E. Sharpe).

Laibman, D. (1997) *Capitalist Macrodynamics: A Systematic Introduction* (Houndmills and London: Macmillan).

Laibman, D. (1999) 'Okishio and his critics: historical cost versus replacement cost', *Research in Political Economy*, **17**.

Laibman, D. (2000a) 'Rhetoric and substance in value theory: an appraisal of the new orthodox marxism', *Science & Society*, **64**, 3.

Laibman, D. (2000b) 'Two of everything: a response', *Research in Political Economy*, **18**.

Laibman, D. (2001a) 'Rising material vs. falling values rates of profit: trial by simulation', *Capital & Class*, **73**.

Laibman, D. (2001b) 'Temporalism and textualism in value theory: rejoinder', *Science & Society*, **65**, 4.

Laibman, D. (2002) 'Value and the quest for the core of capitalism', *Review of Radical Political Economics*, **34**, 2.

Larner, W. and Walters, W. (2002) 'The political rationality of "new regionalism": toward a genealogy of the region', *Theory and Society*, **31**.

Lawson, T. (1997) *Economics and Reality* (London: Routledge).

Lebowitz, M. (1973–74) 'The current crisis in economic theory', *Science & Society*, **37**, 4.

Lebowitz, M. (1976) 'Marx's falling rate of profit: a dialectical view', *Canadian Journal of Economics*, **9**, 2.

Lebowitz, M. (1985) 'The theoretical status of monopoly capital', in Resnick and Wolff, eds.

Lebowitz, M. (1992) *Beyond Capital: Marx's Political Economy of the Working Class* (London: Macmillan).

Lee, C.-O. (1993) 'Marx's labour theory of value revisited', *Cambridge Journal of Economics*, **17**, 4.

Levine, D. (1977) *Economic Studies: Contribution to the Critique of Economic Theory* (London: Routledge and Kegan Paul).

Levine, D. (1978) *Economic Theory*, 2 Volumes (London: Routledge and Kegan Paul).

Likitkijsomboon, P. (1995) 'Marxian theories of value-form', *Review of Radical Political Economics*, **27**, 2.

Linder, M. (1977) *The Anti-Samuelson*, 2 Volumes (New York: Urizen).

Lipietz, A. (1982) 'The so-called "transformation problem" revisited', *Journal of Economic Theory*, **26**, 1.

Lippi, M. (1979) *Value and Naturalism in Marx* (London: New Left Books).

Louçã, F. (1997) *Turbulence in Economics: An Evolutionary Appraisal of Cycles and Complexity in Historical Processes* (Cheltenham: Edward Elgar).

Mage, S. (1963) *'The Law of the Falling Tendency of the Rate of Profit: Its Place in the Marxian System and Relevance to the US Economy'*, Ph.D. Thesis (New York: Columbia University).

Maldonado-Filho, E. (1997) 'Release and Tying up of Productive Capital and the "Transformation Problem"', Paper presented to the 1997 mini-conference of the IWGVT at the Eastern Economic Association, Washington, D.C., April (available at www.gre.ac.uk/~fa03/iwgvt).

Mandel, E. (1968) *Marxist Economic Theory*, Volume 1 (New York: Monthly Review Press).

Mandel, E. (1975) *Late Capitalism* (London: New Left Books).

Mandel, E. (1995) *Long Waves of Capitalist Development*, Second Edition (London: Verso).

Mandel, E. and Freeman, A., eds (1984) *Ricardo, Marx, Sraffa* (London: Verso).

Maniatis, T. (1996) 'Testing Marx: a note', *Capital & Class*, **59**.

Marsden, R. (1998) 'The unknown masterpiece: Marx's model of *Capital*', *Cambridge Journal of Economics*, **22**, 3.

Marx, K. (1867) *Capital*, Volume 1 (Harmondsworth: Penguin).

Marx, K. (1885) *Capital*, Volume 2 (Harmondsworth: Penguin).

Marx, K. (1935) *The Poverty of Philosophy* (Moscow: Cooperative Publishing Society of Foreign Workers in the USSR).

Marx, K. (1963) *Theories of Surplus Value*, Part 1 (Moscow: Progress).

Marx, K. (1967a) *Capital: A Critique of Political Economy*, Volume 1 (New York: International Publishers).

Marx, K. (1967b) *Capital: A Critique of Political Economy*, Volume 3 (New York: International Publishers).

Marx, K. (1968) *Theories of Surplus Value*, Part 2 (Moscow: Progress).

Marx, K. (1971) *Theories of Surplus Value*, Part 3 (Moscow: Progress).

Marx, K. (1972) *Theories of Surplus Value*, Part 3 (London: Lawrence and Wishart).

Marx, K. (1973) *Grundrisse: Foundations of the Critique of Political Economy* (Harmondsworth: Penguin).

Marx, K. (1976) *Capital: A Critique of Political Economy*, Volume 1 (Harmondsworth: Penguin).

Marx, K. (1977) *Capital: A Critique of Political Economy*, Volume 1 (New York: Vintage).

Marx, K. (1978) *Capital: A Critique of Political Economy*, Volume 2 (New York: Vintage).

Marx, K. (1981) *Capital: A Critique of Political Economy*, Volume 3 (New York: Vintage).

Marx, K. (1991) *Capital: A Critique of Political Economy*, Volume 3 (Harmondsworth: Penguin Classics).

Marx, K. and Engels, F. (1982) *Marx Engels Select Correspondence* (Moscow: Progress).

Mattick, P. (1969) *Marx and Keynes* (London: Merlin).

Mattick, P. (1981) *Economic Crisis and Crisis Theory* (London: Merlin).

Mattick, P. (1983) *Marxism: Last Refuge of the Bourgeoisie* (Armonk: M.E. Sharpe).

Mattick, P. Jr (1981) 'Some aspects of the value-price problem', *Economies et Societés*, **15**.

Mattick, P. Jr (1986) *Social Knowledge* (Armonk: M.E. Sharpe).

Mátyás, A. (1985) *History of Modern Non-Marxian Economics*, Second Edition (London: Macmillan).

McMichael, P. (2000) 'Globalisation: trend or project?', in R. Palan, ed., *Global Political Economy: Contemporary Theories* (London: Routledge).

McNally, D. (1988) *Political Economy and the Rise of Capitalism: A Reinterpretation* (Berkeley: University of California Press).

McMurtry, J. (1999) *The Cancer Stage of Capitalism* (London: Pluto Press).
Meek, R. (1956) *Studies in the Labor Theory of Value* (New York: Monthly Review Press).
Miller, A.V. (1969) *Hegel's Science of Logic* (New Jersey: Humanities Press).
Milios, J., Dimoulis, D. and Economakis, G. (2002) 'Karl Marx and the Classics: An Essay on Value', *Crises and the Capitalist Mode of Production* (Ashgate: Aldershot).
Milonakis, D. (1995) 'Commodity production and price formation before capitalism: a value-theoretic approach', *Journal of Peasant Studies*, **22**, 2.
Milward, B. (2000) *Marxian Political Economy* (Basingstoke: Macmillan).
Minsky, H. (1982) *Can 'It' Happen Again?: Essays on Instability and Finance* (Armonk: M.E. Sharpe).
Mittelman, J.H. (2000) *The Globalization Syndrome: Transformation and Resistance* (Princeton, NJ: Princeton University Press).
Mohun, S. (1984) 'Abstract labour and its value form', *Science & Society*, **47**, 4.
Mohun, S. (1985) 'Value theory', in Z. Baranski and J. Short, eds, *Developing Contemporary Marxism* (London: Macmillan).
Mohun, S. (1991) 'Value', in T. Bottomore, ed., *A Dictionary of Marxist Economic Thought*, Second Edition (Oxford: Blackwell).
Mohun, S., ed. (1994a) *Debates in Value Theory* (London: Macmillan).
Mohun, S. (1994b) '*Value, Value-Form and Money*', in Mohun (1994a).
Mohun, S. (1994c) 'A re(in)statement of the labour theory of value', *Cambridge Journal of Economics*, **18**, 4.
Mohun, S. (2000) 'New solution or re(in)statement? a reply', *Cambridge Journal of Economics*, **24**.
Mohun, S. (2001) 'On Two Recent Approaches to Accounting for Value', Paper presented to 2001 IWGVT Summer Symposium, Greenwich, London, July (available at http:/ /www.gre.ac.uk/~fa03/symposium/2001/programme.html).
Mongiovi, G. (2002) 'Vulgar economy in marxian garb: a critique of temporal single system marxism', *Review of Radical Political Economics*, **34**, 4.
Mongiovi, G. and Petri, F., eds (1999) *Value, Distribution and Capital* (London: Routledge).
Moran, J. (1998) 'The dynamics of class politics and national economies in globalisation: the marginalisation of the unacceptable', *Capital & Class*, **66**.
Morishima, M. (1973) *Marx's Economics – A Dual Theory of Value and Growth* (Cambridge: Cambridge University Press).
Morishima, M. (1978) *Value, Exploitation and Growth* (London: McGraw-Hill).
Moseley, F. (1991) *The Falling Rate of Profit in the Postwar United States Economy* (London: Macmillan).
Moseley, F. and Wolff, E.N. (1992) *International Perspectives on Profitability and Accumulation* (Aldershot: Edward Elgar).
Moseley, F., ed. (1993a) *Marx's Method in 'Capital': A Re-examination* (Atlantic Highlands: Humanities Press).
Moseley, F. (1993b) 'Marx's logical method and the "Transformation Problem" ', in Moseley (1993a).
Moseley, F., ed. (1995) *Heterodox Economic Theories: True or False* (Aldershot: Edward Elgar).
Moseley, F. (1997) 'The rate of profit and the future of capitalism', *Review of Radical Political Economics*, **29**, 4.
Moseley, F. (2000a) 'The "new solution" to the transformation problem: a sympathetic critique', *Review of Radical Political Economics*, **32**, 2.
Moseley, F. (2000b) 'The Determination of Constant Capital in the Case of a Change in the Value of the Means of Production', Paper presented to the 2000 mini-conference

of the IWGVT at the Eastern Economic Association, Washington, D.C., March (available at www.gre.ac.uk/~fa03/iwgvt).
Moseley, F. (2001) 'Marx's alleged logical error: a comment', *Science & Society*, **65**, 4.
Moseley, F. and Campbell, M., eds (1997) *New Investigations of Marx's Method* (Atlantic Highlands, NJ: Humanities Press).
Mulberg, J. (1995) *Social Limits to Economic Theory* (London: Routledge).
Murray, P. (1988) *Marx's Theory of Scientific Knowledge* (Atlantic Highlands: Humanities Press).
Murray, P. (1993) 'The necessity of money: how Hegel helped Marx surpass Ricardo's theory of value', in Moseley, ed. (1993a).
Myrdal, G. (1939) *Monetary Equilibrium* (London: William Hodge).
Nagahara, Y. (2000) '*Monsieur le Capital* and *Madame la Terre* Do Their Ghost-Dance: Globalization and the Nation State', *South Atlantic Quarterly*, **99**, 4.
Nagatani, K. (1997) 'Value-Form as a Starting Point of Uno Theory' (available at http://homepage2.nifty.com/nagatani-kiyoshi/my%20works.html).
Naples, M. (1989) 'A radical economic revision of the transformation problem', *Review of Radical Political Economics*, **21**, 1–2.
Naples, M. (1993) 'Unperceived inflation in Shaikh, and Kliman and McGlone: equilibrium, disequilibrium, or nonequilibrium?', *Capital & Class*, **51**.
Napoleoni, C. (1975) *Smith, Ricardo, Marx* (Oxford: Blackwell).
Nelson, A. (1999) *Marx's Concept of Money* (London: Routledge).
Oakley, A. (1983) *The Making of Marx's Critical Theory* (London: Routledge and Kegan Paul).
Oakley, A. (1984, 1985) *Marx's Critique of Political Economy: Intellectual Sources and Evolution*, 2 Volumes (London: Routledge and Kegan Paul).
Ochoa, E. (1984) '*Labor Values and Prices of Production: An Inderindustry Study of the U.S. Economy, 1947–1972*', Ph.D. Thesis (New York: New School for Social Research).
Ochoa, E. (1989) 'Values, prices and wage-profit curves in the U.S. economy', *Cambridge Journal of Economics*, **13**.
O'Hara, P., ed. (1999) *Encyclopedia of Political Economy* (London: Routledge).
Okishio, N. (1961) 'Technical changes and the rate of profit', *Kobe University Economic Review*, **7**.
Ong, N.P. (1983) 'Ricardo's invariable measure of value and Sraffa's "standard commodity" ', *History of Political Economy*, **15**.
Osadchaya, I. (1974) *From Keynes to Neoclassical Synthesis* (Moscow: Progress).
Palan, R. (1998) 'Trying to have your cake and eating it: how and why the state system has created offshore', *International Studies Quarterly*, **42**.
Palloix, C. (1971) *L'Economie Modiale Capitaliste*, 2 Volumes (Paris: Maspero).
Palloix, C. (1973) 'The internationalization of capital and the circuit of social capital', in H. Radice, ed., *International Firms and Modern Imperialism* (Harmondsworth: Penguin).
Panico, C. (1988) 'Marx on the banking sector and the interest rate: some initial notes for a discussion', *Science & Society*, **52**, 3.
Paños, E.F. (2000) 'A re(in)statement of the labor theory of value: a comment', *Cambridge Journal of Economics*, **24**.
Pashukanis, E.B. (1978) *Law and Marxism* (London: Ink Links).
Pasinetti, L. (1977) *Lectures on the Theory of Production* (New York: Columbia University Press).
Petrovic, P. (1987) 'The deviation of production prices from labour values: some methodology and empirical evidence', *Cambridge Journal of Economics*, **11**, 3.

Perelman, M. (1987) *Marx's Crises Theory: Labour, Scarcity, Finance* (New York: Praeger).
Perelman, M. (1993) 'The qualitative side to Marx's value theory', *Rethinking Marxism*, **6**, 1.
Perelman, M. (1999) 'Marx, devalorisation, and the theory of value', *Cambridge Journal of Economics*, **23**.
Perez, C. (2002) *Technological Revolutions and Financial Capital* (Aldershot: Elgar).
Pevsner, Y. (1982) *State Monopoly Capitalism and the Labour Theory of Value* (Moscow: Progress).
Pilling, G. (1980) *Marx's 'Capital': Philosophy and Political Economy* (London: Routledge and Kegan Paul).
Pilling, G. (1986) 'The law of value in Marx and Ricardo', in Fine, ed.
Polanyi, K. (1957) *The Great Transformation: The Political and economic Origins of Our Time* (Boston: Beacon Press).
Popper, K. (1968) *The Logic of Scientific Discovery* (New York: Harper).
Postone, M. (1993) *Time, Labor, and Social Domination* (Cambridge: Cambridge University Press).
Postone, M. (1996) *Time, Labour, and Social Domination* (Cambridge: Cambridge University Press).
Poulantzas N. (1974) *Social Classes in Contemporary Capitalism* (London: New Left Books).
Prakash, A. (2001) 'Grappling with globalisation: challenges for economic governance', *The World Economy* **24**, 4.
Ramirez, M.D. (1986) 'Marx and malthusianism: comment', *American Economic Review*, **76**, 3.
Ramos, A. (1995) 'The Monetary Expression of Labor: Marx's Twofold Measure of Value', Paper presented to the 1995 mini-conference of the IWGVT at the Eastern Economic Association (available at www.gre.ac.uk/~fa03/iwgvt).
Ramos, A. (2003) 'Labour, money, labour-saving innovation and the falling rate of profit', in Freeman, Kliman and Wells, eds.
Resnick, S. and Wolff, R., eds (1985) *Rethinking Marxism: Struggles in Marxist Theory. Essays for Harry Magdoff and Paul Sweezy* (New York: Autonomedia).
Resnick, S. and Wolff, R. (1987) *Knowledge and Class* (Chicago: University of Chicago Press).
Reuten, G. (1999) 'The source versus measure obstacle in value theory', *Rivista di Politica Economica*, **89**, 4–5.
Reuten, G. and Williams, M. (1988) *Value-Form and the state* (London: Routledge).
Reuten, G. and Williams, M. (1989) *Value-Form and the State: The Tendencies of Accumulation and the Determination of Economic Policy in Capitalist Society* (London: Routledge).
Ricardo, D. (1951) [1821] *On the Principles of Political Economy and Taxation* (Cambridge: Cambridge University Press).
Roberts, B. (1987) 'Marx after Steedman: separating Marx from "surplus theory"', *Capital & Class*, **32**.
Roberts, B. (1996) 'The visible and the measurable: Althusser and the marxian theory of value', in A. Callari and D. Ruccio, eds, *Postmodern Marxism and the Future of Marxist Theory: Essays in the Althusserian Tradition* (Hannover: Wesleyan University Press).
Roberts, B. (1998) 'Review of Marx and non-equilibrium economics', *Science & Society*, **62**, 2.
Roberts, B. and Feiner, S., eds (1992) *Radical Economics* (Dordrecht: Kluwer Academic).
Robinson, J. (1953) *On Re-Reading Marx* (Cambridge: Cambridge University Press).
Robinson, J. (1965) *'A reconsideration of the labour theory of value'*, in J. Robinson, ed., *Collected Economic Papers III* (Oxford: Oxford University Press).

Roche, J. (1988) 'Value, money, and crisis in the first part of capital', *Rethinking Marxism*, **1**, 4.

Roemer, J. (1981) *The Analytical Foundations of Marxian Economic Theory* (Cambridge: Cambridge University Press).

Roemer, J. (1986) *Value, Exploitation and Class* (New York: Horwood).

Roemer, J. (1990) 'Review of Duncan K. Foley, Understanding capital', *Journal of Economic Literature*, **27**, 4.

Roll, E. (1992) *A History of Economic Thought*, Fifth Edition (London: Farber and Farber).

Roosevelt, F. (1977) 'Cambridge economics as commodity fetishism', in Schwartz, ed.

Rosdolsky, R. (1977) *The Making of Marx's 'Capital'* (London: Pluto Press).

Rosenthal, J. (1997) *The Myth of Dialectics: Reinterpreting the Marx-Hegel Relation* (London: Macmillan).

Routh, G. (1989) *The Origin of Economic Ideas*, Second Edition (Basingstoke: Macmillan).

Rowthorn, B. (1974) 'Neo-classicism, neo-ricardianism and marxism', *New Left Review*, **86**.

Rubin, I.I. (1972) *Essays on Marx's Theory of Value* (Detroit: Black and Red).

Rubin, I.I. (1979) *A History of Economic Thought* (London: Ink Links).

Rubin, I.I. (1994) [1927] 'Abstract labour and value in Marx's system', *Capital & Class*, **5**, Reprinted in Mohun (1994a).

Saad-Filho, A. (1996), 'The value of money, the value of labour power and the net product: An appraisal of the "New Solution" to the transformation problem', in Freeman and Carchedi, eds.

Saad-Filho, A. (1997) 'Concrete and abstract labour in Marx's theory of value', *Review of Political Economy*, **9**, 4.

Saad-Filho, A. (2002) *The Value of Marx: Political Economy for Contemporary Capitalism* (London: Routledge).

Saad-Filho, A., ed. (2003) *Anti-Capitalism: A Marxist Introduction* (London: Pluto).

Samuelson, P. (1971) 'Understanding the marxian notion of exploitation: a summary of the so-called "transformation problem" between marxian values and competitive prices', *Journal of Economic Literature*, **9**, 2.

Sawyer, M. (1989) *The Challenge of Radical Political Economy* (London: Harvester Wheatsheaf).

Sayer, A. (1995) *Radical Political Economy: A Critique* (Oxford: Blackwell).

Schumpeter, J. (1961) *History of Economic Analysis* (New York: Oxford University Press).

Schwartz, J.G., ed. (1977) *The Subtle Anatomy of Capitalism* (Santa Monica, CA: Goodyear).

Sekine, T. (1975) 'Uno-riron: a Japanese contribution to marxian political economy', *Journal of Economic Literature*, **13**.

Sekine, T. (1997) *An Outline of the Dialectic of Capital*, 2 Volumes (London: Macmillan).

Sekine, T. (1998) 'The dialectic of capital: an unoist interpretation', *Science & Society*, **62**, 3.

Sekine, T. (1999) *'General Equilibrium and the Dialectic of Capital'*, *Chiiki-kenkyu*, Aichi Gakuin University, **37**, 1.

Sekine, T. (2002) 'The dialectic, or logic that coincides with economics', in Albritton and Simoulidis, eds.

Seton, F. (1957) 'The transformation problem', *Review of Economic Studies*, **24**.

Shaikh, A. (1973) *'Marx's Theory of Value and the "Transformation Problem"'*, in Schwartz, ed.

Shaikh, A. (1982) 'Neo-ricardian economics: a wealth of algebra, a poverty of theory', *Review of Radical Political Economics*, **14**, 2.

Shaikh, A. (1984) 'The transformation from Marx to Sraffa', in Mandel and Freeman, eds.

Shaikh, A. (1987) 'Surplus value', in Eatwell, Milgate and Newman, eds.

Shaikh, A. (1992a) 'Value and value transfers: a comment on Itoh', in Roberts and Feiner, eds (1992).
Shaikh, A. (1992b) 'The falling rate of profit as the cause of long waves: theory and empirical evidence', in A. Kleinknecht *et al.*, eds, *New Findings in Long-Wave Research* (New York: St. Martin's Press).
Shaikh, A. and Tonak, E.A. (1994) *Measuring the Wealth of Nations: The Political Economy of National Accounts* (Cambridge: Cambridge University Press).
Shamsavari, A. (1991) *Dialectic and Social Theory: The Logic of 'Capital'* (Braunton: Merlin Books).
Sherman, H.J. (1995) *Reinventing Marxism* (Baltimore: Johns Hopkins University Press).
Sinha, A. (1992) *'The Concept of Value in Marx: A Critique'*, Ph.D. Thesis (Buffalo: SUNY).
Sinha, A. (1996) 'A critique of Part One of *Capital* Volume One: The value controversy revisited', *Research in Political Economy*, **15**.
Sinha, A. (1997) 'The transformation problem: a critique of the "new solution"', *Review of Radical Political Economics*, **29**, 3.
Sinha, A. (1998) 'Hollander's "Marx and Malthusianism": a critique', *History of Economics Review*, **28**.
Sinha, A. (1999) 'Transformation problem', in O'Hara, ed.
Sinha, A. (2000a) 'The transformation problem: is the standard commodity a solution?', *Review of Radical Political Economics*, **32**, 2.
Sinha, A. (2000b) *'Theories of Value from Adam Smith to Piero Sraffa'*, Presented at the Annual Eastern Economic Associations Meetings, Washington D.C.
Sinha, A. (2001a) 'Review of Marx's wage theory in historical perspective: its origin, development and interpretation by K. Lapides', *Review of Radical Political Economics*, **33**, 2.
Sinha, A. (2001b) 'Labour theory of value', in J. Mitchie, ed., *Reader's Guide to the Social Sciences*, Volume 1 (London: Fitzroy Dearborn Publishers).
Sinha, A. (2001c) 'Transformation problem', in J. Mitchie, ed., *Reader's Guide to the Social Sciences*, Volume 2 (London: Fitzroy Dearborn Publishers).
Sinha, A. (2002) *'Reading Sraffa: The Philosophical Underpinnings of Production of Commodities by Means of Commodities'*, Presented at the Fourth Annual Meetings of the Association of Heterodox Economists, Dublin.
Skillman, G. (1999) 'Marx's value-theoretic account of capitalist exploitation: non sequitur or tautology?', *Science & Society*, **63**, 3.
Sklair, L. (2001) *The Transnational Capitalist Class* (London: Blackwell).
Smith, A. (1976) *An Inquiry into the Nature and Causes of the Wealth of Nations* (Oxford: Clarendon Press).
Smith, M.E.G. (1994) *Invisible Leviathan: The Marxist Critique of Market Despotism beyond Postmodernism* (Toronto: University of Toronto Press).
Smith, T. (1990) *The Logic of Marx's Capital: Reply to Hegelian Criticisms* (Albany: SUNY Press).
Smith, T. (1998) 'Value theory and dialectics', *Science & Society*, **62**, 3.
Sraffa, P. (1926) 'The laws of returns under competitive conditions', *Economic Journal*, **36**, 144.
Sraffa, P. (1951) 'Introduction', in D. Ricardo, ed. *The Works and Correspondence of David Ricardo*, Volume 1 (Cambridge: Cambridge University Press).
Sraffa, P. (1960) *Production of Commodities by Means of Commodities* (Cambridge: Cambridge University Press).
Sraffa, P. (1982) 'Introduction' to D. Ricardo, *On the Principles of Political Economy and Taxation* (Cambridge: Cambridge University Press).

Stark, W. (1944) *The History of Economics in its Relation to Social Development* (London: Routledge and Kegan Paul).
Steedman, I. (1977) *Marx After Sraffa* (London: New Left Books).
Steedman, I. *et al.* (1981) *The Value Controversy* (London: Verso).
Stigler, G. (1965) 'Ricardo and the 93% Labor Theory of Value', in G. Stigler, ed., *Essays in the History of Economics* (Chicago: University of Chicago Press).
Strange, S. (1998) *Mad Money: When markets outgrow governments* (Ann Arbor: The University of Michigan Press).
Sweezy, P. (1970) *The Theory of Capitalist Development* (New York: Modern Reader Paperbacks).
Sweezy, P., ed. (1984) *Karl Marx and the Close of his System* (London: Merlin and Augustus M. Kelley).
Szumi, J.S. (1989) 'The transformation problem solved?', *Cambridge Journal of Economics*, **13**, 3.
Szumski, J.S. (1991) 'On Duménil and Lévy's denial of the existence of the so-called transformation problem: a reply', *Cambridge Journal of Economics*, **15**, 3.
Tabb, W. (1999) *Reconstructing Political Economy* (New York: Routledge).
Townshend, H. (1937) 'Liquidity premium and the theory of value', *The Economic Journal*, March.
Uno, K. (1980) *Principles of Political Economy: Theory of a Purely Capitalist Society* (Sussex: Harvester Press).
Van Parijs, P. (1980) 'The falling-rate-of-profit theory of crisis: a rational reconstruction by way of obituary', *Review of Radical Political Economics*, **12**, 1, Spring.
Vasapollo, L. (2002) *An Old Myth: The Transformation of Values into Prices in Marx's Capital* (Rome: Laboratorio per la Critica Sociale).
Virilio, P. (1977) *Speed and Politics* (New York: Semiotext).
Vlachou, A., ed. (1999) *Contemporary Economic Theory: Radical Critiques of Neoliberalism* (London: Macmillan).
Vroey, M. de (1981) 'Value, production and exchange', in Schwartz, ed.
Vroey, M. de (1982) 'On the obsolescence of the marxian theory of value: a critical review', *Capital & Class*, **17**.
Wallace, W. (1975) *Hegel's Logic* (Oxford: Clarendon Press).
Webber, M.J. and Rigby, D.L. (1996) *The Golden Age Illusion: Rethinking Postwar Capitalism* (New York: Guilford Press).
Weeks, J. (1981) *Capital and Exploitation* (Princeton: Princeton University Press).
Weeks, J. (1982) 'Equilibrium, uneven development and the tendency of the rate of profit', *Capital & Class*, **16**.
Weeks, J. (1989) *A Critique of Neoclassical Macroeconomics* (London: Macmillan).
Weeks, J. (1990) 'Abstract labor and commodity production', *Research in Political Economy*, **12**.
Weeks, J. (1999) 'Surfing the global waters of global turbulence: a comment', *Historical Materialism*, **5**.
Weeks, J. (2001) 'Globalize, Globa-lize, Global Lies: Myths of the World Economy in the 1990s', in Albritton, Itoh, Westra and Zuege, eds.
Weiss, L. (1997) 'Globalization and the myth of the powerless state', *New Left Review*, **225**.
Weisskopf, T.E. (1979) 'Marxian crisis theory and the rate of profit in the postwar U.S. economy', *Cambridge Journal of Economics*, **3**, 4.
Wells, J.P. (2001) '*What is the Distribution of the Rate of Profit?*', Paper presented to the 2001 mini-conference of the IWGVT at the Eastern Economic Association, New York, February (available at www.gre.ac.uk/~fa03/iwgvt).

Westra, R. (1996) 'Periodizing capitalism and the political economy of post-war Japan', *Journal of Contemporary Asia*, **26**, 4.

Westra, R. (1999) 'A Japanese contribution to the critique of rational choice marxism', *Social Theory and Practice*, **25**, 3.

Westra, R. (2000) *'Marxist Theory and Creative Thinking About Post-Capitalist Alternatives: A Japanese Intervention'*, Ph.D. Thesis (Kingston, Canada: Queen's University).

Westra, R. (2001) 'Phases of capitalism and post-capitalist social change', in Albritton, Itoh, Westra and Zuege, eds.

Westra, R. (2002a) 'Marxian economic theory and an ontology of socialism: a Japanese intervention', *Capital & Class*, **78**.

Westra, R. (2002b) 'Phases of capitalism, globalizations and the Japanese economic crisis', in J. Busumtwi-Sam and L. Dobuzinskis, eds, *Turbulence and New Directions in Global Political Economy* (Basingstoke: Palgrave Macmillan).

White, J.D. (1996) *Karl Marx and the Intellectual Origins of Dialectical Materialism* (Basingstoke: Macmillan).

Williams, M. (1988) *Value, Social Form, and the State* (Basingstoke: Macmillan).

Williams, M. (1999) 'Why Marx neither has nor needs a commodity theory of money', *Review of Political Economy*, **30**.

Williams, M. (2001) 'Mysticism, method and money in the Marx-Hegel dialectic', *Cambridge Journal of Economics*, **25**.

Wolff, E.N. (1986) 'The productivity slowdown and the fall in the rate of profit, 1947–76', *Review of Radical Political Economics*, **18**, 1–2.

Wolff, E.N. (1987) *Growth, Accumulation, and Unproductive Activity: An Analysis of the Postwar U.S. Economy* (New York: Cambridge Unviersity Press).

Wolff, R. and Resnick, S. (1987) *Economics: Marxian versus Neoclassical* (Baltimore: Johns Hopkins University Press).

Wolff, R., Callari, A. and Roberts, B. (1984) 'A marxian alternative to the traditional "transformation problem" ', *Review of Radical Political Economics*, **16** (2/3).

Wolff, R., Roberts, B. and Callari, A. (1982) 'Marx's (not Ricardo's) "transformation problem": a radical reconceptualization', *History of Political Economy*, **14**, 4.

Woodford, M. (2002) 'Financial market efficiency and the effectiveness of monetary policy', *Economic Policy Review*, **8**, 1.

Wright E.O. (1978) *Class, Crisis and the State* (London: New Left Books).

Wright E.O. (1997) *Class Counts: Comparative Studies in Class Analysis* (Cambridge: Cambridge University Press).

Yaffe, D. (1973) 'Value, price and the neo-ricardians: an introductory note', *Bulletin of the Conference of Socialist Economists*, **2**, 6, Reprinted in Mohun (1994a).

Yaffe, D. (1974) 'Value and price in Marx's *Capital*', *Revolutionary Communist*, **1**.

Zarembka, P. (2003) 'Capital accumulation and crisis', in Saad-Filho, ed.

Zysman, J. (1996) 'The myth of a "global economy": enduring national foundations and emerging regional realities', *New Political Economy*, **1**, 2.

Author Index

Subject Index